THE BENEFACTOR

by Susan Sontag

FICTION

The Benefactor
Death Kit
I, etcetera
The Way We Live Now
The Volcano Lover

ESSAYS

Against Interpretation
Styles of Radical Will
On Photography
Illness as Metaphor
Under the Sign of Saturn
Aids and Its Metaphors

FILMSCRIPTS

Duet for Cannibals
Brother Carl

PLAY

Alice in Bed

A Susan Sontag Reader

SUSAN SONTAG

THE BENEFACTOR

A Novel

Anchor Books
DOUBLEDAY
New York London Toronto Sydney Auckland

AN ANCHOR BOOK
PUBLISHED BY DOUBLEDAY
a division of Bantam Doubleday Dell Publishing Group, Inc.
1540 Broadway, New York, New York 10036

ANCHOR BOOKS, DOUBLEDAY, and the portrayal
of an anchor are trademarks of Doubleday, a division of
Bantam Doubleday Dell Publishing Group, Inc.

The Benefactor was originally published in hardcover
by Farrar, Straus & Giroux in 1963 and in paperback in 1987.
The Anchor Books edition is published by arrangement
with Farrar, Straus & Giroux.

Library of Congress Cataloging-in-Publication Data
Sontag, Susan, 1933–
    The benefactor: a novel / by Susan Sontag.
    —1st Anchor Books ed.
        p.   cm.
    "Originally published in hardcover by Farrar,
    Straus & Giroux in 1963"—T.p. verso.
    I. Title.
PS3569.O6547B46   1991   91-14077
813'.54—dc20   CIP

ISBN 0-385-26710-X

For María Irene Fornés

CONTENTS

Of sleep, every evening's sinister adventure, it may be observed that men go daily to their beds with an audacity which would be beyond comprehension did we not know that is the result of their ignorance of danger.

BAUDELAIRE

If there be anything amiss—let the Dream be responsible. The Dream is a law to itself; and as well quarrel with a rainbow for showing, or for not showing, a secondary arch. . . . The Dream knows best; and the Dream, I say again, is the responsible party.

DE QUINCEY

ONE

Je rêve donc je suis

If only I could explain to you how changed I am since those days! Changed yet still the same, but now I can view my old preoccupations with a calm eye. In the thirty years which have passed, the preoccupation has changed its form, become inverted so to speak. When it began, it grew in me and emptied me out. I ignored it at first, then admitted it to myself, then sought consolation from friends, then resigned myself to it, and finally learned to exploit it for my own wisdom. Now, instead of being inside me, my preoccupation is a house in which I live; in which I live, more or less comfortably, roaming from room to room. Some winters I don't turn on the heat. Then I stay in one room, warmly wrapped in my leather coat, sweaters, boots, and muffler, and recall those agitated days. I have become a rather cranky old man, given to harmless philanthropies. A few friends pay me calls because they are lonely, not because they greatly enjoy my company. Decidedly, I have become less interesting.

Even as a child, there were traits which distinguished me from my playmates. My origins themselves are unremarkable:

I come from a prosperous family which still resides in one of the larger provincial cities. My parents were well into middle age when I was born, much the youngest of three children, and my mother died when I was five. My sister was already married and lived abroad. My brother had just come of age and entered my father's business; he married young (shortly after my mother died) and with equanimity, and soon had several children. I have not seen him for many years. Thus, I had ample opportunity to be alone as a child, and developed a somewhat premature taste for solitude. In that large house, from which my father and brother were chronically absent, I was thrown upon myself, and early evidenced a seriousness, tinged with melancholy, which youth did not dispel. But I did not seek to be different. I did well at school, played with other children, flirted with young girls and brought them presents, made love to the maid, wrote little stories—in short filled my life with the activities normal for my class and age. Because I was not particularly shy, and never sullen, I managed to pass among my relatives as a sombre but likeable child.

It was when I completed my schooling and left the town of my birth to attend the national university, that I first became unable to suppress the sense of being different. In everything one's surroundings are of great importance. Up to now I had been surrounded by my nurse, my father, relatives, friends, all of whom were easily pleased with themselves and me, and lived in comfortable agreement with each other. I was fond of their society. The only one of their traits I found distasteful was the ease and complacency with which they assumed a posture of moral indignation; otherwise they were to me no more and no less than people might sensibly be expected to be. But when I moved to the capital, I soon realized that not only did I not resemble the stolid provincials among whom I had been reared, but I was also unlike the restless cosmopolitans among whom I now lived and with whom I expected to have more in common. Around me were young men and women of my own age, some like myself from the provinces but most from the metropolis in which the university was situated. (I omit the name of this city not to tease the reader—for I have not excised from this narrative certain words and the names of local institutions known to every would-be tourist, so that the reader will soon be able to identify in which city I lived—but because I wish to indicate my conviction that where I lived was not of importance in the matters I shall relate; I make no complaint against my homeland or against this city in particular, which is no worse and perhaps better than most places, a center of culture and the residence of many interesting and gracious people.) At the university, then, were gathered the ambitious youth of my country. Everyone was preparing for accomplishment, some in medicine, the law, the arts, the sciences, some for the civil service and some for revolutions; while I found my heart empty of personal ambition. Ambition if it feeds at all, does so on the ambition of others. I did not come into this sort of relation, part conspiratorial and part envious, with my peers. I have always enjoyed being by myself, and the company of others is more pleasant to me when interspersed with large quantities of the refreshment which I find in myself, and in my dreams and reveries.

Genuinely, I believe, lacking all the usual motives of ambition such as spurred my fellow-students—not even the ambition to displease my family, this being a time of great strain between the generations—I nevertheless proved myself a capable and enthusiastic student. Inspired by the prospect of becoming learned, I enrolled in the most varied courses of lectures. But this very thirst for inquiry, that led to the investigations which subsequently preoccupied me, did not find a proper satisfaction in the divisions and faculties of the university. Do not misunderstand, it was not that I objected to specialization. On the contrary, genuine specialization—the neat and sensitive marking off of a subject, and its accurate quartering and adjacent subdivisions—was just what I looked for and could not find. Neither did I object to pedantry. What I objected to was that my professors raised problems only in order to solve them, and brought their lectures to a conclusion with maddening punctuality. My stubborn commitment to learning was comparable to that of a hungry man who is given sandwiches and eats them in the wax paper, not because he is too impatient to unwrap them but simply because he has never learned or else has forgotten how to remove the paper. My intellectual hunger did not make me insensible to the unappetizing fare of the university lecture rooms. But for a long time I could neither peel off the tasteless wrappings nor eat more moderately.

I studied in this way for three years. At the end of this time I published my first and only philosophical article; in it I proposed important ideas on a topic of no great importance. The article was controversial and excited some discussion in the general literary world, and because of it I was admitted to the circle of a middle-aged couple, foreign born and newly rich, who had an estate in the suburbs and collected stimulating people. On weekends, the Anders provided horseback riding in the afternoon, chamber music in the evening, and long formal meals. Besides myself, the regular guests included a professor who had written several books on the theory of revolution, a Negro ballet dancer, a famous physicist, a writer who had been a professional boxer, a priest who led a weekly forum on the radio called "Confessions and Remedies," and the elderly conductor of the symphony orchestra of a neighboring city (he came sporadically, but he was having an affair with the young daughter of the house). It was Frau Anders, a plump sensuous woman in her late thirties, who really presided, her husband's presence being irregular and his authority nominal; he was often away on business trips; I gathered that their marriage was one of convenience rather than sentiment. Frau Anders insisted on punctuality and deference, but was otherwise a generous hostess, attentive to her guests' idiosyncrasies and skillful in drawing them out.

All of Frau Anders' guests, even the vain and handsome ballet dancer, were virtuoso talkers. At first I was irritated and bewildered by the looseness of their conversation, by their readiness to express an opinion on any subject. These exchanges over a sumptuous dinner table seemed to me no more responsible intellectually than the acrimonious café debates of my fellow students. It took me a while to appreciate the distinctive virtues of the *salon*. Having opinions was only part of it. The more serious part was the display of personality. Frau Anders' guests were particularly accomplished at this display; no doubt that was why they had come together. I found this emphasis on personality, rather than opinions, restful. Already I had detected in myself a certain paucity of opinions. I knew that entering the estate of manhood meant purchasing a set of more or less permanent opinions, yet I found this more difficult than others apparently did. It was not due to intellectual torpor nor, I hope, to pride. My system was simply too busy receiving and discharging what I found about me. And in Frau Anders' circle I learned not to envy others because I had less certitude than they. I had a great faith (it seems a little naive in retrospect) in my own good digestion, and in the eventual triumph of patience. That there is order in this world still appears to me, even in my old age and isolation, beyond doubt. And I did not doubt that in this order I would find a place, as I have.

I ceased attending lectures at the university after acquiring this new circle of friends, and soon after officially resigned. I also stopped writing the monthly letter to my father. One day my father visited the capital on business and took the opportunity to see me. I assumed he meant to reproach me for neglecting my epistolary duties, but I did not hesitate to tell him immediately that I had abandoned my formal studies. I thought it better to deal with his reproaches in one interview than to have him hear the news, which he would interpret as truancy, indirectly. To my great satisfaction, he was not angry. According to his view, my older brother had fulfilled all the hopes he had for a son; for this reason he declared himself willing to support me in any independent path I might choose. He made arrangements with his banker to increase my monthly allowance, and we parted warmly with assurances of his continued affection. I was now in the enviable position of being entirely at my own disposal, free to pursue my own questions (the treasure I had accumulated since my childhood) and to satisfy, better than the university had done, my passion for speculation and investigation.

I continued to spend many hours of each day in rapid voracious reading, though I fear that as I read I did not think much. Not until years later did I understand that here was reason enough to abstain from reading. However, I did stop writing: except for a film scenario, my journals, and numerous letters, I have written nothing since that youthful philosophical article on a topic of no importance. Nothing, that is, until now, when with difficulty I again take up my pen. After reading, my chief pleasure at that time was conversation, and it was in conversation at Frau Anders' and with a few ex-comrades at the university that I occupied those first fledgling months of independence. Of my other interests there seems no reason to speak in detail. My sexual needs were not unduly clamorous, and periodic excursions into a disreputable quarter of the city sufficed to satisfy them. Politics interested me no further than the daily newspaper. In this I resembled most of my generation and class, but I had additional reasons of my own for being unpolitical. I am extremely interested in revolutions. But I believe that the real revolutions of my time have been changes not of government or of the personnel of public institu-

tions, but revolutions of feelings and seeing, much more difficult to analyze.

Sometimes I have thought that the perplexities I encountered
in my own person were themselves symptoms of such a general
revolution of feeling—a revolution not yet named, a disloca-
tion of consciousness not yet diagnosed. But this notion may
be presumptuous on my part. In all likelihood, my difficulties
are no more than my own; nor does it distress me to claim
them as mine. Luckily, being of a sturdy constitution and
serene temperament, I did not endure my inquietude pas-
sively, and have been extracted, through struggle, crisis, and
years of after-meditation, a certain sense from it. However,
I wish at the start to warn the reader that while I endeavor
conscientiously to present a just selection of those events,
it is with no more than the eye and mainly the ear of recol-
lection. It is easier to endure than to change. But once one
has changed, what was endured is hard to recall.

"Strangeness becomes you," my father said to me that kind
May afternoon.

I was, in fact, not as eccentric then as many of the people
I knew—in Frau Anders' salon, on the boulevards, in the university—but I did not contradict him.

"Let it be so, father," I said.

One word more. From my earliest schooling, I was exposed
to the secular intellectual ideals of my country: clarity, rigor,
education of the feelings. I was taught that the way to treat
an idea is to break it into its smallest component parts, and
then to retrace one's steps, proceeding from the most simple to
the complex—not forgetting to check, by enumeration, that
no step is omitted. I learned that reasoning itself, apart from
the particular demands of whatever problem it is applied to,
has a correct form, a style, which may be learned as one learns
the right way to swim or to dance.

If I now object to this style of reasoning, it is not because I share the distrust of reason which is the leading intellectual fashion in our century. My old-fashioned teachers were not in error. The method of analysis does solve all problems. But is that what is wanted always: to solve a problem? Suppose we reverse the method, and proceed from the most complex to the most simple. To be sure, we will be left with less than we started. But why not? Instead of accumulating ideas, we might be better occupied with dissolving them—not by a sudden act of will, but slowly, and with great patience. Our philosophers teach that "the whole is the sum of its parts." True. But perhaps any part also is the sum of the whole; perhaps the real sum of the whole is that part which is smallest, upon which one can concentrate most closely. To assume that "the whole is the sum of its parts" is to assume also that ideas and things are—or can be made to be—symmetrical. I have found that there are symmetrical ideas and asymmetrical ones as well. The ideas which interest me are asymmetrical: one enters through one side and exits through a side which is shaped quite differently. Such ideas rouse my appetite.

But the appetite for thinking must be regulated, as all sensible people know, for it may stifle one's life. I was more fortunate than most in that, in my youth, I had no settled ambitions, no tenacious habits, no ready opinions which I would have to sacrifice to thought. My life was my own: it was not dismembered into work and leisure, family and pleasure, duty and passion. Still I held back at first—keeping myself free of unnecessary entanglements, seeking the company of those whom I understood and therefore could not be seduced by, yet not daring to follow my inclinations toward solitary thought to their conclusion.

During this period of my youth, in the years immediately following my resignation from the university, I took the opportunity to travel outside my native country, and to observe the manners of other peoples and social classes. I found this more instructive than the wordy learning of the university and the library. Perhaps because I never left the country for more than a few months at a time, my travels did not demoralize me. Observing the variety of beliefs in different countries did not lead me to conclude that there is no true right and wrong but only fallible human opinion. However much men disagree about what is forbidden and what allowed, everyone aspires to order and to truth. Truth needs the discipline of custom in order to act. I do not deny that custom is usually narrow-minded and ungenerous. But one has no right to be outraged when, in self-defense, it martyrs the partisans of extreme acts. Any discipline, even that of the most sanctimonious custom, is better than none.

While I was occupied with my initial investigations into what I vaguely thought of as "certitude," I felt obliged to re-consider all opinions which were presented to me. Consequently I felt entitled to none myself. This openmindedness raised certain problems as to how my life was to be guided for the interim, while I questioned content I did not want to lose form. I drew up, for the duration of this period of inquiry, the following provisional maxims of conduct and attitude:

1. Not to be satisfied with my own, or any one else's, good intentions;
2. Not to wish for others what they did not wish for them-selves;
3. Not to spurn the advice of others;
4. Not to fear disapproval, but to observe as much as is feasible the rules of tact and discretion;
5. Not to value possessions nor be distracted by ambition;
6. Not to advertise myself, nor make demands on others;
7. Not to wish for a long life.

These principles were never difficult to follow, since they ac-corded with my own disposition anyway. Happily, I can claim to have observed them all, including the last rule. For although I have had a long life, I have not gone out of my way to provide for it. (I should mention, to give the reader a proper perspective, that I am now sixty-one years old.) And this life, I must also add, I do not recount because I consider it an example to anyone. It is for myself alone; the path I have followed, and the certitude I have found would be unlikely to suit anyone but myself.

The traditional metaphor for a spiritual investigation is that of the voyage or the journey. From this image I must dissociate myself. I do not consider myself a voyager, I have preferred to stand still. I would describe myself rather as a block of marble, acceptably though crudely hewn on the outside, inside which there is a comely statue. When the marble is hewn away, the freed statue may be very small. But whatever the size of the statue, it is better not to endanger it by moving the marble block frequently.

For this effort of hewing away the marble which enclosed me, no experience, no preoccupation was too small. I found nothing to despise. Take, for example, the group of people collected by Frau Anders. It would have been easy to dismiss them as vain and frivolous. But each of them had some perspective on life which was of interest, and something to teach me— the most satisfying grounds for friendship. Sometimes I wished that Frau Anders were not so solely concerned to please and to be pleased. She could have set herself up as a counter-force to her guests' pursuit of their own individualities. Then, instead of revolving around our hostess with compliments and attention, we could have spied on her. She might have asked us to perform and to create in her name, which everyone would have refused. She might have forbidden us to do things, like write novels or fall in love, so that we might have disobeyed her. But good manners forbid that I should have asked more of this woman than she was capable of giving. It was enough that the society I found at her house amused me, without arousing in me many expectations.

As evidence of my friendly conduct as a member of this society, I submit the following anecdote. One day Frau Anders asked me if the lack of financial privation in my life did not open opportunities for boredom. I replied, truthfully, that it did not. I then realized that this rich and still handsome woman was not asking me a question but telling me something, namely, that she herself was bored. But I did not accept her discreet complaint. I explained to her that she was not bored; she was, or was pretending to be, unhappy. This little comment instantly lifted her spirits, and I was pleased to see in subsequent visits to the house that she had become quite gay. I have never understood why people find it so difficult to speak the truth to their acquaintances and friends. In my experience, the truth is always appreciated, and the fear of giving offense is greatly exaggerated. People fear to offend or hurt others, not because they are kind but because they do not care for the truth.

Perhaps it would be easier for people to care for the truth if they understood that truth only exists when they tell it. Let me explain. The truth is always something that is told, not something that is known. If there were no speaking or writing, there would be no truth about anything. There would only be what is. Thus, to me, my life and my preoccupations are not the truth. They are, simply, my life, my preoccupations. But now I am engaged in writing. And in daring to transpose my life into this narrative, I shoulder the dreadful responsibility of telling the truth. I find the narrative which I undertake a difficult task, not because it is hard for me to tell the truth about myself in the sense of reporting honestly "what happened," "what took place," but because it is hard for me to speak the truth in the more pretentious sense, truth in the sense of insisting, rousing, convincing, changing another.

Sometimes I cannot help pursuing various ideas I have of the character and preoccupations of my readers. This weakness I hope to conquer. It is true that the lessons of my life are lessons only for me, suited only to me, to be followed only by me. But the truth of my life is only for someone else. I warn the reader that I shall try henceforth not to imagine who that someone else is, and whether he or she is reading what I have written. This I cannot, and rightly should not, know.

For, to speak the truth is one thing; to write it another. When we speak, we address someone else. When we speak what is best—which is always the truth—still it is to a person, with the thought of a person. But if there is any chance of writing something that is true, it will only be because we have banished the thought of another person.

When we write the truth, we should address ourselves. When in writing we are didactic and admonitory, we must consider that we instruct and admonish only ourselves, for our own failings alone. The reader is a happy accident. One must allow the reader his liberty, his liberty to contradict what is written, his liberty to be distracted by alternatives. Therefore it would be improper for me to try to convince the reader of all that is in this book. It is enough that you imagine me now, as I am, with the companionship of my recollections, in comparative peace, desiring the solace of no one. It is enough that you imagine me now, elderly scribe to my younger self, and accept that I am changed, and that it was different before.

TWO

I don't know how soon it was after the commencement of my visits to the Anders house that I began having a series of dreams that moved and upset me. It was a year, I think, perhaps more. I recall that I had just returned from a brief trip abroad. And I remember how I spent the evening before the first dream. With some others of her circle, I had accompanied Frau Anders to a concert; afterwards I joined a university friend at a café, where I drank somewhat more than was usual for me and argued for the unseemliness of suicide. Toward morning I returned to my rooms in a mood of buoyancy, and without undressing flung myself in bed.

I dreamed that I was in a narrow room which had no windows, only a small door about thirty centimeters high. I wanted to leave and bent down. When I saw that I could not squeeze through the door, I was ashamed that someone might see me conducting such an investigation into the obvious. There were several chains hanging from the wall, each of which terminated in a large metal band. I tried to fasten one of the chains first to some part of my body, but the band was too big for either my hand or my foot and too small for my head. I was in some prison, although apart from the chains the room did not have the appearance of a cell.

Then I heard a noise which came from the ceiling. A trap door opened, and a large man wearing a one-piece bathing costume of black wool peered down at me. The man lowered himself by his hands, hung for a moment, then jumped to the floor. When he stood up and walked, he limped a trifle and grimaced. I assumed he had hurt himself in the jump. I thought it possible that he was already lame; but then it seemed odd for him to have attempted such a feat, for the ceiling was high. And, being lame did not suit the acrobatic fitness of his shiny muscular limbs.

Suddenly I became afraid of him, for I knew I had no right to be in this room. He said nothing, and merely indicated by signs that I was to pass through the small door which I had previously investigated. The door was larger now. I knelt down, and crawled through. When I stood up, I was in another room which looked exactly like the first. The man in the bathing suit was behind me, holding a long copper-colored instrument which looked like a flute. He signalled me to dance by doing a few steps and turns himself. I was afraid again, and asked him why I had to do this. "Because in this room he dances," he said in an even, placating voice.

"But I am not 'he,'" I replied, delighted to be able to reason with him. "I am Hippolyte, a student at the university, but I do not dance." These last words I said more emphatically than I meant to, with perhaps a touch of rudeness. I only meant to appear firm.

He answered with a threatening gesture aimed at my stomach, and the words, "That's a mistake. He dances."

"But why? Tell me why," I protested. "It can't give you pleasure to watch a clumsy man dance."

He made another peremptory gesture, this time not simply

a threat of violence but a hard blow across the calf of my leg with his flute which made me leap with pain. Then, in a tone of great mildness which seemed to contradict the blow, he said, "Does he want to leave this room?"

I knew that I was in the hands of someone stronger than myself, and that I could not afford to challenge the man's peculiar way of addressing me. I wanted to please him. "Can't he leave, if he doesn't dance?" I asked, hoping he would not think I was mocking him.

With that he hurled the instrument at my face. My mouth filled with blood. I felt very cold. "He has lost his chance to dance," he said. I fell to my knees in fear, closed my eyes; I smelled the damp odor of his woolen bathing suit, but nothing happened.

When I opened my eyes the other person in the room was a woman sitting in a tall wicker chair in the corner. She was dressed in something long and white, like a communion dress or a wedding gown.

I could not keep from staring at her, but I knew my gaze was discontinuous, broken, composed of hundreds of frozen gazes, with a tiny interval between each as long as the gaze itself. What interrupted my gaze—the black intervals between the frames, as it were—was the consciousness of something loose in my mouth, and of a painful swelling of my face, which I feared to know more about, as one fears to look at oneself because one doesn't want to discover one is naked. Since, however, the cordial look which the woman turned on me did not reveal any antipathy, I tried to master my embarrassment. Perhaps my look went on and off because it was changing, and the only way I could convey the illusion of a smooth transition from one stage of my gaze to another was precisely by slicing into the gaze, whereas if it had remained continuous there would have been a blur, and a dissolving of my features, and she would have had a disagreeable impression of my face.

I thought of an ingratiating way to approach her. I started to dance, turning around and around. I jumped, and slapped my knees, and waved my arms. But when I stopped to catch my breath I saw that I had not moved nearer. My face felt heavy. She said, "I don't like your face. Give it to me. I'll use it as a shoe."

I wasn't alarmed by this, because she did not get up from her chair. I only said, "You can't put a foot in a face."

"Why not?" she answered. "A shoe has eyeholes."

"And a tongue," I added.

"And a sole," she said, standing up.

"Why do you make silly jokes?" I cried, beginning to be alarmed. I asked her the purpose of the chains on the wall, this room being furnished as the other was. Then she told me a story about the house I was in and why I had been put in the room. I have forgotten this part of the dream. I remember only that there was a secret, and a penalty. Also that someone had fainted. And that because someone had fainted, and others were busy caring for him, I was being neglected, and had a right to demand better treatment.

I told her it was I who fainted.

"The chains are for you," she said. She came toward me. I took off my shoes hastily, and went with her to the wall where she fitted the chains around my wrists. Then she brought me her chair to sit in.

"Why do you like me?" she asked. She was sitting opposite me in another chair. I explained to her that it was because she didn't make me do anything I didn't want to do. But as I said this, I wondered if it were so.

"Then there's no need for me to like you," she replied. "Your passion for me will maintain both of us here happily."

I tried to think of a tactful way of telling her that I was happy but that I still wanted to leave. I was happier with her than I had been in the company of the man with the flute.

The chains felt like bracelets. But my mouth was sore, my feet were perspiring, and my gaze, I knew, was insincere.

I stretched out my legs and placed my feet in the lap of her white dress. She complained that I was soiling the dress and told me that I would have to go. I could hardly believe my good fortune, and so strong was my feeling of relief that the desire to leave the room was now less urgent than the need to express my gratitude. I asked her if I could kiss her before I left. She laughed and slapped my face. "You must learn to take things before you ask," she said sharply, "and dance before you are bidden, and surrender your shoes, and compose your face."

Tears came to my eyes. In my distress I implored her to explain further. She didn't answer. I threw myself on her, with the intention of taking her sexually, and at that very moment awoke.

I got out of bed in a state of elation. After making myself coffee I cleaned my room thoroughly and put everything in order. I knew that something had happened to me which I wanted to celebrate, and for this purpose the gestures of orderliness are always most satisfying. Then I sat at my desk and considered the dream. Several hours passed. At first the dream intrigued me because it was so clear; that is, I remembered it so well. Yet it seemed as if the very explicitness of the dream barred the way to any fruitful interpretation. I persisted. I devoted the entire morning to puzzling over the details of the dream, and urged myself to apply some ingenuity to their interpretation. But my mind refused to cavort about the dream. By mid-afternoon, I suspected that the dream had, so to speak, interpreted itself. Or even, that this morning of mental sluggishness was the real dream, of which the scenes in the two rooms were the interpretation. (I do not hope to make this thought wholly clear to the reader at the present moment.)

Certain features of my own character in the dream—my

crafty humility, my propensity to shame, my posture of sup-
plication and fear, my desire to placate and cajole and endear
myself to the two personages of my dream—recalled to me the
way many people speak of their childhood. But I was not a
fear-ridden child: I don't remember my mother, and my
father never hit or frightened me. "This is not a dream of
childhood," I said, perhaps prematurely.

I paused over the man in the bathing suit and his flute, and
his antagonism to me. I savored my attraction to the woman
in the white dress, and her refusal of me. "I have had a sexual
dream," I said. And I could make little more of it than that,
before the evening.

That evening I had an appointment at a café with the
writer friend I have already mentioned to you, the one who had
been a professional boxer when he was in his early twenties. I
had become more intimate with this man, who was about ten
years older than myself, than with any of the others whom I
met at Frau Anders', despite the fact that he led a life with
many compartments and a costume for each, a life difficult to
grasp in its entirety. By day he sat in his room, dressed in boxing trunks, and wrote novels which were well received by the
critics; for the aperitif hour and the early evening he put on a
dark suit and went to the opera or to Frau Anders' house; and
in the late evening he roamed the boulevards of the city solicit-
ing men, for which purpose he donned various exotic costumes
of an aggressively male character, like that of a hoodlum, a
sailor, or a truck driver. Since none of his novels had sold more
than a few hundred copies, it was through prostitution and
petty thievery that Jean-Jacques earned a modest living. Because he spoke quite openly of his "job" as he called it—he
called writing his "work"—I had often asked him to tell me
of his experiences. He confided more in me, I supposed, because
he sensed something neutral in my attitude, something which
was neither disapproval, nor attraction, nor anything like the

respectful fascination with which his other friends regarded his "job." His indiscretion and my attentiveness, up to the time of my first dream, had been the basis of our friendship.

That night, however, it was I who talked first, he who listened. I told Jean-Jacques of my dream, and it interested him. "Have you ever feared for your sanity?" he asked.

I wondered why he said that, since I understood that the license of dreaming permitted us the most irregular and cryptic fantasies. And I was surprised that this unusual man should find anything in my plain life to stir him to wonder.

"You see," he continued, "I don't dream. I find intolerable the slow leakage of my substance in dreams, so I have staged my life to incorporate the energy that is usually diverted in dreaming. My writing forces from me the dream-substance, prolongs it, plays with it. Then I replenish the substance in the show of the café, in the political intrigue of the salon, in the extravagances of the opera, in the comedy of roles which is the homosexual encounter."

"Up to now I have not dreamt, either."

"But now that you have started," he said, smiling, "you are not going about it in the right way. Your dream contains so much talk, at least as you have related it to me. If you must dream, silence is best. You must be silent if you are absorbed in anything." He laughed. "Perhaps I myself am too talkative to dream."

Jean-Jacques was not only very talkative, but restless, too. He walked and moved rapidly and always seemed to want to go somewhere, yet never seemed in a hurry to be off. His manner of speaking was similar: he talked quickly, hurriedly, but with assurance and conceit. His pronunciation was, if anything, over-distinct. I wondered to myself if he did anything silently —if he wrote in silence, if he made love in silence, if he stole without words.

We ordered two more cognacs. "Do you think I will ever explain this dream?" I asked him.

"You can explain one dream with another," he said thoughtfully. "But the best interpretation of your dream would be to find it in your life. You must outbid your dream."

Finally he reminded me that it was getting late, and that pleasure and business called him. As I paid our bill, he waved and walked away, and I saw him take a golden bracelet from his pocket and attach it to his wrist.

This conversation with Jean-Jacques encouraged me to pursue my dream more intently. In the suspension of all preconceptions which I had adopted as my path to certitude, I could hardly ignore so singular a visitation.

I suppose I had dreamt before my "dream of the two rooms." Perhaps I had dreamt every night. But I did not remember my dreams. If there were shadows of people and situations in my mind when I awakened, as soon as I arose from bed and washed, the shadows vanished, and the day and its tasks appeared to be untrammelled and continuous from the night before when I had lain down. No counter-images waylaid me as I slept.

I had often wondered why I did not dream. Perhaps my personality was assembled late. Nevertheless, the advent of my dreams did not take me completely by surprise. From books and conversations with friends, I was acquainted with the usual dream repertoire: dreams of being trapped in a fire, dreams of falling, dreams of being late, dreams of flying, dreams of being followed, dreams of one's mother, dreams of nakedness, dreams of murdering someone, dreams of sexual conquest, dreams of being sentenced to death. Neither this dream, nor any of those which followed it, failed to include some of these standard dilemmas of dreams. What was odd, and memorable, about the dreams was not their originality but the impression they made on me. My previous dreams, if I had had any, were easily forgotten. This dream and its successors were indelible. They were written, as it were, by a firmer hand, and in a different script.

As I have said, my first recourse was interpretation. It seems that from the beginning I did not accept the dream as a gift but as a task. The dream also provoked a certain reaction of antipathy in me. Therefore I sought to master the dream, by understanding it. The more I thought of the dream, the greater I felt the responsibility. But the various interpretations I conceived did not relieve me. These interpretations, instead of reducing the pressure of the dream on my daytime life, added to it.

The verbosity of the dream, which Jean-Jacques had pointed out to me, alone gave it an entirely different character from what I understood dreams generally to be like. Most dreams show. This dream said.

My vanity was not wounded because the dream, speaking in the accent of command, showed me as without force and pride. I knew that the dream was both voluntary, in that I had imagined it, and involuntary, in that it issued a command I could not understand or answer.

I labored with my dream.

Once, during my travels, I was staying in a mountain village and had observed a woman in difficult childbirth. One wondered how love could ever become her. She was obviously bewildered that by any act of her own she could have brought herself to such great pain. She refused all help—rather, she no longer understood what her relatives and the neighbors and the midwife wanted from her when they tried to help her. She was drowning in herself.

Her husband approached the iron bed and tried to take her hand. She did not push him away. But her senses were turned in an inward direction; only the nerves in the interior side of her skin registered. She was alone in the crammed shell of herself.

There was a period after this first dream when I felt as I have described this woman: weighty, interred. I did not know how to deliver myself. Interpretation was my Caesarean operation, and Jean-Jacques my complaisant physician. Most of this time, you understand, I was quite calm. I was not in pain. This dream was not a nightmare. Nevertheless, this dream changed me. The even tenor of my investigations into the world and its opinions was broken, when I turned to investigate this dream.

The woman who suffered in childbirth had already committed an extreme act: she had slept with her husband and conceived a child. The pain she now suffered was only the logical result of that act. But I seemed to bear fruit without planting anything. This dream was unwanted. It procreated itself.

This dream was my first immoderate act.

THREE

It is hard to explain what happened in the next months. For a long time, no night passed without presenting me some variation on this original dream. Sometimes the woman surrendered to my embrace. Sometimes it was I who played the flute, and struck the bather. Sometimes the woman told me I could go, on the condition that I continued to wear the chains. Sometimes I would not dance for her. Sometimes the bather remained with the woman and made love to her before my guilty eyes. But always at the end of the dream, I wept; and always I awakened with a driving empty elation which ruled the whole of my day.

I did not make much progress in my morning's meditation of the dream. These generous variations on the original scenario made the task of interpretation even more difficult. I no longer knew whether I was master or slave in my dream. Too much was being given for me to understand.

The dream of my imprisonment in the two rooms narrowed my life, so that I thought more, and went out less. Thus, when my father visited the capital again for a few days I forgot to go to see him. Of this absorption by the dream, I do not complain: blessed is the mind with more to occupy it than its own dissatisfactions. But the mind needs the occasional reward of understanding. I was exhausted by my futile efforts to understand the dream, and wondered if I would even know how to act once I did understand. Finally, I began to take seriously the advice of Jean-Jacques, and thought less of how the dream might be interpreted and more of what I should do with it. Since the dream haunted me, I would now haunt the dream. I considered the exercises and prohibitions commanded in the dream. I bought a black bathing suit, and a flute which I painted the color of copper. I walked around the bedroom barefoot. I learned the tango and the foxtrot. I conquered the affections of several reluctant women.

The bridge which I built between my dream and my daytime occupations was my first taste of an inner life. I was not surprised to discover that the claims of an inner life modify one's attitudes to the world, and particularly to other people. The small gallery of characters in my dream now took their place alongside my relatives and my friends. They were perhaps more like the members of my family, whom I no longer saw but whose image I still carried in my head, than my friends in the capital. (For do not the personages of the past have a status similar to the personages of one's dreams? That they existed is confirmed only by turning inward, or by consulting a photograph album or looking at old letters. This autobiographical narrative serves the functions of a photograph album or a collection of letters: already I reread what I have written, and only so far as I confirm by memory that I dreamed these dreams do I recognize what I wrote as constituting my past.) But even the people I knew in the present took on another aspect. I saw them superimposed upon the personages of my dream, or I superimposed the man in the black bathing suit or the woman in white upon them.

Then, one weekend at Frau Anders', the elderly conductor

who came there sporadically to visit the daughter of the house, invited me to spend a fortnight with him in the city where he had his post with the municipal orchestra. I accepted the invitation, for it occurred to me that a change—I had not been out of the capital for months—might provide the stimulus that would crown my efforts of self-mimicry and even dispel the dream. Later I learned that the Maestro had extended this invitation at Frau Anders' request. She was distressed by the mood of thoughtfulness (which she took to be melancholy) I could not conceal during my recent visits and by my increasing abstention from that large ration of shameless flattery which it was necessary at all times to supply her with.

We went by train. When we arrived at his house, the housekeeper showed me to my room; then she served tea and the Maestro, after the most elegant apologies, left for a rehearsal, which I imagine he expected me to ask his permission to attend.

I spent the evening playing records and looking at scores. Although I do not have that facility with a score which allows me to hear with my inner ear the full orchestration as I read, I was sufficiently entertained, and not at all bored.

I went to sleep early, and was rewarded with a new dream.

I dreamed that I was in a crowded city street, hurrying toward some appointment. I was anxious not to be late, but was not sure of my destination. I was not discouraged, though: I thought that if I continued with sufficient energy and display of certitude, I would recognize the place I was to go. Then there was a man walking beside me and I asked him politely for directions.

"Follow him," he said.

The voice was familiar. I turned to inspect my companion and recognized the flute-player in the black bathing suit from my other dream. In exasperation I struck him with what, I believe, was his own flute. He groaned and fell, and rolled down the steps of a Metro entrance. Then I remembered he was lame and regretted my fury, for I could not claim that this time he had menaced me or seemed to intend me any harm.

Fearful that he would emerge, brandishing his flute in anger, and pursue me, I began to run. At first I had to exert myself, but soon the running became easier. My panic subsided, for it was as if someone were helping me. I was running on a large black disc, which was revolving faster than I could run, so that I was losing time. I felt my hair becoming stiff and heavy on my scalp. I jumped off the disc, and stood in the street again. At first I was extremely dizzy; then I felt quite calm. I must have had, at this point, that semi-awareness of the dream-state itself, common in dreams, which inspires a complacent passivity before events. At the same time that I stood in the street looking for an address which I had forgotten, I saw myself very clearly further down the conveyor belt of the dream, safely at my destination.

At some point in this part of the dream I bought some cigarettes. I remember that the brand I requested was "face cigarettes," and that the proprietress of the *tabac* told me she had only "musical cigarettes." I assured her that these would be equally satisfactory, and paid for them with some warm unfamiliar coins which I had in my pocket.

Then I was arriving somewhere, a large atelier where a rowdy party was in progress. The red tile floor was littered with still burning cigarettes. I stepped carefully for fear of burning myself. I was barefoot.

The hostess was Frau Anders, who was sitting on a stool and leaning with her elbows on a slanted drawing board. She was overseeing the party, and did not seem to mind that some of her guests were breaking glasses and others scribbling on the walls with lipstick and pieces of charcoal. She did not see me come in and I avoided meeting her eyes, for I owed her some debt which I was afraid she might confront me with and demand that I pay. Someone proposed a game, and I accepted with the idea that by joining the game I should show myself co-operative and of good character and at the same time be more inconspicuous.

I understood we were going to play charades. But all we were asked to do was to bend over from the waist and touch the floor with our hands, "making an inverted U," as the leader of the game described it. Vaguely indecent thoughts passed through my mind—rising to a definite state of sexual excitement—but I could find no grounds for legitimate embarrassment, since I saw that all around me the other guests had already assumed the difficult posture, and were playfully chatting with each other between their legs.

There was a concert going on in the next room, and I was saying something about it to my neighbor in the game, the Negro ballet dancer. As we were talking, he began to spread, to unfold until he was prone upon the floor. He closed his eyes and sighed. Others near me followed suit, sliding to the floor, their bodies touching and overlapping, everyone sighing; they all looked so happy, I felt suddenly peaceful and happy myself. A feeling of great lightness maintained my body above the others.

"Hippolyte can hold the position longest," I heard Frau Anders declare. "Hippolyte has won the game." Her voice interrupted my mood of tranquillity, and for a moment I was annoyed. I did not see why in so pleasant a game anyone need be designated as the winner. This seemed to me just the virtue of the game, that there were neither rules nor goal. But after all, if it is a game, it must end, I then thought, and was pleased that, still somehow in keeping with the spirit of this mysterious and delightful game, I had won inadvertently, without striving. So warm a feeling of love did I feel for my prostrate companions on the floor that I was not embarrased over my winning and their losing, nor did I fear that they would think I had not deserved to win. I felt quite clearly that they all wished me to win, or at least—since their eyes were closed and they did not register any awareness of Frau Anders' announcement—that they wished to be where they were. Their heavy contented position on the floor was as apt and desired by them as my weightless approval, suspended above them, was by me.

Of course, I had thus attracted Frau Anders' attention despite my efforts to avoid it. But now, I knew, she would be pleased with me. And so she was. She put her arm under my stomach to raise me to a standing position, led me to a couch, and then sat on my lap.

"Frau Anders," I said into the space between her heavy breasts. "Frau Anders, I love you." She embraced me tightly. "Let those mock who will," I cried, caught up in a mounting enthusiasm. "I am not like the others, who accept your hospitality only for the celebrities whom they can meet at your house, for I am not ambitious. I do not care for your money, for I am rich. I will not touch your daughter, for I have you. Come away with me."

She held my neck more tightly. "Tell me you will always love me," I said, forcing her to look at me. "Tell me that you will do all that I wish."

"Now," she whispered.

"Not in front of all your guests!" I replied. I could hardly believe that I had aroused this proud woman so quickly, or that she could be so thoughtless of her duties as a hostess.

She pointed to the drawing board. We tiptoed across the floor. She leaned backwards on the hard table. For a moment I was numb with embarrassment. "Draw me," she whispered, pulling my head toward hers. Then I recovered myself, and told her it could not be done here. I told her we would go to my room. I had only to find my shoes.

We both squatted and began to search for them on the

floor among the bodies of the guests. We did not find them. I now regretted that I had placed any conditions upon this happy sexual encounter which had been so imminent only a moment before, and began looking for my shoes less conscientiously, as if by this means the search might be abandoned without regret. But now it was Frau Anders who insisted, crawling on the floor, that I must have them.

"Look," she said. "I have found some of your hair." In her right hand she held a piece of my black hair which seemed congealed and shiny. I begged her not to distract herself with that.

"And here is another piece," she said loudly, lifting up a larger tuft. Again I implored her not to concern herself about my hair. At the same time, I did not believe it was mine. I felt my head. Everything seemed perfectly normal.

But when she told me that it couldn't have come from any of the other guests, because no one had hair as black as mine, I thought she might be right. And since she insisted that she would not have this mess on her floor, I had to help her. Still squatting in the middle of the floor, we collected a small pile of it, she remarking continually at the blackness and quantity of my hair in a way which conveyed an unmistakable tone of disgust.

"You have spoiled everything," I shouted, feeling my cheeks flush with shame. I decided not to stay in this place another minute, clambered to my feet, ran to the door, and awoke.

When I awoke from my dream, my room was still dark, and the black sky outside my window just starting to purple. Nevertheless I dressed and went downstairs where I saw a light under the door of the conductor's study. Emboldened by the bizarre liberations I had lived through in my dream, I knocked without hesitating and found the Maestro at his desk.

"Come in, Hippolyte," he said cordially, removing his spectacles. "I am not working, only writing a letter since I cannot sleep."

"Perhaps the rehearsal has overstimulated you," I ventured politely.

He ignored my comment and said, "Hippolyte, will you give me your opinion, as a friend and as a younger man to one much older? Do you feel that a great difference in age between two people who love each other is important? You no doubt know," he continued, "of my attachment to young Lucrezia Anders, and you may have guessed—if you are indeed as sensitive as I believe you to be—that it is to her that I am writing."

I sensed that I had the Maestro's permission to pause lengthily before making my reply, and that any answer, however wise, if delivered quickly, would be offensive to him. I paused, thinking of how I should reply.

"Well, Maestro, I have had a dream," I finally said. "I learn very much from my dreams, and in this dream I saw that both attraction and repulsion exist between youth and age. If an older person pursues too shamelessly, the younger will be repelled. Youth must woo and age must yield."

He frowned. "I take it you are advising me to be less ardent. But frankly I am afraid to visit the Anders' house less often, or to write fewer letters to my shy darling. The only respect in which I am confident I can outdo a younger man is in the tenacity of my wooing. Reserve is a great gamble for an older man. It can be misinterpreted as debility."

"Perhaps there's no chance you will be misinterpreted," I said, trying to be helpful. "May I ask if you are her first lover?"

"Alas, no," he said. "Our estimable hostess has seen to Lucrezia's education long before my advances were sanctioned."

"And do you think that at the present moment you alone enjoy her favors?"

He paled and I could observe that the question was distasteful to him. "I do not know my rivals," he said. "And surely

these are unnecessary questions from someone who frequents
the household more than I do. Although"—he collected himself—"Frau Anders tells me that you have been acting strangely
of late, that you withhold yourself and do not call as regularly
as before. Is there some young woman who occupies your time?
I should not burden you with an old man's problems." He put
on his glasses again. The lenses were thick, and made his eyes
look round and empty. "You must have problems of your own
that you would like to discuss with me," he continued. "In fact,
my little remarks just now—which I know you will treat in
the strictest confidence—were less an expression of my own
thoughts and problems than they were—I hope you are not
offended—directed to make you repose an absolute confidence
in me and promote a more intimate atmosphere between us.
I had intended to bring this up tomorrow, perhaps at lunch,
though I really should not be distracted before the concert,
so perhaps this is a more propitious occasion. There is something troubling you, Hippolyte. And if I can be of any. . . ."

His thin monotonous voice stopped. I had been watching
the dawn break through the window behind the Maestro's desk.

"No sir," I said. "There is nothing. Except, perhaps, too
much solitude."

"But it is your solitude which is the result, I am sure, of
some inner unhappiness; and not the solitude which causes
your present manner, a manner which distresses all your friends.
Allow me to. . . ."

"My solitude is entirely voluntary, I assure you."

"I beg your pardon but. . . ."

"Let me tell you, Maestro," I exclaimed, "that I am having
experiences of a purity, albeit of a great narrowness, such as
cannot be shared. Only in myself—only in himself I might say,
if you permit the locution—do I savor them."

He tried to soothe me, and only succeeded in being patronizing. "My young friend, ever since I first saw you in Frau

Anders' drawing room I have felt you had the makings of an artist. But we artists," he smiled at his generous gift, this 'we,' "we artists must avoid the temptation to isolate ourselves, to lose contact with the. . . ."

"I am no artist, dear Maestro. You mistake me." I decided to patronize him in return. "I have no inner burden which I wish to unload upon a passive audience. I do not wish to contribute one jot to the fund of public fantasy. Perhaps I have something to reveal, but it is of so intensely private a nature that it could not possible interest anyone else. Perhaps I will reveal nothing, even to myself. But I know I am on the trail of something. I am crawling through the tunnel of myself— which takes me farther and farther from the artist's base craving for applause." Since he refused to be offended at my pointed words, I continued. "I am looking for silence, I am exploring the various styles of silence, and I wish to be answered by silence. You might say," I concluded gaily, "that I am disembowelling myself."

I detest what are called looks of understanding. "Dear Hippolyte," he said, without even trying to understand what I had said, "all young artists go through a period of. . . ."

I stood up and walked to the door, determined to take this very morning's train back to the capital. I became inexcusably hilarious at that moment; it was the excitement of the new dream. "Maestro," I shouted at him as he rose to follow me, "Maestro, does Lucrezia give you pleasure? Does she make you jump?" He scowled with disbelief at my rudeness, and stood still. I sped down the hall and took the stairs two at a time, roaring with laughter. "Does she make you dance, old man?" I called over my shoulder. "Do you wave your baton? Do any of the instruments play for you alone?"

Once back in the city, I unwearily went about my new project, the seduction of Frau Anders. The source of energy tapped in my new dream, which I fondly denominated "the dream of the unconventional party," was not illusory. That zest which had begun inauspiciously with my rudeness to the Maestro continued. I felt more lively than I had in months. And I had need of much energy. For while I was courting my patronness with all the smiles and winning words I could muster, she professed to see only the evidence of my recovery from melancholy. It took the most shameless, the least subtle glances to refine her neutral complicity into a state of sexual awareness of my intentions. Flattery had become for my mistress a drug administered in such large doses that her system had become immune to anything less. To convert flattery into, seduction it was not enough merely to sleep with her. The sexual act itself was to her like the gift of a rare *objet d'art* or a bouquet of flowers, or a verbal compliment. Only with difficulty, with the crudest insistence, could she brought to understand the sexual act as a gesture different from these. The point had to be made again and again that she was not being flattered, not being given anything at all. The despair of my campaign was that she did not believe anything had changed between us!

I realize there was something contradictory in the management of our affair. I wished to make Frau Anders realize that my love for her was not something that was her due. Nothing was more frustrating to me than that she should take my feeling for her, the surprising and unexpected command of my dreams, for granted. The only way in which I could shake her exasperating self-assurance was by insinuating to her that she was not altogether desirable to me. I dropped remarks on the difference in our ages, her tendency to gain weight, the stridency of her laughter, her color blindness, the imperfections of her accent —none of which in fact was the least unattractive to me. I did not wish to humiliate her. Therefore I only insinuated these things, always short of the point of conviction. You see my dilemma. I am not an unkind person. But I regretted that she was deprived of the pleasure of knowing herself the recipient of a love different from, and stronger than, what she wanted to arouse.

I did not wish gratitude from Frau Anders, you understand —only seriousness. It was not enough that she pleased me in bed. I hardened myself against her easy responsiveness. Thus in the newly opened but complacent arms of my mistress I found a portion of pleasure but not happiness, and she found in me happiness but little pleasure.

You may conclude that our affair did not take me outside the curious questions which preoccupied me, but rather provided me with new material. My feeling for Frau Anders was an exploration of myself. Our affair ran parallel to the successive editions and variations on my second dream, "the dream of the unconventional party." Sometimes I lost the bending-over game, sometimes I never reached the party, sometimes the irate man in the bathing suit pursued me, sometimes Frau Anders gave up the search for my hair and lay, voluptuous and adorable, in my arms. In order to wait for the secret and unpredictible cues from the dreams, I had to impose a rigid discipline on our liaison. It was only by keeping some reserve with Frau Anders, that I managed to continue my feelings at their height. The art of feeling, as of erotic performance, is the ability to prolong it; in my case duration depended on my ability to refresh my fantasies. To insure privacy, I did not let her do me favors. Neither did I move into a house on her estate, as she wished me to do; and in all I insisted on discretion and tried to maintain as correct an exterior as possible. The role of the lover of a married woman has its conventions, like any other role, and I wanted to observe them. Unconventionality for its own sake does not attract me. Such differences from other people as I do display force their way to the surface of action from the depths of my character without my being particularly pleased at the result.

My mistress' unconventionality was, by contrast, entirely superficial. The lies entailed by her frequent adulteries had been perfunctory; nothing except truth could disturb the life of the salon and its incessant conversation. Having the fortune to live in a milieu where unconventionality was encouraged and appreciated, she was, outwardly, unconventional. Inwardly she was full of respect for society's law; only it hardly ever applied to her. No wonder that consistency always surprised her, the arbitrary never.

Thus she was not surprised by the ebb and flow of my desire for her, according to the secret tides of my dreams. Nor did she complain when for a week or more at a time I occupied myself in the city, and endeavored not to think of her. These activities often kept me in my room, where I felt most at liberty. Besides reading and meditating on my dreams, they included various exercises which I practiced for the care of my body, and such cerebral amusements as tracing hieroglyphs, memorizing the names of the two hundred and ninety-six Popes and Anti-Popes, and corresponding with a Bolivian mathematician on a logical problem on which I had been at work for several years.

The dream-life which was never absent from my thoughts subsided into curious variations on my nights with my mistress—no new dream yet, but a lengthy entr'acte as it were. I found that the excitement of my dreams surpassed that of my meetings with Frau Anders. It was never she who aroused my sexual feelings. Such feelings were born in me and perished in her. She was the vessel in which I deposited the substance of my dreams. But this did not make her any less important to me. To me she was unique among women. The puzzles and variations in erotic technique proposed by my dreams were solved on her body—on hers, and on no other. This I took as a good omen for our affair, which, however, I had determined would last no longer than it should.

When, finally, the energy of my dreaming was attenuated and it occurred to me to break off our connection, I found myself with less energy to be cruel than I had counted on. I even contemplated leaving the city without telling her. Luckily, just at this time, Frau Anders' husband returned from one of his long business trips abroad and—to her surprise—asked her to accompany him on the next. She urged me to forbid her to go. This was the first of her infidelities, she told me, in which she wanted to tell her husband everything. But I, pleading respect for her reputation and comforts, declined to rescue her permanently from her conjugal bonds.

Thus I was entirely at liberty in my adopted city, for the first time in six months. I returned to the seduction of Frau Anders in my dreams, until one night a new dream revolved into my view.

FOUR

In the dream I was standing in the cobblestone courtyard of some building. It was noon, and the sun was hot. Two men, wearing long pants and naked to the waist, were violently locked together. At times they seemed to be fighting; then it seemed to be a wrestling match. I wanted it to be a wrestling match, even though there were no spectators other than myself. And I felt encouraged in believing this by the fact that the two men were of equal strength; neither could force the other to the ground.

To insure that this was sport and not private violence I decided to wager some money on one of the wrestlers, the one who looked somewhat like my brother. But I couldn't find a booth where I could place my bet. Then both men suddenly fell. I was frightened. I suspected that this had been a personal fight, even a fight to the death. There were several other spectators now. One of them, a child, nudged the prostrate men with a stick. She poked her stick in the face of the one who resembled my brother. Both men, pale and motionless, had their eyes closed.

I realized that I knew a secret of which the other spectators were ignorant and tried to compose my face, lest I give the secret away. The effort made my face very warm, and I decided I was doing myself an injury by being so discreet. I wanted to tell my secret to another person, and looked about for someone I knew. I recognized the man in the black bathing suit, and it seemed to me that he was my friend. Reassured, I smiled and beckoned to him. He approached me, but made no gesture of salutation. But he was only pretending not to know me.

"The outcome remains quite clear," I whispered into his ear. I felt as if we were fellow conspirators. Although his head was turned away from me, I was sure he was listening.

"That's because they are dead," he said.

"The contest was unfair," I replied. There was an idea which I was struggling to express. "At least one of them must be alive. The other may or may not be dead, as he chooses."

He turned and put his face next to mine. "In a moment," he shouted, "I am going to dispose of the bodies."

"Don't shout," I answered boldly. "Shouting has never made me understand anything."

He yawned in my face. I reflected that I had no right to demand courtesy from this man, and should have been grateful that he did not abuse me.

He had something with him that looked like a large drum. He slit open the skin of this drum with a knife. Then he lifted the wrestlers one at a time and stuffed them into the drum, hoisted the drum on his back, and carried it out of the courtyard. I watched his efforts, and saw that the load was much too heavy for one man, lame at that. But I determined to let him labor alone since he would not acknowledge me.

When he was gone, however, I regretted not offering to assist him. I felt I had been harsh and spiteful. The fault swelled to the size of a sin, and I wanted to be absolved of it. No sooner had I entertained this thought than I was entering a small building with bronze doors and a low roof. I was surprised at how easy it was to find a church. Inside, I looked about for the man in the black bathing suit, in order to apologize to him. I could not find him.

I went to a side altar, with the intention of lighting a candle. On the altar there was a statue of the Virgin, and astride or rather straddling the shoulders of the Virgin sat a priest who was nodding gravely and blessing the people who passed in the aisle with a pink flower he held in one hand. I noticed the flower particularly because ever since I entered the building I had been aware of a strong sweetish odor, and I now supposed that the smell came from the flower. Then I saw that it could not, because the flower was artificial, made of alabaster. More curious than ever, I left the altar and went looking, without success, for the choir boys swinging their brass incense-holders. It then occurred to me that the smell was not provided for the pleasure of the worshippers but to conceal a bad odor which I could not yet detect. I decided to remain in the church until I discovered where the smell came from. I should have liked to sit quietly in a pew, but I felt that I should be more useful to the church if I moved around and acquainted myself with the monuments and statues, for I dimly remembered that this was an ancient building and contained much that was worth seeing for anyone, like myself, who is interested in architecture.

At some point later in the dream, I discovered that the smell came from the central sanctuary where, lying in state, was the corpse of a bearded man wearing a gold crown. People milled about the coffin and bent down to kiss the king's nostrils. This is why there was no one to watch the wrestlers, I thought. I approached the coffin respectfully, and tried to imitate the others. But when I bent over, I was felled by a great weight in my body. As I rolled and turned on the floor, unable to get up, an old man sternly admonished me. "There is a room for that sort of thing," he said. He conferred with the others briefly. "Put him in the room," another said, "before he does it here."

I thought they meant they were going to take me to the confessional.

Someone else said, "Put him in the chair." I was seized forcibly and seated in a black electric chair such as I had seen in American gangster films. With horror I realized this was not for a confession. But while I waited, trembling, for the switch to be thrown, the chair seemed to rise with me in it. I dared to look down and saw that the chair was still bolted to the floor. It was I alone who was soaring, rising higher and higher in what was now an immense cathedral with rose and blue windows. I was rising toward an opening in the vault still far above me, buoyed up by a dense wet substance which lapped about my face.

"It's only a dream," I called to those below me, who were now tiny black figures on the great cruciform stone floor. "I'm having a religious dream." I rose still higher until, just as I had pierced the cathedral roof, I awoke.

This dream, arriving as I reposed from my calculated felicity with Frau Anders, informed me that I was not to have rest also from my labors of investigation. In certain ways, I found the dream puzzling. This new dream, perhaps because it was the most recent, seemed to offer matter more challenging than the torments and delights of what I had interpreted as my erotic dreams of the past year. Was not my first dream, "the dream of the two rooms," about two species of love and domination, in both the masculine and the feminine styles? And did not my second dream, "the dream of the unconventional party," furnish me with a direction for my erotic life in the person of Frau Anders? But what did this third dream—the wrestlers, my old friend the bather, the king, the cathedral, the ascent— dictate for me to do?

Certainly, this dream was no less enigmatic than its predecessors, despite the odd fact of my having shouted into the dream, as it were, an interpretation before I awoke. This could not be what the dream really meant, but must be interpreted along with what else lay within the brackets of the dream.

Still, the remark could not be denied a certain privileged position in the order of dream thoughts. Besides it was, so clearly, "a religious dream," the dream of a devout person, lame with guilt, hungering for absolution.

I did not wish to deny an obvious erotic sense to all the dreams. But in this dream, the sexual was joined with more abstract longings for union and penetration. The sexual was acted out with scenes of death and with palpable images of excrement—for how else could I interpret that hidden smell, and that repulsive substance which enveloped me at the close of the dream? A distasteful conjunction, I admit! But while I shall try to put the matter decorously in order to spare the reader any undue embarrassment, it is necessary to write unsparingly and truthfully.

The widening thematic range of my dreams plunged me into a new melancholy. The enterprise which I had undertaken was, I now saw, enormous. You understand, my dismay did not arise from the fact that I barely recognized the oppressed principal actor in the dreams as myself. I was not looking for my dreams to interpret my life, but rather for my life to interpret my dreams. But I now saw this was a more formidable undertaking than I had anticipated. I had acted on my dreams, well and good. But the mere execution of the dream images, the process whereby I inscribed them on my life, was not enough. Perhaps, I thought, the dreams not only instructed me to do something —like seduce a woman; but also to do nothing—except concentrate on purging myself of some impurity, which might be the dreams themselves. I could no longer single out the erotic in my interpretation and acting-out of the dreams.

Here I took my cue from the setting of this latest dream. After all, where throughout history have the indescribable longings and anxieties of man been invested? Surely not in the communion of bodies, but in the exaltations of the spirit. No doubt the first religious men were as perplexed as I, since they knew no name for what they experienced.

It was in this manner that I conquered the sentiment that my dreams had marked and defiled my daytime life. I concluded that my dreams, being susceptible to many interpretations, were no less susceptible to the religious one: namely, that something which one might, for want of a better name, call religious had erupted within me. This did not in itself afford me pleasure, for I am not a credulous person nor given to postponing my happiness to another world. Neither do I crave the dubious prestige of the name "religion" to make my spiritual efforts respectable in my own eyes. Nevertheless I know that I am a person capable of devoutness. Yes, definitely, I would say that, in certain circumstances, I enjoy nothing better than being devout.

I have said that my first reaction to the dream was melancholy. Further reflections promptly turned my melancholy to thoughtfulness, and I experienced a marvellous calm. One of my reflections was about thoughtfulness itself: I realized that I had never really thought except when I wrote or talked. Now I resolved to become more silent, without becoming morose. This was easier without Frau Anders about; she had the habit of interrupting my silences to ask me what I was thinking. Being at times a sociable person, however, I continued to frequent my café and attended some parties, but certain friends, heirs to the solicitousness of Frau Anders, remarked the difference and judged that I was again unhappy.

One of my friends, the priest who conducted the radio program, undertook to cure my melancholy by taking me on long walks in the famous woods which lie on the outskirts of the city. He was a kindly alert man whose conversation I esteemed, for the clergy in my country is better educated than it used to be. (There is always something touching in the tardy efforts toward self-improvement of an institution or a feeling in decline.) I accepted his ministrations with interest, because of the recent turning of my thoughts toward religious schemes. What he told me, after a series of talks, was that my dreams represented the revolt of my conscience against a religious vocation which I had suppressed.

"I do not mean," said the good Father Trissotin, "that I believe you should aspire toward the priesthood." I blushed and assured him that I would not take his words other than as he meant them.

"What I mean," he continued, obviously relieved, "is that you should go to confession. Our talks are only a preparation for that step, for which you already yearn in your dreams. It is there that you will find yourself purged."

I must explain that I have always respected the church which baptized me and which only a million and a half citizens of my country disavow to the extent of belonging to another religious community. There is no doubt that the church has performed much good, and even today when I see the little priests hurrying through the city on motorcycles, their black cassocks trailing in the wind, I generally pause to watch them. They cannot harm those souls in distress to whom they minister: the dying; the pious housemaids; the pregnant girls, abandoned and remorseful; the criminal, the insane, the intolerant. I have a congenital susceptibility, some might call it a weakness, for those who profess the cure of souls.

Also I enjoy religion aesthetically. As my dream indicates, I am attracted by the slow ceremonies of the cathedral. I respond to incense, stained glass, genuflection. I like the way the Spanish kiss their thumbs after making the sign of the cross. In short, I welcome gestures which are repeated. I suppose that part of the reason my dreams intrigued me was that every dream was a recurrent dream. Thus, every gesture in the dream gained the status of a ritual.

But I do not see how one gesture can suppress another. And I did not want to be appeased.

"Confess rather than express, my son." Father Trissotin's rosy face was set in a look of concern.

I have already said that I was prepared to admit that something religious had erupted within me. But I did not like Father Trissotin's well-meaning assumption that my dreams were something of which I would necessarily want to rid myself. However, I thought it best to keep this objection to myself, and decided to challenge my friend on the appropriateness and efficacy of the confessional.

"Do you really think," I said finally, "that a confession would rid me of my dreams?"

I did not intend to take up with him the question of the value of my dreams. But he seemed to anticipate my inward reservation. "I believe," he said, not at all portentously, "that you are possessed, if not by God, then by the devil. You have freely admitted to me the perverse and arbitrary impulses by which you have lately been governed, and you attribute these to your dreams. But you cannot simply hold your dreams responsible. What if they are sent by the devil? It is your duty to combat them, not yield to them."

When I did not reply immediately, I could see that he took my silence as a good omen for the success of his counsel. "All dreams," he added gently, "are spiritual messages."

"Perhaps these dreams are a message," I said. "I have often thought so myself. But I believe they are a message from one part of myself to another." Father Trissotin shook his head disapprovingly. I continued: "How dare I *not* answer the sender of these messages with my own body? I say my body, since the dreams are grossly, indecently preoccupied with the fate of my body. How dare I employ an intermediary instead? Especially the one you propose, a priest, someone trained in the arts of neglecting the body."

"Don't trust your own clarity," he said. "The body is more mysterious than you think."

I was silent again. It would have been ungracious of me to challenge Father Trissotin on these grounds, his vocational disavowal of his own body giving him immunity from embarrassing rejoinders. Though he might proselytize in intimate libertine circles, like Frau Anders', as well as over the radio to the mass of his countrymen, most of whom cared far more for the outcome of the annual bicycle race than for the salvation of their souls, he risked nothing. He always spoke across the unbesiegeable moat of his own chastity.

"You have been given a message which you cannot read," he continued with marvellous confidence. "If you were illiterate, you would not hesitate to appoint a scribe to conduct your correspondence."

"Ah," I answered, "in such a case it would be I still who dictated the letters. But when I accept the advice of priests, I accept a form letter. And while I admit my dreams may not be as original as they seem to me, I cannot yet give up the idea that an answer that is different, that is mine alone, is expected of me."

With that Father Trissotin looked at me with pity, and said: "You are being naive. The illiterate peasant never knows if the scribe really puts down his words exactly as he dictates them. It must often happen that the scribe thinks he knows better than his client. He has, after all, more experience in anticipating the reactions of those who read letters." He went on: "You are just such an illiterate in spiritual transactions, and the priest an experienced scribe. All letters are form letters, are they not? Letters of hope, of love, of spite, of hypocritical solicitude. . . . Why not seek out the most expert form your message can take, since your purpose is not just to be understood but to have a certain effect on the person receiving your letter?"

"Perhaps," I replied, "I do not want to have any effect at all." I could not restrain myself from explaining to him. "You assume, Father, that I wish to rid myself of the dreams, and you recommend to me the agency of the confessional for this purpose. But, no! What I want, if anything, is to rid my dreams of me."

He seemed almost defeated by my obstinacy for he delivered, in a troubled tone, a most impersonal answer. "God gave you your soul to be saved."

I would not permit this evasion. "Father, let me continue my explanation," I said, directing my steps to a bench by the fountain. We sat in a gloomy truce-like silence for a moment and watched the children playing. Then I roused myself and said, "What I mean is this. I see the confessional as a devious means to answer a message which comes from myself. It is the long way around, like stepping out of one's front door onto the highway to reach the back door. Or going to the airport to hire a plane to travel from the attic to the basement." He stared with displeasure. I went on: "It's not the distance, you understand, which I object to in these maneuvers. For in an oddly designed house, it could indeed be very far from the front door to the back door, from the attic to the basement. But why go out of the house?"

Hearing my own words I doubted my ability to convince Father Trissotin, for I have observed that the most direct path for one person appears intolerably roundabout to another.

"To choose a priest to answer my own message, seems to me. . . ." I paused, not wishing to be indelicate, "it reminds me—if you will permit my frankness, Father—of the not entirely rational conventions of sexuality. I mean," I concluded, somewhat anti-climactically, "that I cannot altogether see the reason for coupling when anyone can procure for himself an equally intense and purer pleasure alone."

With that he was, after all, shocked, and recalled an appointment with his bishop or with someone at the radio station, I do not remember. The afternoon was almost over, but I sat for a while in the park, thinking of what we had said.

Perhaps I should have recounted some of my earlier meetings in the park with Father Trissotin; but this to me is the most interesting because it was the least doctrinal. In earlier sessions, Father Trissotin had assumed I needed theological instruction, and had expounded the claims and glories of the Church. He had even given me a rosary, which I always took with me when we had an appointment, but otherwise kept in a drawer with my cuff links. For all my good will, however, I had not listened too patiently to Father Trissotin. I did not believe in his form letter, nor understand how he could believe in it. Which form? The proliferation of religions throughout the world irritates me. How can one worship the divine in so many postures? While Buddha reclines on his side on one elbow, Christ strains at the cross. They cancel out each other.

While these thoughts were wrestling in my mind, I was watching a little girl playing with a large rubber ball. Ever since I have been myself no longer a child, I have enjoyed the company of children. I felt it would relieve me to talk with a child, and since this one was nearest to hand, I began to watch her movements more attentively. When the child's ball rolled down the pathway a good distance away from her nurse and she toddled after it, I got up and followed her.

I shall not insult my reader's character by reassuring him as to the purity of my motives. For the fact was that I did not know what I would say to the child or do with her.

She was a pretty child in a pink frock, about four years old. I walked behind her in order to watch her run. When she reached her ball, she hugged and talked to it. But again it slipped out of the grasp of her short plump arms and rolled away. This time I went ahead of her and picked up the ball.

"It's mine!"

"I know," I replied. "What do you think I'm going to do with it?"

"Give it back to me?" she said doubtfully.

"Don't cry, little one. Of course I shall give it back to you. But what do you suppose I shall do with it first?"

"Eat it."

"And then?"

She giggled. I was delighted. I longed to toss my fantasies at her, like the ball, and hear them bounce back at me in her childish accents. But I did not want her to take the ball from me, as she was at that moment trying to do.

"No, no. Not yet." I held it out of her reach. "Tell me, little one, what is the first thing you remember?"

"I want my ball."

"Do you remember anything?"

"Once I went to the zoo."

"Anything else?"

"I remember my name. Do you want to know what it is?"

"No."

"I remember where I live, too. Do you want to know that?"

"Do you remember your mother?"

She laughed heartily. "Silly! How can I? She's at home!"

"I don't remember my mother, either," I said.

"Is she at home?"

"No, she's dead."

"I know lots of dead people," the child replied. "Millions. Millions and millions. Millions of them."

"Where are they?"

"My father keeps them in his office. He goes every day to talk to them."

"Is he a doctor, your father?"

"No, he makes money. That's what he does."

"Does your mother often scold you?"

"No. Only my nurse. She scolds me when I go away from the bench."

"Would you like your ball back?"

"Aren't you going to eat it? Is it too big?"

I wanted to please the child, so I said, "No, I breakfast on bigger things than this every day. I eat tigers and acrobats and doorknobs. This morning I ate a black chair."

It was better than any confessional to see her laugh. "Did you? I don't believe it. You're pretending."

"No, I swear. It's true. Would you really like me to eat your ball?"

"Can I have it back then?"

"Perhaps. Look." I took out my pocketknife and made a small incision in the fleshy rubber of the ball. The ball crumpled in my hand. Then I crammed the rubber in my mouth and made the motions of chewing.

"Oh, you did! You did! Let's tell the nurse."

"No, you must go now." I turned so she could not see me, and spit the rubber into my hand.

"I want to eat the ball, too."

"No, you must get another one."

"Is the ball dead? Did you kill it with your knife?"

"No, the ball is inside me. It will take a long time for it to come out, so you must get another in the meantime. But I have a present for you." I saw the nurse looking anxiously up and down an adjacent path.

"A present!"

"Yes, it's a rosary. A good priest gave it to me. And now you can pray for your ball." I put it into her hands. She took it hesitantly, and then smiled when she looked at it more closely.

"I think I would like to have my ball, too."

"Good-bye, little one."

"The rosary is black," she said in a puzzled tone.

"Good-bye, little one." And I left her, in the middle of the path, peering between the beads.

FIVE

I came to spend more time with Jean-Jacques. He seemed to understand better than others what preoccupied me. But I did not encourage him to interpret my dreams. He had his life, which I assumed to be suitable for him; I had mine. To keep myself alert to his influence, I began a notebook in which I recorded some of our meetings and conversations. Here are several entries.

"May 21. It is Jean-Jacques' cheerfulness that attracts me most to him. He tells me, 'I hate plots that illustrate the death of love, the failure of talent, the mediocrity of society.' This refusal to be dreary is admirable. Why, for instance, are there so many novels about parents—the giants of our childhood who cut off our feet and shove us, limping, into the world? He is right: the writer may celebrate or mock, he must not stare or whine. I am rereading his first two novels, and I find them very good, although a little over-written. The one about the boxer is especially fine. He has made something sublime out of the agonies of the arena."

"May 23. No wonder Jean-Jacques is so prolific; he writes five or six hours a day, and rewrites very little; that baroque style of his dictates itself to him in the first draft, he tells me. But why does he never draw upon his exploits of the night as the subject for a novel? Not out of prudence. I have never known anyone so careless of his reputation. . . . I think I understand this seemingly uncharacteristic reticence. By keeping the day and night separate, his acts are not hectic. His life is not dismembered, because he has found the seams in a piece of whole cloth and calmly unstitched them. Thus I find all his acts mysterious and graceful. . . . I, too, want my life not to be dismembered. But I am not willing to separate the day from the night. 'You wish to unify,' Jean-Jacques says to me. 'I practice the arts of dissociation.' "

"July 13. I am methodical, secretive, honest. Jean-Jacques is lavish, indiscreet, dishonest. This contrast is the basis of our friendship."

"August 4. I am annoyed with Jean-Jacques for bothering to tell me I am not a writer, and inform him that I have never thought that I was. But his reasons for thinking this of me are not the obvious ones. You can't write, he says, because you are a born specialist, the sort of person who can do only one thing. Writing is not that thing, he concludes. Is it dreaming? I ask, somewhat facetiously. He does not reply, he only smiles."

These are several journal entries of that period. Although I realized that, in Frau Anders' absence, I should not neglect my sexual needs, the pleasures of spectatorship came to interest me more than my own performance. From spending only my late afternoons with Jean-Jacques, I began to accompany him on his nightly rounds. It was a mild spring and a voluptuous summer.

We would meet at his café at aperitif time. He would have just emerged from his regimen of writing, and always greeted me with a vacant and distracted look. I soon understood that this merely signified the slow return of his attention from its lunar voyage of withdrawal. By the second vermouth he would be chatting gaily about old furniture or the opera, or I would be leading him into the maze of my latest reflection about my dreams.

When his energies had returned, we would leave the café and go to his hotel. Jean-Jacques was permanently and comfortably installed in a large, atelier-sized room on the top floor. For a while I liked just to sit on the bed and watch him shave and dress. He was very conscious of clothes, perhaps because he was plain-faced, lean, and even a little nondescript. "I have the face of a stock broker," I once heard him mutter to his image in the mirror. The choice of his apparel for the evening was as carefully considered as if he were an actor making-up in his dressing room, which in a way he was. Sometimes he felt boisterous, and assembled a real costume, such as the red kerchief, striped shirt, and tight black pants of an *apache*. Generally the choices were more delicate—it was a question of the slimness of the pants; leather jacket or turtleneck sweater, rings, military or dandyish; the boots or the pointed shoes.

Later, when the fascination of his dressing had become more familiar to me, I used to amuse myself looking among the objects in his room. Jean-Jacques was a collector. On tables, and on the floor, under the bed and in corners of the room, were boxes of strange treasure. In one box were hundreds of turn-of-the-century picture postcards of music hall dancers. There were files of newspaper clippings about prize-fighters and wrestlers, autographed photos of film stars, and confidential police reports (I never found out how he got hold of these) on cases of armed robbery committed in the capital in the last twenty years. In other boxes there were fringed scarves, fans, seashells, feather boas, cheap jewelry, miscellaneous carved chessmen, wigs. It seemed that whenever I came he had installed something new in his room—another Epinal print, a

Boy Scout hat, an *art nouveau* mirror with a snake design, a beaded lamp, a piece of cemetery statuary, a circus poster, a set of marionettes representing Bluebeard and eight wives, a white-and-green wool rug with the shape and design of an American dollar bill. When I tired of looking and touching, he would play records for me: an aria from an obscure melo-dramatic opera of the last century, or an old java. I did not share these enthusiasms. Since I knew Jean-Jacques to have the most scrupulous judgment in all the arts, his love of these exaggerated, trivial, and vulgar artifacts was a mystery to me. "My dear Hippolyte," he would say, "you will never under-stand, but sometime I will explain it to you anyway." I do not think of myself as a solemn person, but Jean-Jacques made me feel so.

When he had finished dressing we would go down, past the deaf old concierge who never failed to shout some cheerless obscene compliment to Jean-Jacques. Once in the street, Jean-Jacques walked stealthily but steadily, and I followed at a distance. Usually he had to wait no more than an half-hour before someone, silently, joined him. If he were concerned solely for his own pleasure, it might be a truck-driver, an immaculate Italian business man, an Arab, or a student; the main requirement was that his partner be evidently manly in his appearance and tastes. For this purpose, he could venture almost anywhere in the city and might remain with whomever he found for the entire evening. But if he were out to be paid, he was confined to certain neighborhoods and cafés where he would find the confirmed homosexuals, invariably middle-aged or elderly, to whom he appealed as a rough type, and who would be eager to pay him for some minutes of his virile company. He and his companion would merely go off to the *quais* and disappear beneath a bridge; or if the financial prospect were more promising Jean-Jacques would take the man to his own room, and would not return to the route he patrolled until an hour or two later.

I therefore cannot speak with much knowledge of what Jean-Jacques did for his own pleasures; on these excursions, understandably, he went alone. But on the several nights a week which he would set aside for business, I would often accompany him through the entire evening. While he was off with a client I would wait for him in various cafés which were the specialized territory of the male prostitute—of the delicate-featured young boys, the toughs and bandits like Jean-Jacques, and the transvestites. Gradually I, too, became known and came to sit at tables of the waiting, gossiping sisterhood of men, the peroxided and beringed friends of my friend. They did not talk to me much, although their regard was always amiable; polite conversation in that circle, conversation that was not about their vocation, was unthinkable. Their sentences were expletive, never expository. They had no opinions. They knew only two emotions, jealousy and love, and their talk, which was often spiteful, was only of beauty. *Folles de nuit*, madwomen of the nights, was what they jokingly called themselves. A genuine whore is rare; most whores are businessmen. But these whores really loved their clients. They had gone too far in demonstrating their love for the bodies of their own sex to feel the detachment which a female prostitute customarily feels toward men. They were so proud of their ability to give pleasure that they did not allow themselves to feel rejected when, after making love, their clients reviled them.

When I was not sitting in such cafés the nights of that summer I too walked the streets—observing further how men employ themselves for their pleasure. I frequented the other public stations of this transient lust, where I learned to recognize the more disguised homosexuals who sought each other in the urinals and the back rows of cinemas. I cannot think of a more perfect example of understanding without words than these faultless encounters. Not a word was exchanged, but some mysterious chemistry of attraction drew them together to grasp each other in public places—they never seemed to make a mistake—and to consummate the sexual act with such swiftness that it was as if each man worked singly at a task which could only be performed alone, the other invisibly assisting.

Once I came upon such a scene already in process, among a number of men in a *pissoir*. There was perfect silence. A tall Arab in an ill-fitting blue suit had seized the member of the man urinating beside him. That man seized that of his neighbor, and so on down a line of men, none of them in the least effeminate-looking, all responding as though to a prearranged signal. It was like a dream, in that the strange had become easy, the willed merely necessary. And then, as quickly, the line was broken, the dancers abandoned the rhythm; it was over and the men walked out, hitching up their pants.

Another time, in a Metro lavatory, I witnessed the scene from the beginning. It started with jokes, and a fight between an African and a dark well-dressed man over an insult which I had not heard. They began to grapple with each other and others gathered around shouting words of encouragement, until the fight—which I soon realized was a delicate pretext—spread to the spectators and each man was pushing and shoving his neighbor, calling out obscene insults. One cried, "You wouldn't dare!" and another, "I challenge you to repeat that outside!" and another, "Let me out of here!" But no one left. The shoving and shouting continued at the same level—the African and the businessman were already on their knees—and I joined in, taking care neither to exceed nor to fall short of my neighbors in vehemence. I wondered why the shouting prolonged itself since it was so repetitive, and they seemed to be growing less rather than more angry. Then another man dropped to his knees, then another. Now the spirit of the encounter had taken over, flushing away the dark uncertain scraps of each man's personality. Silence came to each in turn, like the serial extinguishing of candles. And on the cold tile floor the act of love was performed in haste but dexterously, with economy and professionalism.

When I began to acompany my friend the writer, I had no opinions about his activities, and even if I had felt licensed to urge him to a less perverse and promiscuous life, I would have held my tongue. Jean-Jacques, however, would not allow my silence. Though I did not attack him, he was resolute and ingenious in his own defense, or rather the defense of the pleasures of disguises, secrecy, entrapments, and being-what-one-is-not.

Several times that summer, he tried to overturn my unspoken objections. "Don't be so solemn, Hippolyte. You are worse than a moralist." While I could not help regarding this world of illicit lust as a dream, skillful but also weighty and dangerous, he saw it simply as theatre. "Why should we all not exchange our masks—once a night, once a month, once a year?" he said. "The masks of one's job, one's class, one's citizenship, one's opinions. The masks of husband and wife, parent and child, master and slave. Even the masks of the body —male and female, ugly and beautiful, old and young. Most men, without resisting, put them on and wear them all their lives. But the men around you in this café do not. Homosexuality, you see, is a kind of playfulness with masks. Try it and you will see how it induces a welcome detachment from yourself."

But I did not want to be detached from myself, but rather in myself.

"What is a revolutionary act in our time?" he asked me, rhetorically, at another meeting. "To overturn a convention is like answering a question. He who asks a question already excludes so much that he may be said to give the answer at the same time. At least he marks off a zone, the zone of legitimate answers to his question. You understand?"

"Yes, I understand. But not what bearing it has—"

"Look, Hippolyte. You know how little audacity is required today to be unconventional. The sexual and social conventions of our time prescribe the homosexual parody."

I could not agree. "It takes courage to parody the normal," I said. "Courage and a great capacity for guilt. I don't see the humor in these proceedings that you do, my friend. Surely it would be easier for them—I exclude you, Jean-Jacques, because you're not like the others—if things were as you say."

"You're wrong," he replied. "The price is not as exacting as you think."

"Doesn't the transvestite who roams the streets yearn for his family whom he can no longer face because he has plucked his eyebrows?"

"Hippolyte," he said in an exasperated tone. "I am very angry that you speak of them—and exclude me. And thus you try to please me!"

"But you aren't like them, Jean-Jacques. You choose. They are obsessed."

"So much the worse for me," he said. "No," he continued, "to pretend one thing is only not to pretend something else. But to be obsessed is not to pretend at all. The sun does not play at rising every morning. Do you know why? Because the sun is obsessed with its tasks. All that we admire in nature under the name of order, and the basis of the confidence we repose in her regular movements, is obsession."

The idea struck me as true. "Then obsession, not virtue, is the only sensible ground for trust."

"Right," he said. "Which is why I trust you."

Then I thought, that is why I cannot trust you, Jean-Jacques. But this I did not say.

You see, even if I did not trust Jean-Jacques I honored and admired him as a mentor and companion in the search for the self. But so much of taste and habits of character separated us. Because he was absolutely committed to his work, writing, he could afford to be unreliable in every other way—and to ornament his life with games, strategies, and artifacts. These strange rites he practiced with himself were not mine.

"You and I are very much alike," he explained to me on another evening of that ambulatory summer.

I expressed surprise.

"Only," he continued, "you will not succeed and I will. I am prepared to carry out my character to the extreme—"

"So am I," I interrupted.

"I am prepared to carry out my character to the extreme, which is a variety of character. You know nothing of varying yourself. You wish your character to be concentrated and clear, but you will find that when you have boiled away the water you have reduced yourself to an acid that is too strong for your own nostrils, not to speak of the world's. You will burn away, while I—I am diluted through and through."

Of course I protested.

"I know," he went on, "that you think my life adventurous. How little you know of risk! You are the adventurer, the one taking risks, because you are not clear about what territory you are surveying, your body or your mind. If you mistake one for the other, you will stumble."

I listened intently. Although not a vain person, I enjoy hearing my friends talk about me.

"My life is bizarre but tractable," he went on. "Yours is too resolute and full of dangers. . . . It's well to be serious, but not to understand seriousness as making a demand on you."

"If you mean," I replied, "that I do not have your catholicity of taste, that is true."

"There are many demands," he said. "Seriousness is only

one of them. But I like you, Hippolyte," he added, smiling, and put his arm around me. "You have character, like an American temperance tract or the great unfinished cathedral in Barcelona. Everything you do is you. You are incapable of being otherwise. That is why I . . . collect you."

Whatever I wanted from Jean-Jacques, it was not for him to find me merely amusing. I suppose this was the first moment I resented him.

"I *want* to be myself, more than anyone else in the world," I declared firmly.

"And so you are, dear Hippolyte," he said, smiling and propelling me toward the door of the crowded café where we sat that August evening. And just to show me that he could act out of character, that he could surprise me as I could never surprise him, that night he took me home with him to bed.

This impromptu sexual encounter did not change our relationship. We parted as friends. But although the experiment was never repeated, I was dismayed at Jean-Jacques' flippancy and vowed to be more on guard against him.

I was never tempted to discuss Frau Anders with my friend, but then it is natural for me to be discreet. Jean-Jacques, however, was most indiscreet with me. He always had a new story to tell me about his latest conquest, or his latest enthusiasm. He discussed his sexual escapades—as well as his impoverished childhood, his boxing career, his thefts, everything except his writing—prodigally, without reserve; and I learned to my surprise that he was often impotent. Throughout these confidences I forebore remonstrating with him about his unnatural tastes and exaggerated life, for while I did not agree with Jean-Jacques' curious theory that homosexuality was both guilt and humor, revolt and convention, it has never been my aim to interfere with other people's happiness. This, you will remember, was one of the maxims I had decided upon early in my intellectual adventures. And Jean-Jacques seemed to me a happy man.

Perhaps though I should have guessed that his cynical virility was partly sham. There was something in Jean-Jacques' small eyes and high forehead, a look of ill health—but no, this was misleading. He was in perfect health. I, in contrast, have the look of good health that derives from a well-fed childhood, and the reliable body that makes the appearance true. The reader may have gathered that I do not experience difficulties of Jean-Jacques' sort, however bizarre the situation, though I would not be surprised to learn that I miss certain peaks of satisfaction in the course of my unruffled potency.

Neither have I ever suffered during long periods of sexual abstinence. In Frau Anders' absence, I busied myself with reading and correspondence, with an occasional participation in the life of Jean-Jacques' night, and in continued meditation on my dreams.

I made an inventory of my possessions. I had a modest acceptable wardrobe—nothing to pare away there. I thought of selling my books, but I had not freed myself from the habit of reading a good part of each day. The furniture was another matter. All but the most necessary furniture—a bed, a chest of drawers, bookshelves—I gave away to student friends. Even the chair went, for I could sit on the bed. I also disposed of the few paintings which I owned, and the flute which I had purchased after my first dream. Eventually I got rid of the bed, too, and slept on a mat which I rolled up and put in the closet in the daytime.

I was also concerned with the proper maintenance of my body, which I do not neglect and am never tempted to despise. Then I liked to take long walks, and found that any change of scene revived my too easily depleted energies. To supplement my walks, Jean-Jacques suggested a program of exercises of the type practiced in the Orient which I could do in my own rooms. The purpose of these exercises had nothing to do with the vain purpose of strengthening the body. They had nothing to do with the body, apart from the aim of reaching perfect control over it. They aimed, through the body, straight to the mind, to produce an alertness without content, a state of shimmering weightlessness. But it was mainly the idea of the exercises which attracted me; perhaps this is why I did not become proficient at them. I never did succeed in attaining control over my digestion and anal sphincter, so that I could vomit, excrete, and increte at will. Even after I stopped doing the exercises, however, I often imagined myself doing them, wearing a close-fitting bathing costume of black wool.

I did practice regularly one less strenuous exercise, of my own invention, in which I performed on an invisible electronic instrument. I sat very still, trying to find the right posture, the right disposition of my arms and legs—in order to touch all the invisible nodes and start the current flowing. Sometimes it was not an electronic instrument which I played but an impalpable wind instrument, such as a flute: then I had to search for where I was to put my mouth, where the stops were, and what to play.

A less successful expression of my concern for my body was with diet experiments. I knew that some religious sects forbid their members to eat sour, pungent, or spicy foods, and all meat and intoxicating drink. I decided to see if these rules applied to me. Some weeks I would eat nothing but rice and fruit, while for certain periods I would eat only the forbidden foods. In neither case did I notice any significant change in my body's sensations.

It then occurred to me that there was no reason to reproach myself for not doing all the exercises. After all, what is their function? The exercises are a method of eliminating thought, of devoting oneself to the utmost void. But was not this the purpose that was served by my meditation on my dreams?

The substitution was confirmed by what the exercise book, which Jean-Jacques lent me, recommends to the adept after the body is mastered: to be perfectly still, select a spot, and concentrate on it. This act of concentration is the real climax of the exercises. Concentration upon a particular spot rules out other thoughts; the mind is opened, and the light shines within. According to the exercise book, the concentration spot may be either a small, centrally placed part of one's own body or a small object in one's room. But was not this what I had been doing? I had something better than my nose or my navel, or a landscape on the wall. I had my dreams.

I now turned back to my dreams with a new demand. If I was to concentrate on my dreams as an analogue to fasting or exercising, I wanted them to be bare and taciturn. But in this I was disappointed; they were not laconic but full of conversations. I wondered what I might do to curb the loquacity of my dreams.

I dared to hope that one day my dreams would be altogether silent, as Jean-Jacques had once suggested. But for this large improvement, I felt I needed models. I found such a model in one of my favorite recreations, the temple of public dreams, the cinema. Films had already begun to talk at this time, but in out-of-the-way theatres I could still see old movies which were blessedly silent. The reading of medical books provided another model, in the chapters on aphasia. I wanted to emulate those who hear the voice, the sound of speech, but not the words; to an aphasiac, the words do not pronounce themselves. Though I was far from being able to put this into practice in my dreams, I came to understand that words coerce the feelings they attempt to embody. Words are not the proper vehicle for a general upheaval which destroys the old accumulation of feeling.

I suppose I could be considered a stubborn person, but my stubbornness is not superficial or ostentatious. It lies deep down, and behaves like deference and humility. At least I was not entirely literal-minded, the most common cause of stubbornness. If I were, I would not have continued to talk with my friends.

"Hippolyte, my dear," Jean-Jacques said to me one early evening, as we walked along a boulevard, "you have taken a vow to be absurd. Not just one vow, even. Many vows. You make vows like a greedy pauper buying recklessly on the installment plan. You're becoming more and more deeply in debt to yourself, and you are already bankrupt. What's the point of encumbering yourself so?"

I explained to Jean-Jacques how misleading was his metaphor. "I am not interested in buying or possessing anything," I said. "I am only interested in postures."

"Then I tell you to break your posture and dance. You look at yourself too much. That's the beginning of all absurdity. Look about you. The world is an interesting place."

I replied that I waited for my dreams to be explained to me.

"There are no explanations," he said, "just as there should be no vows and promises. To explain one thing is to make another thing—which only litters the world the more. What blank useless things your explanations will be when you finally settle on them!"

"But you, Jean-Jacques, your life is filled with useless passions and contradictory pleasures."

"It's not the same," he said. "Let me tell you a story which will explain. I know two pacifists. One is a man who believes that violence is wrong and acts in a way that accords with his beliefs. He has committed himself to being a pacifist, and so he is. He acts as a pacifist because he is one."

"And the other?"

"The other man abjures violence in all situations and therefore knows he is a pacifist. He is a pacifist because he acts like one. Do you see the difference?"

I did not, and it is never my habit to claim more understanding than I have.

"Look," he said. "I am a writer, yes? You know that I write every day. But I might not write tomorrow, from tomorrow on I might never write again. I am a writer because I write. I do not write because I am a writer."

I thought I understood then, and was disheartened by the distance which Jean-Jacques was putting between us. "But you said you were going to tell me a story," I said, pushing aside my melancholy thoughts. "You have only introduced two characters."

"Oh, the story is that the man who was a pacifist because he acted like one killed his wife yesterday. I was in court this afternoon when he was arraigned."

"And the other?"

He laughed. "That one, he's still a pacifist."

"And you find some . . . beauty . . . in the murderer who violated his principles?" Again I was baffled.

"No beauty. Only life. Don't you see, that man had never acted out of principles. He had taken no vows—and neither have I. Therefore nothing I do is useless or contradictory, as you thought a moment ago. It is you who are scattered and dismembered."

"Language does that to me," I murmured, half to myself. "My dreams are too talkative. Perhaps, if I didn't speak—"

"No, no, don't tamper with yourself any more than you have! It's much simpler. All you have to do is speak without trying to prolong the life of your words. For each word that is spoken, another word must die."

"Then I must learn to destroy."

"Not destroy either!" He was becoming exasperated with me.

"Life will take care of itself, unless it is diluted by too much life."

"I want to improve the mixture, but you tell me I am brewing an acid."

"Exactly," he said. "But I know it does you no good to tell you these things. Oh, I could tell you many things. . . . Listen, if I tell you something, will you promise not to seize on it as a candidate for your damned set of rules for yourself? Please."

I promised.

"One should always be submerged. But never in one thing." He paused. "Now, doesn't that sound like a rule?"

I acknowledged that it did.

"But it isn't, it needn't be. Imagine that submergence is not a rule or a vow on which you act, making you diversify your tastes and affections, but something you discover each day about yourself. Each day you—rather, I—discover that I am engrossed, submerged, in something or someone."

"But don't you think about what to do with your discoveries? Doesn't it happen that one overwhelms the rest and makes you want to change your life?"

"Why should I change my life?" he said. "Why can't I have everything I want? You see," he smiled roguishly, "how the bees come straight to my honey."

Was this another scene of seduction? Better to change the subject! "And I believe," I spoke slowly and solemnly, "that one should always be submerged. Like you, Jean-Jacques. But the rest cannot be decided. My temperament is more serious than yours, as I think we both agree, but do not caricature me as a man who decides everything while feeling nothing. I assure you I am a man of feeling." I thought tenderly of Frau Anders.

"No, little Hippolyte, you do not decide anything. You linger atrociously over your dreams. You let them influence your acts, only because you have decided to be the man-who-dreams. You are like a man who discovers a log across his path, and instead of pushing aside the log he calls in a construction company to widen the entire road.

"You will trip," he called after me as I left him.

SIX

"No," I said to myself one day. "It's very clear, I have not yet done with Frau Anders. I am waiting for her."

Frau Anders returned, strangely irritable, from accompanying her husband on the business trip which had evolved into a world tour and second honeymoon. I had never known her like this. "How dead the world is," she cried, "how dreary the people in it! I used to be so gay, so eager for life. Now I can barely lift my head from the pillow in the morning." I urged her to come away with me, to leave her husband and his money, her daughter, and her salon.

Perhaps it was the intensive company of her husband with whom she had spent so little time in the past years: she agreed. Frau Anders wanted a final interview with her husband so she could denounce him for driving her by his neglect into her various adulteries, but I forbade melodrama. She would not at first be dissuaded, but I pressed the point, for I realized that if we were to live together I had to assert my authority at once. Eventually and somewhat to my surprise—she was by nature an imperious woman—she agreed to this as well. We waited until her husband left on another trip. She told her daughter she was visiting a relative in the country where she was born. Our exit from the city was clandestine. No one except Jean-Jacques knew I accompanied her.

When we began to travel, I learned that my mistress had an unlimited capacity for boredom. She required continual entertainment, and took up cities like facial tissues, to be used once and thrown away. Her appetite for the exotic was insatiable, for her only purpose was to devour and to move on. I did my best to keep her amused, and at the same time worked at refashioning her idea of our relationship. Before her trip I had been, as I have already indicated, extremely frustrated. Frau Anders did not understand our affair, or my feeling for her. I knew that our relationship was more serious than she thought it was—and I regretted not being able to give pleasure when it cost me nothing but the truth, an easy premium. She must have been aware of my lack of romantic interest in her, but I wished she had been aware of how deeply, though impersonally, I felt her as the embodiment of my passionate relationship to my dreams. Through my willful match-making dreams, she had stirred me sexually as no woman had ever done before and, perhaps, since.

After some months of hasty expensive touring Frau Anders was sufficiently appeased and confident in me to rest for a while. We settled in a small island, where I spent the days near the boats talking with the fishermen and sponge-gatherers and swimming in the warm blue sea. I am very fond of islanders, who have a dignity which city-dwellers have lost and a cosmopolitanism that country-dwellers can never achieve. In the late afternoon, I returned to the house we had rented to take the waning sun with my mistress. In the evenings we sat by the dock, at one of the three cafés on the island, drinking absinthe and exchanging comments with the other foreign residents about the splendor of visiting yachts. Occasionally a policeman, wearing his cape and patent-leather cockade hat, strutted past, and the foreigners' conversation halted in order to admire his vanity. My senses became very acute on the island, with this reliable diet of sun, water, sex, and empty talk. My palate, for instance: the evening meal, soaked in olive oil and crushed garlic, came to have an exquisitely varied tang and odor. And my hearing, too. When at ten o'clock the island's electricity was turned off and kerosene lamps were lit, I could distinguish at a distance of many miles the sounds of the different bells, the heavier bell worn by the donkey from the shriller ring of the goat bell. At midnight, at the final tolling of the monastery bell from the hill behind the town, we would retire.

Away from the ingenious conversation of her guests in the capital, and discovering (and at first resisting) my own need for solitude, Frau Anders was openly bored. I suggested that she try to meditate, now that there was silence. The idea seemed to revive her spirits. But a few days later she confessed to me that the effort was not bearing fruit, and begged my leave to write. Reluctantly I agreed. I say reluctantly because I had little confidence in Frau Anders' mind, and considered that her best qualities—her sweetness, her stubbornness—flourished only because they had escaped her own detection. I feared that the effort of assuming the identity of a writer might deprive her of the scant realism about herself which she possessed. "No poetry," I said firmly. "Of course not," she replied, offended at my insinuation. "It is philosophy alone which claims my interest." She decided to communicate her insights to the world in the form of letters to her daughter who, at the time we left the capital, had discarded the elderly conductor for the middle-aged physicist.

"Dear Lucrezia," she would sigh on the veranda as we lay sunbathing. This was the signal that her epistolary efforts were about to resume. She would go indoors to take up her scented note paper and fountain pen with red ink, and set down several pages of her reflections. Upon finishing she would come outside again and read the letter aloud to me. Generally she refused all my sincere efforts at emendation.

"Dear Lucrezia," began one letter I remember. "Have you ever noticed that men feel called on to prove that they are men, while women do not have to assert their femininity in order to be counted as women? Do you know why this is so? Permit me, with a mother's and a woman's wisdom, to instruct you. To be a woman is to be as human beings were meant to be, full of love and serenity"—here she stroked my thick hair consolingly—"while to be a man is to attempt something unnatural, something that nature never intended. The task of being a man overstrains the machine"—I beg the reader to note how she confounded the natural and mechanical metaphors —"which is continually breaking down. The violence and rashness and schemes, all pathetic pretenses, by which a man persists in his vain enterprise of proving himself are known and esteemed as 'acts of manliness.' Without them he is not a man. Of course not!"

I will admit that if I am to be patronized as a man, I would rather it were by Jean-Jacques, whose haughtiness was at least tempered by the habit of irony that is second nature to all who play games with their sexual identity. Yet how could I be angry with Frau Anders? Her impudence was so naive, so endearing, so funny. And even if I had been angry I would have foreborne, thinking I had no right to judge this woman, having never known my own mother.

"Money, dear Lucrezia, clogs the spirit. False values begin with the worship of things. It is the same with reputation. What should we ask of society more than indifference, more than the freedom to pursue our pleasures?" This was the theme of another letter, which charmed me by its attempt to emulate my own indifference to possessions and reputation, which I had by this time often demonstrated to Frau Anders.

"Do not be afraid of your body, dear Lucrezia, the loveliest body in all the world. Dare to cast aside all false prudery and seize your pleasures as your wise mother counsels you. Oh, that mothers always instructed their daughters thus! What a garden the world would be, what a paradise. Do not let the dead hand of religion inhibit your sensations. Take, and it will be given to you. Disregard all those around you who measure themselves out, saving and spending! Dare to ask for more."

As she read these lines to me, I recalled that placid blonde girl whom her mother imagined as a great courtesan. I felt sorry for Lucrezia, and angry at her mother for continuing at a distance to play the procuress for her, if only with theories. But in this quick judgment I was subsequently to be corrected, for in later years I learned that Lucrezia had never been an innocent girl corrupted by a worldly mother. If anything, as Lucrezia later explained to me, it was the other way around: it was the daughter's libertine adolescence which had incited her more affectionate, innocent mother into her own career of erotic freedom. At the time about which I write, however, I saw Lucrezia only through the eyes of her mother's hectic admonitions, as before I had seen her through the elderly conductor's desire. I judged her accordingly, as the victim of both.

"There is only one communion, dear Lucrezia, the communion of instinct. For two thousand years instinct has labored under the pretentious dictates of the spirit, but I see emerging a new nakedness which will free us of the old chains of legality and convention. Our senses are numbed by the heavy weight of civilization. The dark people of the world know this wisdom; our pale race is finished. Man with his machines, his intellect, his science, his technology will give way before the intuition of women and the sensuous power and cruelty of black men."

But enough—I shall not tire the reader further. And I do not wish to give the impression that my feeling for Frau Anders was totally dissipated by our living together in greedy proximity.

In the privacy of the bedroom I tested her theories and found her more compliant than ever. I was a vigorous lover (despite my pale flesh) though, as I have said, I found her ardors too easily satisfied. I began to complicate our relationship. There was a young fisherman on the island who followed my mistress around like a lost dog, and I made my absence of jealousy very clear to her. Once she began to doubt her hold over me she doubled her solicitude, and I basked in the peace of the flesh if not of the spirit.

After one winter on the island, I proposed one day that we decamp. Soon we headed further south to the exotic lands Frau Anders professed to admire. Along the way there were many purchases of "native goods," but I wanted to travel as much as possible unencumbered by baggage, and suggested that they be mailed to my rooms back in the capital. I took these packages, elaborately wrapped by Frau Anders, to the post office myself, and sent them to a non-existent address.

One day we arrived in a city of Arabs, and on my urging prepared to settle there for a time. We toured the native quarter with a fourteen-year-old boy who had accosted us outside our hotel. It was in the annual month of abstinence prescribed by their religion, during which all believers are required to be sexually continent and to fast between sunrise and sunset. The boy watched without expression as we drank glasses of delicious mint tea in the sultan's palace (now open to tourists) and consumed the sticky honey cakes sold in the market place. Frau Anders tried, unsuccessfully, to coax the boy into eating them. To divert her attention from this impiety, I suggested that she get the boy to give us a prohibited pleasure, since he would not allow us to give him one. She asked him where we might procure some of the narcotics for which the city was noted. He looked cheerful for the first moment since we had engaged him, and led us to the native equivalent of a pharmacist's shop where we purchased two clay pipes and five packets of coarse green powder, which we took back to the hotel and sampled. I do not approve of narcotics—at least I have not known the need for them, never having appraised my senses as jaded—but I was curious to see what effect they would have on my mistress. Promptly she lay down on the bed and began to giggle. The sexual invitation was unmistakable. But I wanted to see something new and, seizing her by the arm, I told her that we must go out, that the city would be her lover tonight, that it would appear to us distended, in slow motion, more sensuous than any city she had known. She allowed me to raise her from the bed. After putting on her best frock and fussing over my tie, she went slowly, partly leaning on me to steady herself, to the elevator.

The sunset gun was sounding. We hired a carriage to take us to a shabby wooden building by the harbor which housed a bar where sailors and the more disreputable foreign tourists gathered. The barman, a tall well-built Arab, pressed my hand as I paid for our first round of drinks. The band played javas, flamenco, polkas; we sat at a table and watched the dancers. An hour later, the barman came over and introduced his wife to us. The woman, also Arab, but red-haired as well, put her arm around Frau Anders' bare shoulder and whispered something in her ear. I noted the sly embarrassed look which my mistress gave the woman, followed by a vacant, slightly smug glance directed at me.

"They have invited us to have a drink with them after the bar closes, dear Hippolyte. In their apartment above here. Isn't it delightful?"

I agreed that it was.

So after the noise ended and the last chalk sums written on the wooden surface of the barman's counter were added up and paid for or charged, we retired to the dark lodging upstairs. More drink was offered, which I refused. I did not assist in the seduction of Frau Anders by the barman's bulky pock-marked wife. It was an easy task. All I did was to give my consent at a crucial moment when my mistress wavered, out of fear, I suppose, that I might be jealous and reproach her with our adventure in the morning. The barman and I sat in the parlor and he recited some poetry to me, accompanying himself on the guitar. I could not give his performance my full attention, my ear being repeatedly diverted by the sounds that I thought came from the adjacent room. Perhaps I was a little jealous, after all.

Next morning—or rather, afternoon—Frau Anders was claiming a satisfaction with her adventure which I could see was less than sincere. As usual, in moments when she was aspiring to an emotion she did not altogether feel, she thought of her daughter. "Dear Lucrezia," she began at the narrow hotel writing table. "Love transcends all boundaries. I have long known, and encouraged you to discover for yourself, that the love between two persons of widely differing ages is no barrier to the mutual fulfillment of both. Let me add to that counsel, dearest child, that love knows no boundary of sex either. What is more beautiful than the love of two manly men, or the love of a refined woman of our northern climate for a slim dark girl of the pagan world? Each has much to teach the other. Do not be afraid of such leanings when you find them *genuinely* in your heart."

This letter I burned the next day while Frau Anders was out shopping. I wrote to Jean-Jacques, a letter full of tiresome dissection of my mistress' character, but thought better of it and tore it up. A letter for a letter. I repented of these fits of censoriousness to which I was subject still, despite all my good resolutions. Once again I tried to think of what was beneficent in Frau Anders' nature, to herself and to me.

That she was thriving, there could be no doubt. It even seemed to me that she was more attractive. For a woman of about forty (she would never tell me her exact age) she was good-looking in any case. Now she was blossoming under the southern sun and the heat of her narcotic fantasies, becoming artless in her dress and allowing me to see her without cosmetics. This did not make me desire her more, for I found her compliance to my every whim fatiguing. But I became more fond of her, as my passion depleted itself.

I thought I would give my passion one last chance by making her privy to my dreams. She listened in lazy silence, and after I had related several of my treasures, I regretted what I had done. "My darling Hippolyte," she exclaimed. "They are adorable. You are a poet of sex, you know. All your dreams are mystically sexual."

"I think," I said gloomily, "they're all dreams of shame."

"But you have nothing to be ashamed of, darling."

"Sometimes I am ashamed that I have these dreams," I replied. "Otherwise there is nothing I am ashamed of in my life."

"You see, darling!" she said affectionately.

"Prove to me that I may be proud of my dreams."

"How?"

"I shall tell you something," was my calm answer. "What would you think if I told you that every time I embrace you my care is not for your pleasure, or even for mine, but only for the dreams?"

"Fantasy is perfectly normal," she said, trying to conceal her hurt.

"And what if I told you that my share in the fantasy is no longer enough, that I need your conscious cooperation in my dreams, in order to go on loving you?"

She agreed to do what I asked of her—had I hoped otherwise?—and I showed her how to enact the scenes from my dreams when we made love. She played the man in the bathing suit, the woman in the second room, herself as the hostess of the unconventional party, the ballet dancer, the priest, the statue of the Virgin, the dead king—all the roles of my dreams. Our sexual life became a dream rehearsal, instead of a dream reprise. But for all my careful instructions and her willingness to please me, something did not work. It was her very willingness, I think; I needed an opponent rather than an accomplice, and Frau Anders did not act toward me with the certainty demanded by my dreams. This theatre of the bedroom did not satisfy me because, while my mistress lent me her body to carry out the varied roles of my fantasies, she no longer knew how to patronize me.

But can another person ever participate in one's dreams? Surely this was a foolish, youthful project on my own part, and I cannot blame Frau Anders for its failure. I have also thought since, in reflecting on these events, that in her own way Frau Anders did become engrossed in my preoccupation. It is true she suffered from it—knowing herself loved not as a person but as a *persona*—yet she did not defend herself by finding me ridiculous. She had come to love me too much. And the fact I was not afraid of her ridicule does not diminish the credit due her for transcending her storehouse of clichés to accept, if not understand, me. Fortunately I am not the kind of man who fears ridicule, at least outside my mysterious dreams; but I know enough of the world to recognize it.

Since she had consented to take my dreams seriously, I thought it only just to repay her in kind. But I must confess that I could not match her naive seriousness; my own efforts to convert her fantasies into deeds made me laugh sometimes. I cannot excuse the morbid levity that possessed me then. You must understand that I did not mean to be cruel, though my acts might be so interpreted.

We began, largely at the initiative of Frau Anders, to spend our evenings in the native quarter. It was now summer, and even an afternoon at the wide handsome beaches which adorned the city did not keep us cool through the evening. Since my mistress dispensed money lavishly at bars and cafés, we were always warmly received. She continued to occupy her days with the erotic good-naturedness induced by kif and with her exuberant letters to Lucrezia, who was now having an affair with the Negro ballet dancer, and presiding over her mother's salon with a success she only modestly hinted at in her own letters. Frau Anders was not that out of touch that she was incapable of being piqued at the news, and it seemed to make her restless and occasionally irritable.

I decided it would be good for her to taste more fully the exotic passions she rhapsodized over. There was a merchant who accosted me one evening as I was returning to the hotel with a new purchase of kif.

"Your wife, monsieur?" he began. "My son has greatly admired her. He will not touch a morsel of food."

"My wife would be delighted," I said somewhat nervously. The man's candor—a quality which I admire above all others —disarmed me, but his utter lack of ceremony suggested an unseemly impatience which hinted at violence should his wish be thwarted.

"How much?" he said.

"Sixteen thousand francs," I said, having no idea of an appropriate figure. The reader must think of the value of the franc as it was thirty years ago.

"Oh, no, monsieur," he replied, backing away and gesticulating eloquently. "That is too much, much too much. You Europeans set too high a value on your women. And besides, I make no commitment as to how long my son wishes to enjoy the company of your wife."

I decided it was well to adopt the firmest tone, since it was impossible not to bargain with these people. "I must tell you," I said, "that in exactly one week I intend to leave this city to return to my country. Should I depart without my wife, I shall count the eight thousand francs which you shall pay me tonight, when my wife and I visit your house, as a down payment on the balance of eight thousand which you shall pay me one week from today."

He drew me into a white doorway. "Five thousand now—and —perhaps—if all goes well—another five thousand in a week."

"Seven thousand now, and the same—if all goes well," I replied, pulling my arm from his grasp.

We settled at seven thousand that night, and six thousand in a week. It seemed to me fair that a week or less with my mistress should be more expensive, being less tiresome, than the indefinite purchase of her person. Nevertheless I protested gallantly that her worth was far greater than this insignificant sum.

"Assure me that you will make your son promise not to hurt her."

"I promise," he said genially.

It seemed to me obvious at the time that there was no son at all. My merchant friend was merely being gallant himself; seeing my attractive but aging mistress in the company of a reasonably good-looking young man, he wished to assure me that she would not be making a disadvantageous exchange. I, however, thought it improbable that a young Arab would desire an expensive middle-aged European woman, no matter how earnestly his dark flesh yearned to triumph over white. I assumed, then, that the stout greying merchant wanted her for himself. Why was I so sure? The month of abstinence being over, who knows what strange fantasies demanded to be executed. I already knew well there is no predicting sexual tastes: had I not wanted Frau Anders myself? Had she not proved attractive to as unlikely a person as the barman's wife? So it was that on the boat home I decided that it was a virile white-toothed Arab youth who desired Frau Anders, and that she had yielded with joy, relieved to be rid of her tiresome Hippolyte with his dreams and dissatisfactions. At least I hoped so. I did not like to think that there might have been violence and terror and rape and mutilation of that ever-hopeful body.

When she did not return to our city immediately after my own return, I liked to think that she was happy—there is later evidence for this—and that she learned the truth of the brash sentiments in her letters to Lucrezia. For nothing that she wrote was untrue. But Frau Anders had the ability to make truths untrue when she said them. Her letters were rhetoric; I had enabled her to act.

Perfumed and in ignorance of her destiny, I delivered her to the merchant's door. She stepped in before me, and the door closed silently behind her. I wondered if this would prove a lesson to her as to the true worth of those ceremonial courtesies to women which falsify the relationships of European men and women. If men preceded women through doorways, or if there were no order of precedence, it would not have been so simple.

I waited on the cobblestoned street before the house. In a half-hour the merchant came out bearing a discreet-looking envelope containing the seven thousand francs and kissed me on both cheeks. I lingered a few moments after he went in again. There was no sound.

Apparently, all went well. In a week my friend was at the dock with another envelope, more kisses, reassurance as to Frau Anders' health and contentment, and poetic compliments to her person.

I sailed directly for home.

SEVEN

After returning from the city of Arabs, I thought only of how best to make use of my freedom. I wished for a powerful desire or fantasy, which could be fulfilled as I had fulfilled that of Frau Anders. I wanted to shed my skin. In a way I had done this, by disposing of my mistress; but I had accomplished more for her good than for my own. The sale of Frau Anders was, perhaps, my only altruistic act. And as with all altruisms, I suffered from certain twinges of guilt. Was the act correct? I asked myself. Was it well-performed? Did I not have some secret, self-serving motive?

I thought of resuming my old diversions with Jean-Jacques. We met, and he inquired, "What has happened to our amiable hostess?" I had made the mistake of confiding in him before my departure, but I was determined not to repeat the error. He received my silence playfully. "You surprise me, Hippolyte. I would have predicted it would be Frau Anders who would return, and you who would stay." I did not allow myself to be provoked into explanations. "Will you share with me none of the fruits of your southern journey?" he said finally. His irony troubled me. I dreaded our incipient intimacy.

Fortunately, the following dream intervened.

I dreamed I was at a garden party. The grade of the hill on which the party was being held made the tables and chairs stand somewhat crooked. I remember best an extremely small wizened old man who sat in an infant's high chair, drinking tea out of an earthenware jug, spilling it on his shirt, and mumbling inaudibly.

I asked someone who the old man was, and learned that he was R., the multimillionaire tobacco king. I wondered how he had become so small.

Later I was told the old man wanted to see me. Someone guided me up the hill, through the stone gates, down a gravel path, and into a side entrance of the large house. I was led through a series of deserted basement passageways. The only person we encountered was a servant stationed by a door which interrupted a long, wide, institutional-looking corridor. He wore a green vizor and sat reading at a small table, which held a lamp and some magazines. As we approached him, he jumped to his feet and opened the door for us with a bow. The door was not heavy nor was it locked.

I was impressed with this ostentation, and envied the luxuries which the old man's fortune could provide for his family. We entered the old man's room, which had all the trappings of a sick-room. I stood at the foot of his bed, in an attitude of respect, thinking of the bequest which he might make me when he died.

"Send him around the world," he said to the youth standing beside me, the one who had led me into the house, and who I now understood was his son. "It will do him good."

The son beckoned to me. I thanked the old man profusely and followed the son out into the garden where he told me to wait, and left. I stood there alone for a while, not in the least impatient, for I was relishing the sense of being cared for, of being deployed by some benevolent power. I thought of Frau

Anders, and that I would tell her, if I met her on my travels, how well I had been understood by the old man.

A grey cat came by, which I picked up in my arms and fondled. I was repelled by the cat's strong odor. I flung it on the ground but it remained by my side, so I picked it up again and put it in my pocket, thinking I would wait until I found a place to dispose of it.

A score of people had collected near me, and I joined them. We were all waiting for a doctor to arrive, who was to question us. "We do this every Sunday afternoon," one of the party explained to me. The doctor came down the slope, and we sat down on the grass in a circle. He passed around sheets of paper for each of us to fill out—name, identity card number, weekly earnings, profession—and to sign. I was dismayed at this requirement, for I did not have my papers with me, and I had neither profession nor salary. Watching the others busily filling out their forms, I realized my presence was illegal. I was sorry to miss whatever was to happen, but I was afraid of being detained or perhaps even refused a passport. I left the group.

I decided to return to the house and was heading in that direction when I met the millionaire's son. He told me to adjust the large bath towel which I realized was all I was wearing, and led me to another part of the garden where I was given a shovel and told to dig. I began earnestly enough, though the towel which was knotted around my waist kept coming loose. The ground was hard and the digging strenuous. And when I had dug a fair-sized trench, water began seeping into it. Soon the trench was half filled with muddy water. There seemed no point in continuing, so I stopped digging and threw the cat in.

Somehow, though, I seem to have kept the cat with me and carried it from the garden. Then I met Jean-Jacques and gave him the cat which he tossed away in disgust. "Dogs!" he shouted at me.

"Don't be angry," I answered.

"Have you forgotten it's time for your operation?" he said. I became afraid, for I now did recall something about an operation, though it seemed to come from a previous dream.

"Everything is too heavy," I said, to distract him. "Besides," I added ingratiatingly, "I'm asleep."

"Shark balls!" he said, and laughed coarsely.

I could not understand how I was continuing to provoke him. "There's nothing unhealthy about that," I continued. "I get up very early."

"Go on your trip and leave me alone," he said.

But instead of leaving me, as I expected, Jean-Jacques became very large, and I faced an enormous pair of feet and could barely see the head which soared above me. Alarmed and perplexed, I considered how I might cajole him to return to normal size. I threw a rock at his ankle. There was no response. Then I looked up at the giant, and saw he was no longer Jean-Jacques but a malevolent stranger who might step on me, and I did not dare continue trying to attract his attention.

At that moment I was aware that something was wrong with my body, and looking under the towel I saw to my horror that, from the middle of my ribs to my hip, my entire left side was open and wet. I couldn't understand how I had failed to notice it before. This butcher's view of myself was revolting. I wrapped the towel around me even more tightly and, with both hands pressed against my side to prevent my entrails from falling out, I started to walk. At first I felt dignified and brave, and I determined to ask help of no one.

It was dusk now. People were hurrying home through the streets, on foot and on bicycles. It grew darker. I had to find a hospital, for I felt weak now from the loss of blood and could barely walk. I also thought of trying to find the mansion of my aged patron, where I would lie down in the garden, for I dared not go inside and tell the little old man how I had failed to carry out his advice. There was a doctor there, I remembered, although I was not sure that he was not a consul or some passport official. Yet finding the mansion seemed out of the question. I was lost. There was no one to ask directions from; night had fallen and the unfamiliar streets were empty. I pressed my left side, holding back my tears of humiliation. I wanted to lie down, but I was reluctant to dirty my white towel on the pavement. The feeling of heaviness on my left side increased. I was draining away and struggled to lean toward the right. It was then that I died. At least, it became completely dark.

"This dream is too heavy," I said to myself when I awoke, in an effort to be cheerful. Whenever I woke up still submerged in a dream, I would try to recover my equanimity as quickly as possible. It was not easy, for this dream told me all too plainly how burdened I was and how I despised myself. Who am I to aspire to being free? I thought. How dare I go about disposing of others, when I cannot even dispose of myself. Yet I am free, except for the languishing captivity of my dreams. I cursed my dreams.

After a melancholy morning, I managed to slough off my heaviness, but it was only through the most extreme posture of resignation to the dream. I said to myself: if I am burdened, so be it. And I was reluctant to consider a more hopeful interpretation of the dream.

But someone to whom I related this dream, Professor Bulgaraux, a scholar whose special field of study was ancient religious sects, thought differently. "According to certain theological ideas with which I shall acquaint you," he said, "this may be interpreted as a dream of water. You dug a ditch and it filled with water. And in the end, you were not heavy. You were—how shall I say?—liquefying."

It was a comforting thought, but I was not convinced. "Do you think I should travel, as the old millionaire advised?"

"You have been travelling, have you not?"

I nodded.

"Now you must digest what you have learned, and then expel it. There is guilt in your bowels."

I did not answer, but considered sadly that he might be right.

"You credit yourself with a detachment which you do not yet possess. You are right in listening to your dreams and accepting them—how could you refuse?—but wrong in condemning the self that is revealed in them. I could show you, if you will listen to me."

At first I did not understand this invitation, and felt wary of revealing myself once again. I may have made a mistake in telling my dreams to this man. God knows what he believed! I had been told that he practiced incantations and tried to summon dream-sending demons, all of which is repugnant to any person of sense. However I would not convict him of charlatanry without giving him a full hearing. I respect an authentic mystery, while I deplore the attempt to mystify. I had to find out whether Professor Bulgaraux really believed in what preoccupied him.

"It is rumored," I told him one day over a glass of sherry in his book-lined apartment, "that you are not content with the vocation of a scholar, but in your private life actually subscribe to the beliefs you study."

"Yes, it's true. Or partly," he replied. "I do not believe, alas. But I know how these beliefs truly apply. I am prepared to carry them out, and to teach others how they may be carried out."

"To teach me?" I asked.

He looked at me thoughtfully for a while. "You say your dreams concern you more than anything else?"

I nodded.

"Let me read you the theogonic myth of a sect about which I am lecturing and writing a paper at the moment. It occurs to me that their doctrines apply particularly well in your case."

He took down several volumes bulging with paper slips, opened one, and began to read in his dry, rather nasal voice. I will summarize as best as I can. According to this sect, there was originally one god, a self-sufficient male deity named Autogenes. He was not entirely alone, though. In creating himself, by a super-abundance of the creative gesture he had also brought into existence a certain number of angels and powers. But he created no world. His own being, and that of the angels and powers who reinforced his being by knowing and acknowledging him, was sufficient. He only was; he knew nothing of himself. Then it happened that this all-sufficient god came to know one thing—that he was known. And then he wanted to know himself; he became dissatisfied with merely being. This constituted his fall. He united with one of his female attending angels, Sophia. The issue of that union was a child who was both male and female named Dianus.

The sect which adhered to this myth flourished about two thousand years ago. Its earliest devotees regarded Dianus as a usurper, a pretender, an evil god whose birth signified the corruption of the original godhead. But when the sect began to spread and win converts, the newer members tended to regard Dianus as the principal god, and to relegate Autogenes to the status of an ineffectual guarantee of the divinity of Dianus. More and more it was to Dianus that they turned. To him they could pray, in the hope of their salvation, while Autogenes remained distant and inaccessible. Dianus, unlike Autogenes, was not an altogether aloof god. But he had some of the traits of his father. Most of the time he slept on top of a mountain. Periodically he ventured forth among human beings to be worshipped, assailed, and martyred by them. Only in this way could he continue his divine sleep.

"Of course," observed Professor Bulgaraux, "I do not give credence to the magical arts which this sect practiced. Members of the Autogenist fellowship used to brand each other inside the lobe of the right ear. You may examine my right ear, Hippolyte. You will find only a small mole which I have had since birth."

Not understanding the application of this myth to me, I challenged the value of myth itself. "Such tales are just a sop for the credulous, picturesque concessions to those who cannot stand the shock of a naked idea."

"Are your dreams merely allegories?" returned Professor Bulgaraux. "Do you believe that they present themselves to you as stories because you can't bear the shock of a naked idea?"

"Certainly not! My dreams are no more or less than the story they tell."

"Would you be content to regard your dreams as poetry, if poetry be opposed to truth?"

"No."

"Then reflect, Hippolyte, and see if you do not find more than attractive poetry in this obscure mythology."

I agreed to try, and found that there was as much truth, and a truth quite similar in content, in the Autogenist myth as in my dreams. Were not my dreams about the ideal of self-sufficiency, and the inevitable fall into knowledge? If I had begun to feel martyred by them, was this not ingratitude? However painful they were, I needed my dreams—the metaphor for my introspection—if I was ever to be at peace. I liked very much that part of the myth which explained that the periodic martyrdom of Dianus was necessary not for the salvation of men, but for the comfort and health of the god. Here was god-making in its most dignified and candid form. Similarly, I was learning to regard my dreams not as producing any knowledge useful for others, but for myself, my own comfort and health alone. Here was dream-interpreting in its most dignified and candid form.

In the Autogenist account of the creation of man, I found another clue to my dreams, particularly this last one, which I called "the dream of an elderly patron." The Autogenists believed that the human race is not created by the aloof father-god, nor by the somnolent and lovely Dianus. Rather man owes his generation and allegiance to Sophia, the female agency, who took the form of a serpent; and as proof of this their teachers pointed to the shape of the human viscera. Our internal configuration in the form of a serpent—that is, the shape of the intestines—is the signature of our subtle generatrix. I was delighted with the idea. I would not have thought that among the body's juices and bones and crowded organs churning and pumping, there was room for such an extravagant symbol—much more imaginative than the banal identification of the brain with thought, or the heart with love. When, in this last dream, I dreamed that my entrails were falling out, was I not dreaming that I was losing the signature of my humanity? It was a warning to me—of the guilt in my bowels, as Professor Bulgaraux put it.

I decided to lay aside my intellectual reservations, and hear further what Professor Bulgaraux had to say. If I was to escape the insupportable view that the dreams were an ultimately senseless burden foisted on me by my own malice toward myself, I would have to be purged of any residual attitudes by which I stood condemned in my own eyes. . . . No matter that this was another "religious" interpretation. At least Professor Bulgaraux, unlike the good Father Trissotin, did not urge me to submit my dreams to judgment, but encouraged me to go on as I had been doing—grooming my life for the judgment of my dreams. If this was heresy, so be it. The most exacting forms of spirituality are usually found among heretics.

I thought I was already acquainted with all the heterodox movements available to the searcher for truth in this city and, as I have already indicated to the reader, I am not addicted to group enthusiasms. There are too many ill-thought-out sects in our century, too many partial revolutions inspired by little more than the vogue of being revolutionary. Yet I do not condemn heresy as such, if it be sincere enough, and I came to believe that Professor Bulgaraux really meant what he said.

On his invitation, I visited his apartment several times in the next month to hear him expound the views of the Autogenists. He had in his possession an ancient codex which had been found in an urn buried in a cemetery in the Near East. For many years he had been deciphering and preparing it for publication; these private seminars were, ostensibly, about the contents of the codex. Though there were always other auditors, a few curious academics and some middle-aged women with foreign accents whose occupation I could not determine, the meetings had a very different character from the university lectures I had once attended with such naive zeal for enlightenment. A few simply took notes. But to those who listened eagerly to Professor Bulgaraux's words without paper and pencil in their hands, he made a point of interspersing personal remarks, showing his auditors how these ideas applied to each of them. As I looked about the room, I saw women who reminded me of Frau Anders. It stirred me to realize that Frau Anders might well—if she had ever heard of this group—have become one of Professor Bulgaraux's disciples. What was he expounding if not the idea of being liberated through contradicting one's settled life and unleashing one's deepest fantasies—the very thing which I had done when I disposed of Frau Anders?

I don't mean to give the impression that he sent the ladies

off to murder their husbands, or eat candle wax, or steal from church poorboxes, or drink the semen of their poodles. However, the incitement to action which he offered was not a subtle one. I found it in remarkable agreement with my own instinct in these matters.

"Moderation is the sign of a mixed spiritual state," he said. But any act, he continued, might be performed moderately or immoderately. There are moderate murders and immoderate walks along the river.

You see, the Autogenist cosmology and plan of salvation entailed a whole code of conduct, or rather anti-conduct. Man was created by Sophia, the subtle generatrix, out of dark matter in which only a spark of Autogenes' pure light remained. But man, whom the Autogenist scripture calls "the subjacent dregs of matter," nevertheless can, by various rites of purification, ascend to heaven. Man can return to the bosom of Autogenes, if he becomes "light"—meaning, Professor Bulgaraux explained with a glance intended just for me, as much the absence of weight as luminousness. This purification does not take place through self-denial but through total self-expressiveness. Thus the Autogenists held that men cannot be saved until they have gone through all kinds of experience. An angel, they maintained, attends them in every one of their illegal actions, and urges them to commit their audacities. Whatever might be the nature of the action, they would declare that they did it in the name of the angel, saying: "O thou angel, I use thy work! O thou power, I accomplish thy operation." "They called this perfect knowledge," continued Professor Bulgaraux, "performing such actions as their critics blushed to name."

"There is no need to name them," cried one of the ladies of the enrapt circle. "Or to blush at naming them," I added to myself.

The Autogenist view that good and bad are only human

opinion had nothing in common with the familiar modern disenchantment with morality. They intend this view as a means of salvation. As the result of moral distinctions is that, through them, we gain a personality, that is to say a weight, so the purpose of defying the moral law is to become weightless, to free the person from being only himself. Individual personalities must be neutralized in the acids of transgression.

Looking at Professor Bulgaraux's broad bespectacled face, his unkempt beard, his egg-stained vest, his baggy wrinkled suit, I could not determine whether I saw before me a paragon of anonymity or merely an unsuccessful zealot in all his picturesque and particular squalor. But if he had something true to teach me it did not matter what he was himself. "What is this personality that you advise us to lose?" I asked him at the last meeting I attended in his apartment. This was the only time that I dared to allude publicly to his more than scholarly attachment to the beliefs of the Autogenists, to take for granted that these were indeed his own beliefs.

"Lose it, and you will understand."

"Tell me how," I asked.

"Do you still dream?"

"More than ever."

"You've lost it," he cried, and each of the dozen or so other auditors rose from their upholstered chairs to shake my hand and congratulate me.

Yes, I still dreamed. Would that it were as simple as that! Nightly I lay in the sarcophagus of sleep, the man in the black bathing suit carved in stone on the coffin lid. But, like Dianus, I awoke restless, expectant. Sometimes it seemed as if my dreams were a parasite upon my life, other times that my life was a parasite on my dreams. I wanted to find the heart of my preoccupation. I wanted to escape from this personality which hedged me in, and clashed so sorely with my dreams.

The divorce between my life and my dreams I came, through Professor Bulgaraux's instruction, to see precisely as a result of this thing—call it personality, character—which everyone around me seemed to cultivate and take pride in. I concluded that "personality" is simply the result of being off balance. We have "characters" because we have not found our center of gravity. A personality is, at best, a way of meeting the problem of imbalance. But the problem remains. We do not accept ourselves for what we are, we retreat from our real selves, and then we erect a personality to bridge the gap.

Is not to have a personality just to define our points of vulnerability and strength? A personality is our way of being for others. We hope that others will meet us half way or more, gratify our needs, be our audience, soothe our fears.

But how to escape having a personality? I should have liked to be Chinese for a while, to see if their fabled impassivity feels different, lighter, on the inside. But I could not change the color of my skin or the geography of my heart. Narcotics were equally out of the question. They had never supplied me, even temporarily, with this sense of imperturbability and lightness.

There is one well-advertised way of experiencing this loss of personality—the sexual act. For a time I went often to prostitutes because I expected they would not pretend to be persons; at least their calling forbids it. In the carnal maneuvers of two people who have not been and will not be introduced to each other, a certain silence and lightness may prevail. But one may not count on it. The odor of personality—a photograph on the wall, a scar on the woman's thigh, a certain print dress in the closet, an appealing or contemptuous look on her face—is always seeping in. I learned not to expect too much from sexuality. Nevertheless, I understood why sexuality, like crime, is an imperishable resource of the impersonal. Properly performed, these acts do blunt the sense of self. It is, I think, because the end is fixed: in sexuality, the orgasm; in crime, the punishment. One becomes free precisely through those acts which have an inescapable end.

But for this purpose there is something even more valuable than sexuality and crime—and I testify from the experiences which I relate to you of a life at times libertine, a life in some respects criminal. That is the dream. Could it be that my dreams, which had been often a source of anguish and heaviness to me, were in fact the transparent medium whereby I would lose my tiresome personality? I had thought of the dreams as a foreign body in my flesh, against which I fended as best as I could. Now I was inclined to see them as a blessing. The dreams were grafted on my life, like a third eye in the middle of my forehead. With this eye, I could see more clearly than I ever had before. Jean-Jacques had warned me against my dreams, and my seriousness. Father Trissotin had urged me to confess and rid myself of them. Frau Anders had submitted to my dreams, but had understood them only as fantasies. Now Professor Bulgaraux had suggested to me that I might be proud of them. If I was losing something in the dreams, it was something I should be happy to lose. I was losing myself—losing the serpent that is inside, as shown in my last dream, "the dream of an elderly patron," which ended so graphically with the loss of my very entrails. I was becoming free, if only to be more exclusively a man-who-dreams. I knew that I did not yet understand the nature of freedom, but I had hopes that my dreams, with their painful images of enslavement and humiliation, would continue to elucidate it for me.

Most people consider dreams as the trash-bin of the day: an occupation that is undisciplined, unproductive, asocial. I understand. I understand why most people regard their dreams as of little importance. They are too light for them, and most people identify the serious with what has weight. Tears are serious; one can collect them in a jar. But a dream, like a smile, is pure air. Dreams, like smiles, fade rapidly.

But what if the face faded away, and the smile remained? What if the life on which the dreams fed withered, and the dreams flourished? Why, one would really be free then, really lightened of one's burdens. Nothing can compare with it. We may wonder why we seek so meager a daily portion of that divine sensation of absence and soaring which rises from the commerce of the flesh to erase the world. We may well say of sexuality: what a promise of freedom it is, how astonishing that it is not outlawed.

I am surprised dreams are not outlawed. What a promise the dream is! How delightful! How private! And one needs no partner, one need not enlist the cooperation of anyone, female or male. Dreams are the onanism of the spirit.

EIGHT

I started keeping a journal in which I wrote down my dreams, ventured to interpret them, spun reveries around them. This work was made possible by the new leisure I obtained by giving up reading. I had discovered that the taste for print, and the ability to read rapidly, depend on a trained mental passivity. It would be an exaggeration to say that the bookish man does not think. But he thinks only up to a point; he must arrest his thoughts or else he could never pass beyond the first sentence. Because I did not want to miss even the faintest whisper or echo of my dreams, I determined to discontinue the habit of crowding my mind with the printed dreams of others. One day I cleared my room of most of my books and donated them to the public library of my native city. I retained as souvenirs some *lycée* textbooks on the inside of whose covers classmates had scribbled various affectionate or insulting messages. I also kept a Bible, a handbook on semaphore signals, a history of architecture, and the inscribed copies of his works which Jean-Jacques had given me.

I was no longer so ingenuous or so eager to share my ideas with others. You must not imagine that I had entirely lost the capacity to confide in my friends. But I had lost the confidence that they might teach me something I did not already know. Thus I saw less of Jean-Jacques, who continued to treat me as a novice in any matter we discussed.

Young Lucrezia had succeeded her not greatly lamented mother as my companion and prospective mistress. (No one, not even her husband, exerted himself greatly over Frau Anders' disappearance.) I worried about my growing tendency to irascibility, and made a considerable effort to be less demanding of Lucrezia than I had been of her mother. This was made easier by the fact that she was not in love with me, nor I with her. I was happy when with Lucrezia, but she was a luxury that I was not sure I deserved. Nothing really interested me as much as my presumptuous dreams. And I felt a certain reluctance, perhaps it was selfishness, to initiate Lucrezia into my secrets.

However, the waning pleasures of friendship, as well as thinking and writing about my dreams, were not at that time all of which I was capable. I was a young man still, and it was natural for me to translate part of my restlessness into activity. Amidst all my inner perplexities, I also wanted to live more actively— with the proviso that I not bind myself to any useful, remunerative, or self-advancing occupation. It was thus that, in place of a life of action, I settled for a brief career as an actor. Through the group of people formerly collected by Frau Anders and now presided over by her daughter Lucrezia, I met a number of independent film-makers and began to work with them. My first job was rewriting scripts for a young photographer who was doing some short films on night life in the capital. Four were made: one about the barges that ply up and down the river, one about two lovers on the Metro at midnight, one on the prefecture of police, and one on the Arab quarter near the university. Then I wrote a screenplay of my own, about a nun. It was filmed, though the changes and excisions did not have my approval. Work on this script took over a year; I write very slowly. During this time I also had several small acting parts.

Eventually, as an actor rather than a writer, I graduated to the commercial cinema. This was the first decade of sound films, and although foreign directors can claim pre-eminence during the silent period, at this time my country's cinema was, I think, the best. I never had or aspired to leading parts, but I at least avoided being typecast. I played the butler and the jilted suitor in two romantic comedies, the older brother in a family melodrama, and the patriotic schoolteacher in a film about the conscription of schoolboys at the close of the First World War.

In performing a role I liked to imagine myself inserting a surreptitious footnote to the audience. When I was supposed to play a good-hearted lover, I tried to insert a promise of cruelty in my embrace. When I played the villain, I hinted at tenderness. When I crawled, I imagined I was flying. When I danced, I was a cripple.

The need to contradict, at least in my private thoughts, seems to have grown on me during that period. While in my daily comportment I rarely contradicted the wishes of others, except when I was entirely convinced that I was in the right, every word I heard made me think of its opposite. This was why acting was so felicitous an occupation for me. Acting was a happy compromise between word and deed. A role could be condensed into a single word or phrase; a word or phrase could be expanded into a role. "Butler!" "I do not love you." "Liberty, equality, fraternity"—to give but a few examples. And while I played the role, enunciated the word or phrase, I could think of its opposite with impunity.

Eventually, of course, I could not help but wish for roles which would themselves exemplify these contradictions. I wanted to play a fat African, whose flat cavernous nostrils twitch in disgust at the floral scent of a white woman. I wanted to play a painter, blind from birth, who hears the murmur of colors in his paint-tubes and considers himself a musician. I wanted to play a rotund and genial politician who, when his prosperous country's farmlands are afflicted with drought, sends the nation's grain reserves as a gift to the starving millions of India. Such roles, unfortunately, are not often available. There is a need for more writers to create them. Jean-Jacques could have written parts like these, if he had wanted to; but his art was in the service of other ideals— an idea of comedy, both measured and extravagant, which I have always been either too solemn or not finely tuned enough to appreciate.

Why did I not write such roles myself? you may ask. And why did I give myself to acting? Though I was approaching my thirtieth birthday, it was not that I suddenly felt the lack of a profession. No, the truth was that I was enjoying myself (I am capable of enjoying myself in many ways). I must not omit, however, that the enjoyment was somewhat tainted by vanity. Vanity surely played a part in my preferring acting in films to the theatre. But I enjoyed the fact that in a film the role and my performance were indissoluble, one and the same; while in the theatre, the same role has been and will be performed by many actors. (Are the films in this respect more like life than is the stage?) Also—another incentive to vanity—what one does in a film is recorded and as imperishable as celluloid; while performances in the theatre are without record.

I also preferred the cinema to the theatre because there is no audience present except one's working colleagues, and no applause. In fact, not only is there no audience, there is really no acting either. Acting in films is not like acting in a play which is, whatever the interruptions of rehearsal, in performance continuous, cumulative, and replete with consummated movement and emotion. What is called acting in the films is, on the contrary, much closer to stillness, to posing for a sequence of still photographs like those in monthly *roman-photos* read by shop girls and housewives. In a film every scene is subdivided into dozens of separate shots, each of which entails no more than a line or two of dialogue, a single expression on the actor's face. The camera creates motion, animates these brief frozen moments—like the eye of the dreamer inhabiting and at the same time being a spectator to his own dreams.

I find the cinema a much more rigorous art than the theatre; and one which gave me a profound analogue to the way of behaving whose initial model came from my dreams. I don't mean that watching a film, in a darkened theatre which one can enter on the spur of the moment without prior appointment, is like entering a dream. I am not talking about the dream-like freedom which the camera has with time and space. I speak here not of the spectator's experience but of the actor's: in acting in the films, one must forget passion, and replace it by a sort of extreme coldness. This is easy, even necessary, because the scenes are not filmed consecutively; the actor before the camera is not propelled by the quasi-natural emotions which accumulate in the course of any single performance of a play.

The only advantage I could see which the theatre has over the cinema is that one can repeat the same role night after night—more times than the number of takes a director requires before he is satisfied that he has a shot he can print. And while in each take the actor tries to improve his performance (a period corresponding to rehearsals in the theatre), once the actor has done it correctly the shot is concluded. In the theatre once the actor has learned to do it correctly, he is ready to begin to do it over and over as long as there is an audience for the play. This is the final analogue between acting and my dreams. Those things we do well are those we do over and over, and best are those which have themselves an es-

sentially monotonous form: dancing, making love, playing a
musical instrument. I was fortunate in that the activity of
dreaming had for me this character. There was enough time
and repetitiveness for me to become good at it. I became a
good dreamer, while I never became an outstanding actor.

Through my cinemaphile friends, I made the acquaintance of
Larsen, the well-known Scandinavian director, who was casting
a film based on the life of a fascinating personage in my
country's history. This person, whom no doubt most of my
readers can identify, was a nobleman, of ample fortune and
aristocratic title, who as a young man fought alongside the
devout peasant girl who freed the nation from a hated invader,
and somewhat later in life was denounced as an apostate,
heretic, and criminal. For his apostasy, for heresy, and for
crimes which included having lured to his castle, violated, and
murdered hundreds of children, he was tried and sent to the
scaffold. Before his execution he repented fully and most
movingly of his crimes, and was forgiven by the Church and
mourned by the populace.

I read the script, and expressed strong interest in the project.
Larsen had me audition for the role of the confessor who is
assigned to the nobleman after his arrest. He liked my performance and engaged me. I would have preferred a smaller
part—say, one of the judges—which would have taken less of
my time, but Larsen insisted that my face was exactly as he
imagined the face of the zealous priest who procures the
nobleman's repentance.

Work on this film occupied me for the next half year. We
went on location to the south, and most of the film was made
in a small farming village in the neighborhood of the nobleman's castle, the very castle, now in ruins and visited only by
truant schoolboys and adolescent lovers, to which he had
brought his victims many centuries ago. Social life in this town

was dull. I had a tender affair with the mayor's daughter, whom I used to meet clandestinely in an abandoned barn on the edge of the town. I also passed time with the village priest, arguing about religion and politics. But it was difficult to escape the company of my colleagues. There was only one small hotel in the town, and the actors and entire production staff lived there. It became virtually a dormitory. The director, cameraman, script girl, and cast would meet each morning for breakfast to discuss the day's shooting, and in the evening sit together in the parlor to listen to the hotel's radio, one of the few in the entire town, for news of the civil war which was raging at the time in the country to the south.

I got along with the other members of the company, in particular with Larsen and his pleasant young wife. The one exception was the make-up man, who on the first day of the shooting schedule took a dislike to me. We were to begin with a scene in which the nobleman is led through the village to the place of execution; the cameraman wanted morning light, so the cast had to arrive at six o'clock to be made up in order to get the first take no later than nine. I arrived promptly, but the moment I sat down in the chair in the basement room of the grain warehouse where our props and costumes were stored, and the man in charge of make-up examined my face, he grimaced and began complaining under his breath. For an hour he labored over me to apply a small amount of rouge and powder, for, he told me, I was a hopeless case: I had a type of skin, not too rare but thankfully uncommon in the acting profession, which resisted the application of make-up. "Your skin is matte," he said.

"This is my only face," I replied sarcastically.

"The director won't like it. But he can't blame me."

"Nobody will blame you," I told him.

I had been told something of the sort by make-up men in other films in which I had worked, but never in so surly a manner. Needless to say, my non-absorbent face caused no difficulty that morning.

The actual making of the film went smoothly, though it is difficult to see progress when one proceeds so piecemeal. We worked in a jungle of ladders, scaffolding, cables on the floor, lights and gauze shades for the lights, mimeographed copies of the script, stacks of free cigarettes, and bottles of wine for the crew. We seemed, as befitted a historical spectacle, a multitude. Besides over two score of staff, film crew, and principal actors, extras were recruited from the town, as well as tanned bare-chested men and boys in khaki shorts and sneakers to haul the camera, lights, and props about, and to bring lunch to us while we were shooting. The only still point in all this activity was Mme. Larsen, the director's wife, who spent most of each day in a corner of the set knitting first a beige sweater and then a blanket.

There was some trouble with the investors in the capital, who had chronic doubts about the film's commercial soundness. Everyone on the set learned to respect Larsen's scowl when he was brought his mail at four o'clock each afternoon, sat apart to read it, then stuffed it in the back pocket of his knickers. He also was frequently called to the hotel for long-distance telephone calls. Whatever pressures were being put on him, though, I felt it was principally due to his own indecision that it took as long as it did (seventy-three days of shooting spread over a period of four and a half months) to finish the film. We arrived with a complete shooting script, but he was con-tinually making changes, and much of the breakfast conferences were wasted in debate over sexual motives and theological ideas. I played a modest role in these discussions, and can take some credit for keeping the film from turning into an anti-clerical tract. For Larsen, who had written the script, could not decide how to represent the nobleman. Some mornings he would threaten to halt production so he could rewrite the whole middle of the script, to show that the nobleman was entirely innocent of the extraordinary crimes of which he was accused. At least, he wanted to exonerate the offending nobleman—as a man broken by the torments which an overscrupulous conscience imposes upon an unconventional sexual temperament.

"He must have been a very passionate man," mused the director. "Antoine," he said, turning to the actor who was playing the nobleman, "you must get more of that into your performance."

I demurred. "I imagine him as very serene," I said. "Such a great quantity of victims testifies to an immensity of appetite which amounts to indifference."

Everyone at the table disagreed with me. "How could anyone be so cruel!" exclaimed the short-haired young woman who was playing the patriot. "Think of all those little children."

I tried to explain. "I don't think the nobleman illustrates the extreme of cruelty of which human nature is capable. He illustrates the problem of satiety. Don't you see? All acts are undertaken in the hope of their consequences. What passes for being satiated is simply the arrival at the consequences— the fulfillment—of one's act. But sometimes the moral atmosphere becomes clogged. There is a backlog of consequences. It takes a long time for the consequences to catch up with the act. Then one must go on repeating oneself, and boring others, in the interval between act and consequences. This is when people say, he is insatiable. And sometimes—very rarely to be sure—there are no consequences, and one has the impression of not being alive at all."

"You're trying to exonerate him, too," said the script girl.

"No, not at all," I replied. "I would be the first to agree that he should have been executed. For who would act as he did except for the purpose of incurring punishment? It's just that he was very literal-minded. He repeated himself—that is, his crimes—extravagantly. He became a machine. The only questions for me"—I turned to address Larsen—"are these. With each repetition, with each revolution of the machine, did he become less oppressed, until it was as nothing for him eventually to confess and to be sent to his death? Or would he have been satisfied with one murder, if he had been caught?"

"Go on," said Larsen. "I see you have given the matter much thought."

"What does it mean for someone to murder three hundred children, when one murder more than suffices most people?" I said. "Did this man have three hundred times the capacity for murder that you and I have? Or does it not rather suggest that for him one murder could only weigh one-threehundredth of what it does for an ordinary person?"

I do not remember the rest of the discussion, except that I was over-ruled when I made some specific suggestions for changing the script. My colleagues, understandably, did not share my desire to reshape this fascinating subject in the langorous style of my dreams. But I would still argue that Larsen's interpretation was lacking in imaginativeness. To my taste, he devoted too much of the film to the nobleman's association with the adolescent patriot; and in the final scenes he failed to do justice to the astonishing procession in which the sodomist and mass murderer was followed to the scaffold by hundreds of weeping citizens, many of them the parents of his tiny victims.

Why did they weep? Could it be because his crimes had somehow the odor of sanctity? More exactly, that the nobleman was a convert to certain heretical religious ideas, which prompted and even sanctified his abominable crimes? And that peasant girl, the national heroine of my country—I argued that his association with her did not partly redeem him, as Larsen would have it. On the contrary. Was not the girl herself brought to trial and burned at the stake? The virgin and the child-murderer, these two persons so opposite in the judgment of history and apparently connected only by the exploits of battle, did have something in common, namely heresy, the principal charge (be it remembered) in both trials. Both were accused of heresy first, of insurrection and crime only secondarily. Is it possible that both were punished for something never disclosed in either trial? According to Professor Bulgaraux, who sent me several convincing letters on the subject, both were volunteer scapegoats of an underground cult whose doctrines bear some resemblance to the ideas of the Autogenists.

But if this is so, then one must say that of the two it was the nobleman who better fulfilled the sacred mission of defiling himself in the eyes of the world. The peasant girl, though she wore men's clothing and heard voices and went into battle, could not avoid being made into a saint by the Church which condemned her. But no church, however imaginative, could canonize the nobleman. Thus to make his crimes issue from sexual distress, as Larsen would have it, showed the greatest lack of moral tact. His crimes were monstrous because they were real, whatever the motive. Don't exonerate him, I urged Larsen. Respect his choice and don't try to turn evil into good. Let nothing be interpreted. No part of the modern sensibility is more tiresome than its eagerness to excuse and to have one thing always mean something else!

By these reflections, I was moved to adopt a new attitude while before the camera. For once in my brief acting career, I played a role without duplicity. I played the priest as though I had nothing but his words in my head, his compassion and horror inscribed on my face. When I pleaded with the nobleman to repent, I truly prayed that his crimes could be undone and all the little children be restored to their mothers. I hoped that the actor who played the nobleman thought of those crimes as real. How else could he pretend to commit them, repent of them, or die for them?

My performance in this film was my last work as an actor. It is not for me to say whether it was my best, though the reader may perhaps have an opportunity to judge for himself, since the film is still often shown by film societies. All that is important to mention now is that my new attitude toward acting, in which I wanted to be without reservation or inner distraction the character I was playing, had abolished the value of acting for me. There was no point in being someone else, if I were really to be someone else. For then I might just as well be myself. Besides, the work was demanding and left me less time than I wished for the occupations of solitude.

I returned to the capital after the conclusion of the film, and took a room near the great market in the center of the city. This was furnished, or rather unfurnished, in the same way as my old place. Lucrezia became again my constant companion, and I shared with her the ideas about good and evil which arose from my audiences with Professor Bulgaraux and my part in the film about the nobleman. She had a quiet, independent intelligence and could never have needed any liberating counsel from her mother. One day, however, something happened which changed our friendship, or rather, prevented our friendship from changing. She had come to my room directly from the hairdresser, and after admiring her coiffure and thinking of taking her into my arms, I had offered her a drink and we had begun to talk.

"Hippolyte," she said, breaking into our conversation which was about the Offending Nobleman, as Lucrezia and I called him, "do you ever think of Mother?"

"Yes," I replied truthfully, "I do."

"I know Mother liked you very much." I reached for her

hand, sympathetically. "Do you think it's very wicked of me not to miss her?"

"I'm sure she is happy, wherever she is," I said.

"I do hope so," said Lucrezia. "Because I have received a letter which purports to be from her—although Mother had always a rather elegant script and this letter is unevenly written, on soiled brown paper. This letter, Hippolyte," she grasped my hand warmly, "contains many curious reproaches, directed to you as well as to me."

"Tell me about them," I said.

"Oh, Hippolyte, I didn't think Mother loved you." She brushed some moisture from one eye.

"But surely you knew. . . ."

"Yes, yes," she said hurriedly. "But I didn't know you went away with her. She says she is so angry with you she will not come back. She says that she imagines I, too, am happier without her. And that she is very happy where she is. Oh, my dear, she does not sound at all happy, does she?"

"I think she has every reason to be happy," I said, "if the fulfillment of a powerful fantasy ever brings happiness."

"Only it would be most unlike Mother to be happy, Hippolyte. She is not that sort of person. Perhaps it isn't Mother, after all. The person who wrote the letter signs herself 'Scheherazade.' "

"It is your mother, I am sure."

"But do you know how she is living now? The letter doesn't give any details."

"When last I saw her," I explained, "she had entered the household of an Arab merchant who greatly desired her. This seemed to be the perfect solution to her perennial dissatisfactions. You remember, do you not, the letters she wrote you?"

"Yes! Were you with her when she wrote those embarrassing letters, Hippolyte? Did you read them? Oh, but I'm becoming jealous again! The letters were very touching, weren't they?"

"Your mother wanted to try a way of life entirely different from the one she led here, Lucrezia, but she didn't have the courage to discard this life by herself. She had to be helped."

"Pushed."

"She wanted to be pushed."

"Oh, Hippolyte, sometimes I wish you would push me!"

"You are not at all like your mother," I reminded her.

"Yes," she said, "that's true. I don't long for the primitive, as Mother did. Life in this careful city is already too primitive for me."

"Does your mother ask for money?"

"She hints at ransom. She says she's a prisoner of love. That sounds as if we could coax her to come back."

"Would you allow me to donate the sum of thirteen thousand francs toward her return?"

"Hippolyte, that will pay for ten returns! Why so much?"

"Because that was the amount for which I sold her. I did not dare take less, for fear the merchant would not value her properly."

And for a while the conversation turned to the question of how money may operate to create value as well as to measure it.

"I am very fond of money," Lucrezia said in a self-congratulatory tone. "While Mother, who is more generous than I, will only give the money to her lover. Perhaps she will buy him a herd of camels with it."

Frowning at her snobbery, I said, "I give you the money in her name." I went to a drawer, and handed the sum to her, still in the merchant's envelope, with a feeling of relief. I should never have liked it to appear that money played anything but an aesthetic role in that curious incident.

"I begin to think you were very fond of my mother," Lucrezia said, taking off her gloves to count the bills, and then putting them in her bag.

I became annoyed. "She was most generous with herself to me," I said.

"Nonsense!"

I was astonished at the way Lucrezia persisted in this scene of jealousy which I could not believe was sincere.

"What do you want from me, Lucrezia?"

"Nothing," she said, reddening. It embarrassed her to discover herself seeking intimacy instead of conferring it.

When she said she wanted nothing from me, I resolved to give nothing more than I had thus far. For some time I had been in doubt about my friendship with Lucrezia. My restrained conduct with her testifies to that. I was not unaware that there was something unseemly in my inheriting the daughter after enjoying the mother; and considerations of good taste, although not in the way they did with my friend Jean-Jacques, have always weighed strongly with me. Now I saw that there was no reason for us to be more to each other than we already were. Who knows what perverse impulses lay behind Lucrezia's feeling for me, which I had up to that point taken for granted, being accustomed at that age and state of good looks to the attention of women.

Lucrezia and I continued talking until dark, and then went out to stroll by the river. We were speaking then, as I recall, of how coarsely praise and blame are distributed in the world. We agreed that many bad things are commonly praised, and many good things are censured.

"Do you admire effort?" I asked. "Do you esteem feelings which correct themselves, and behavior which does not rest until it is different?"

"No," she replied, "I don't admire effort. I admire excellence, which is less accomplished when it results from effort. And less graceful, too."

For a moment, I wondered why I was set on rejecting the affection of this intelligent woman with whom I shared so

many ideas. Whenever we disagreed, as now, I enjoyed her
even more.

"And beauty?" I asked. Lucrezia had blonde hair, china-blue
eyes, and very fine features.

"Oh, yes. I forgive anything that is beautiful."

"I don't see why we should praise beauty," I replied thoughtfully. "It's too easy to learn from the world what is beautiful
and what is not. We should allow ourselves to find beautiful
anything which holds our complete interest—those things, and
only those things, no matter how disfigured and terrifying."

"In short," she said quizzically, "the only thing you admire
is what preoccupies you."

"I admire the preoccupying. I respect the preoccupied."

"Nothing else! Where is love? Fear? Remorse?"

"Nothing else."

After this conversation adjourned, I dismissed Lucrezia from
my thoughts as anything other than a graceful and urbane
friend. The spectre of her mother had risen between us, and
I could not bear the thought of there being any rivalry between
the two women, either in Lucrezia's mind or in mine. Although
we continued to meet, often to go to the films together,
Lucrezia accepted the stasis in our friendship and turned her
amorous interest to more promising candidates.

For the months that followed, I find more dreams in my
notebooks and a greater serenity in their interpretation. My
effort was less, my attention greater. I still pursued the same
preoccupations, but I learned from the dreams how to pursue
them better. The dreams taught me the secret of perpetual
presentness, and freed me from the desire to adorn my life
and my conversation.

Let me explain. Imagine that something happens—say, an
act of assault—and someone comes in immediately afterwards.

"What happened?" asks the visitor.

"Help!" Moans, cries, and so forth.

"What happened?"

"They . . . came . . . through the window." More moans.

"And then?" says the visitor.

"They . . . hit me . . . with an axe."

In these first moments, the bleeding victim is not interested in persuading anyone of the reality of the event. It has just occurred, and he cannot imagine how anyone could doubt it. Should anyone doubt the story, he has his wounds to show. No, even this would not occur to him. Should anyone doubt the story, he would not care, as long as a doctor is sent for. His wounds would be companions enough.

It is not until later, when the wounds have begun to heal, that the victim wants to talk. And as the event becomes more distant in time, the victim—healed and restored to the bosom of his family—gives it dramatic form. He embellishes his narrative and sets it to music. He puts drums in the background. The axe gleams. He sees the whites of the man's eyes. He tells his children that the attacker wore a blue scarf. "And he sprang through the window with a great noise," says the aging and healthy victim to his children. "He raised his arm and I was terrified and. . . ."

Why has he become so verbose? Because he no longer has the companionship of his pain. He has only an audience, whose attentiveness he doubts. In telling the story he is attempting to convince his audience that "it" really happened, that it was like this, that he felt violent emotions and was in great danger. He craves reassurance. He also learns he can collect from the telling—money, respect, sympathy. With time, the event is not quite real to him, to whom it happened. He believes less in the reality of the assault; more real to him are all the ways he has found to describe it. His narrative becomes persuasive.

But in the beginning, when the assault was real, when it did not occur to him to persuade anyone, his narration was laconic and honorable.

This is what I learned from dreams. Dreams always have the quality of being present—even when, as I am doing, one relates them ten, twenty, thirty years after. They do not age, or become less credible; they are what they are. The loyal dreamer does not seek his hearer's credence, he does not need to convince his hearer that such and such amazing thing happened in the dream. Since all events in the dream are equally fantastic, they are independent of the assent of other people. This reveals, by the way, the falsity of that line which people of taste insist on drawing and redrawing between the banal and the extraordinary. All events in dreams are extraordinary, and banal, at the same time.

In dreams, assaults happen. We kill, we fall, we fly, we rape. But things are as they are. We accept them in the dream; they are irrevocable, though often without consequences. When someone disappears from the stage of the dream, one does not in the dream wonder where he has gone. Anyone relating his dream who says, "The clerk left me at the counter. I believe he went to consult his supervisor about my request," is telling the dream wrong. He is not being honest: he is trying to persuade. One says, "I was at the counter talking to a clerk. Then I was alone."

I should like to describe my life to you with the same evenness that one recounts one's dreams. Such a narration would be the only honest one. If I have not entirely succeeded in doing this, at least I continue to aim at this goal as I write. I have tried not to extract from my life any excitement which it does not yield of itself, or to over-stimulate the reader with names and dates, with tiresome descriptions of my own person and appearance, of those whom I knew, with the furniture of rooms, the progress of wars, the swirl of cigarette smoke, and other matters which took place concurrently with the encounters and conversations I have reported. That only one passion, or one idea, be made clear is task enough to fill a hundred volumes—and beyond my powers to do more, in these pages, than to suggest.

NINE

One day I had a visit from Frau Anders' husband. Let me correct myself: from Herr Anders. Now that his wife was gone, he certainly deserved the recognition of his own identity. Yet her husband he remained to me, even then, for all I knew of him (mainly from Frau Anders) was that he had a keen sense of smell, that his hobby was taxidermy, and that she suspected he had never been unfaithful to her. Their daughter Lucrezia took no notice of his existence.

I was dismayed when I saw who was at my door, for I anticipated a storm of reproaches, at the least a tale of loneliness and misery. If he had really loved her, how could I show Herr Anders that his wife's removal to the land of her desire was as beneficial for him as it was for her? But he didn't seem irate, only uncomfortable. I begged him to come in.

Without ceremony, for he had the manners of a busy man, he told me what he had come to say. I learned that he believed that his wife had retired to a nunnery; there was no question in his mind that her holy vows must be respected. When I asked him how he had gained this impression, he told me of a letter which he had from her six months after her departure. He also told me—and seemed surprised that I did not know it—that in this letter Frau Anders named me her trustee in the world, the executor as it were of her mundane estate, her intermediary. Although this tale of the nunnery struck me as a rather malicious joke on the part of Frau Anders, I felt I had to go along with her wishes, and asked him how I might fulfill my duty.

Herr Anders had a message to transmit to his wife, but since he did not know her whereabouts, he asked me to communicate with her. He wished to remarry.

"But," I replied, somewhat disconcerted, "I don't know exactly where she is. Several years have passed and. . . ."

"Please!" He gazed at me imploringly. "I know I may divorce her on the grounds of desertion. But I want her to know. Do you understand? I don't want to marry without her consent, and her blessing."

I didn't understand, and therefore did not know what to say. "If God has given her a better life," he added softly, "I don't want to interfere with her happiness." It occurred to me that Herr Anders thought he was becoming religious.

I was silent a moment more. The husband of my lost mistress regarded me quizzically; a look of apprehension, which shaded off into animosity, appeared in his face. "You are concealing something from me," he said bitterly. And at that he settled himself more firmly against the wall (I had no chairs in the room, and did not dare invite him to sit on the floor), and awaited my reply.

I decided to tell him a portion of the truth. "Yes, I am concealing something. For myself, I would tell you all. But I have an idea that your wife would wish it otherwise. Else, why would she not have told you herself where she is?"

"Tell me," he said.

"Is it your impression"—I began cautiously—"that your wife

ever displayed any of the customary signs of a religious vocation?"

"Why do you ask me that? I must believe that she did, and that I was too blind to see. Possibly you do not know that she is a convert. I would not like to have that fact broadcast about, by the way. Certainly, she was very fretful and discontented, especially in the last year or two of our life together, and that is a sure sign of being on the verge of a great decision." His look became challenging. "Why? Do you think one can be devout, and not have a vocation for it? Is there some insincerity of which you suspect my wife? Is that what you're trying to tell me?"

"No," I replied. "Not insincerity, not that at all. But I speak of certain tastes, inclinations, and ideas which perhaps you did not suspect. . . ."

"Speak up, man," he shouted. "What has she done? I will not be held liable for any of her idiocies or extravagances!"

"No, no," I said soothingly. "You don't understand. And how could you? I know I have not been clear. What I mean is that—"

"If you don't speak plainly, I'll—" He was becoming purple in the face and gripped his hat tightly.

"Did she tell you what kind of nunnery she had retired to?"

"No!"

"And how do you imagine it?" I asked cautiously.

"I don't imagine anything! What do you want from me?"

"In your mind's eye," I continued, "do you see nuns, bare white-washed cells, crucifixes, orisons at five in the morning, a portly Mother Superior, a bell that sounds in the parlor when visitors ring to gain admittance?" He made a noise of strangled rage, so I finished quickly. "Well, it is not like that at all," I said. "You see, Frau Anders is not particularly Catholic. If she is in a nunnery, it is one of the faith of Islam."

"*If* she is in a nunnery! Why do you speak in such a craven manner? Don't spare me." He took out his handkerchief. "Islam!" He breathed heavily, sank down on his haunches, and sat on the floor. "That's incredible. Disgraceful. No wonder she didn't dare tell me. Have you told anyone of this?"

"No."

"Paganism! My God! Why isn't atheism good enough for her? It's good enough for everyone else! Why, she might as well have stayed a Jew!"

I was becoming annoyed with his indignation. What a tiresome man he had revealed himself to be! Nevertheless, I felt bound to make the truth available to him, if Frau Anders wanted it so. "Shall I give you her address?" I said after a moment. "I have the address where I last saw her."

"I don't know if I want it now. . . . Yes, give it to me. I may write her. It seems to matter much less now," he subsided in a murmur. "If you only knew how much I admired her."

For all his pomposity, he did seem terribly distressed as he rose to his feet and put on his hat. I reached in my wallet, took out the address of the merchant and copied it for him.

"One more word," I said, as we stood at the door. "Have you been happier without her? You can speak candidly to me."

"Insolent man! I know what you have been to her." He glared at me. Then he began to laugh, violently, until the tears came to his eyes. "I have never been happy. Never! Never! Never!"

Later I heard from Lucrezia that Herr Anders had written to his wife at the address I had given him, asking for an annulment, that she had replied to him, granting it, and that soon after he indeed remarried. I often wondered if he were happy now, for I believe that there is no one who cannot be made happy by some means. Was Frau Anders happy? I inclined to think so. At least, she was alive, reasonable, and willing to stay where she was. I must confess that, knowing nothing more of her fortunes, I envied her. She had achieved her freedom, which coincided with the fulfillment of her fantasy, while I remained chained to the interpretation of mine. While Frau Anders was off in the desert disporting herself with her Moslem lover, I stayed in my room, an ear pressed to my pillow, listening to my dreams.

Frau Anders wanted to be liberated, so I had torn her from her old life and confined her in a new one. I wanted also to be liberated by being confined. That is why I had enjoyed my work in the cinema. Acting in films gave me a sense of being absolutely used, deployed—and this I knew was the model of my salvation. But my own needs were such that an external change of life—the choice of a domineering mistress or an enslaving vocation—was not enough. The enslavement had to be an inner one. Were my dreams, then, the authority I sought? I had tried to obey them, but their demands were so contradictory.

All around me I saw my friends expressing preferences, making choices. Even Herr Anders knew when the game was up, and how to provide for himself. I would not put myself above the chance of happiness, for which I was even prepared to sacrifice some of the demands of my dreams.

It is only in this way that I can explain a relationship which I began that year with an earnest young woman named Monique. Friends had introduced us with the thought that we would be compatible, because (apart from my work in the cinema, which my friends thought, correctly, I pursued in the spirit of an amateur) I still had the undeserved reputation of a man of ideas, in short a writer who happened not to write, and Monique herself was a literate, appreciative person. I believe our friends also thought that Monique would be a good influence on me, because she had a reliable character, and a generous uncomplicated view of life. She came from a poor but decent family with many children; her father was a clerk in the Ministry of Finance and her mother was a schoolteacher; she had grown up in the capital and knew no other life than that of large boulevards, crowded apartments filled with cooking smells, first balcony seats at the theatre, offices staffed by fretful men in shirtsleeves sitting at typewriters and helpful women in heavy stockings who went back and forth from filing cabinets. By profession, she was a functionary in good causes. She had worked for several years for a small left-wing weekly. Now she was employed by an organization dedicated to the emancipation of colonial peoples, for which she wrote articles, sent out mailings, and made speeches. I noticed soon that Monique's radical political opinions had not damaged her faith in official institutions. Marriage, the civil service, the courts, the press, the schools, the army—about none of these was she seriously disillusioned. It never occurred to her that her passion for justice could not be transmitted along the established lines of communication and through the established institutions, which she maintained were not bad but only misinformed. Since, as the reader will recall, this was a decade in which political discontent among well-meaning Europeans often took the form of much more radical commitments than they intended, it was remarkable that Monique, with her moralizing temper, did not join the Party—where, at least for a time, she would have been much happier, that is, much more thoroughly used. At first I found Monique's intransigence charming. But I soon began to suspect that her unfashionableness was more a question of muddle than integrity. The same traits appeared in her personal habits, which were a mixture of bourgeois conscientiousness and proletarian bad taste. Her private passions were children, *haute cuisine*, and celebrities; and although she had had several abortions and usually served me no better fare than overseasoned meat and stale cheese when I ate at her apartment and no famous person wanted to marry her, these affections remained undiminished.

I do not mean to sound patronizing towards Monique, for I was not nor had I the right to be. In her astounding capacity for preserving her passions and convictions intact, despite their objective fate in the world, did she not curiously, and instructively, resemble me?

We met at a time when I was feeling rather lonely, and ill at ease with myself. Despite my apparent confidence in my own judgment and tastes and in the meandering way of life which I had chosen for myself, I did succumb to moments of doubt, and to harsher moments when I even pitied myself for my condition of exile from the ordinary routines of the community. Here I was, after a decade of adult life, having educated myself and engaged in conversation with many interesting people; having had a mistress and learned how to make her happy, even at the price of losing her to myself; having pursued a career. Yet I knew that I had really given myself to none of these activities, that only one, which I could share with no one—my dubious pursuit of wisdom through my dreams—really mattered to me. I was experiencing the dilemmas and distractions of the utterly self-elected man. (These, if nothing else, I shared with the artist—as opposed to the professor, the politician, the general, the bureaucrat, the wife.) No one appointed me to devote myself to my dreams. And I had to bear my own doubts as to the value of my vocation, as well as the casual disapproval of my friends and relatives who thought me an eccentric wastrel. Was I even qualified? I sometimes asked myself. Was I wasting my time? Was I giving pleasure to anyone, even to myself?

Monique, dear Monique, Monique of the large hands and unfurrowed brow, restored to me a measure of confidence in myself, although I know this was not her intention, for we quarreled often and strenuously. She was critical of the way I lived, of the bareness of my room, my lack of interest in politics, my distant relationship with my family. Through her criticisms of me, so ingenuous and self-righteous that I could take them seriously without becoming offended, I began to sort out what was necessary to my vocation of self-investigation and what was superfluous or exaggerated. I also discovered several hitherto unremarked inconsistencies in myself. For one thing I had always dressed carefully, neatly, in clothes made by a good tailor who was recommended to me by my father when I first moved to the capital. How could I reconcile my taste for clean and well-pressed grey suits, grey socks, black shoes, a foulard, and a hat (rather than sweaters, odd pants, ascots, and the like) with the sparseness of my furnishings and the austerity of my diet? I suspected that the diet and the bare room had become an affectation, and allowed myself to be persuaded by Monique to move to a furnished apartment near hers, and also to engage a maid to come in and clean for me twice a week. I, in turn, convinced Monique that she could not admire good food, and prate of the glories of the national cuisine, if she did not make an effort in her own home. Together we bought some cookbooks and spent many pleasant hours shopping for herbs and concocting provincial specialties in her kitchen which she ate with only a bit more relish than I. . . . My fits and starts and waverings—and, dare I say? yearnings—for a more normal life seem pathetic to me now. But I meant them sincerely, and it testifies at least to the lack of arrogance, if not to the intelligence, with which I pursued my search.

I enjoyed my new apartment; I learned that I was not made to live in only one room. For me there was pleasure, as well as a further step in my self-elucidation, in the person of Monique. But I was never sure why Monique was drawn to me. Did she want me for myself, or for the celebrities I knew in the film world and elsewhere? She introduced me to her ex-lover, a burly African revolutionist in exile named Tububu, and the three of us spent many evenings debating the possibility of a just revolution and the transformation of society through political means. I, in return, introduced her to Jean-Jacques, whose books were becoming well-known; she disapproved of him as reactionary and selfish, and he was amused by her. I also brought her together with Larsen, the Scandinavian film director, and observed that she would have discarded me in a moment for him, had he shown any interest in her.

Love-making with Monique was athletic, unsubtle, and bare of fantasy. Though I felt no desire to inform her about the cinema of my inner life, I became quite fond of her. Some of my emotion was a brotherly tenderness, aroused by our mutual efforts at self-improvement; some of it was a lover's feeling, more selfish and mercurial. I felt unmistakable pangs of jealousy in the presence of Tububu, whom otherwise I liked, and when I realized she aspired to a romance with the happily-married Larsen. But I could not bring myself to reproach Monique for her emotional unfaithfulness to me. The love of the famous, like all strong passions, is quite abstract. Its intensity can be measured mathematically, and it is independent of persons. Monique did not reject me as such. It was simply that I did not rank as high as others on the gauge of fame.

Our conversations with Tububu clarified my ideas about revolutionary acts, which had begun to form themselves during the talks I had had with Jean-Jacques. For, as I have intimated, I sometimes fancied myself as an agent in a revolution not yet named, and I was eager to match my non-political ideas against any political ones.

"You are finished, you white people," exclaimed Tububu. "You have the capacity neither for conscienceless violence nor for change." I could not help staring at the deep symmetrical scars slashed on his black cheeks, as if these proved he knew something I could never know.

Monique protested gallantly. "I know your peoples' grievances are just," she said, "but surely the country which gave birth to the ideals of liberty, equality, and fraternity cannot long remain an oppressor."

Perhaps Tububu was right. Certainly Monique was being naive. In darker countries, justice may be secured by communal violence; where the oppressor is a foreigner, violence is at least plausible. But other things than political justice are in store for Europe, and here violence is a form of ineffectual suicide. Look at the history of my country in the last two centuries. First there was a revolution which overthrew the Church and invented a new cult, the worship of Reason personified by a goddess. There have been other revolutions since. Only last year petitions were signed, newspapers confiscated, a general strike called. Students scribbled slogans on the walls, the police marched on the parliament screaming anti-Semitic slogans, two cabinet ministers took refuge in a foreign embassy, the paratroopers came from the south. You know how little resulted from all this commotion. New textbooks were issued in the schools, new faces appear in the newspapers. Several cafés, the meeting-places of subversive elements, have been closed. There are more frequent street-checks of identity cards by the police. Otherwise things remain much the same.

In Europe such public upheavals no longer change anything, however much the revolutionary option in its political form may still hold among darker peoples. We may look forward to more appropriate, and more dangerous, revolutions than political ones. Perhaps the revolutions of the future will all be revolutions of single persons, exemplifying not the cult of reason but the cult of privacy whose worship is personified by a puppet. . . . Needless to say, I could not win Monique over to my ideas. The acts of the private self did not seem important to her, except as she might measure them by public standards —even as the charm of the private person needed the public certificate of fame to affect her.

An incident I might tell illustrates this difference between us. We were on our way to her apartment one afternoon: someone spat from a window above us, and the gob of spittle landed on the sidewalk a step ahead of our feet. Our reactions contrasted nicely. "How can people do things like that!" exclaimed Monique. "Thank you," I called upwards.

"What do you mean?" she said to me, indignantly. "That man has no consideration for other people, and this is the source of all unfairness."

"Nonsense," I said, "he has just distributed a precious part of the very substance of his body, and thereby rearranged, however trivially, the order of the universe. He has made something happen, with the greatest economy and the smallest possible means. For that model act, we must be grateful, not squeamish."

"I still think it's disgusting." Monique never really listened.

"That's the trouble with those revolutions you and your colleagues are fomenting. Too lavish an expenditure of means, too gross an effect."

My point was confirmed when, shortly after this incident, Monique became pregnant. I urged her to have the child, and assured her I would support it. Such a large outcome—another human being to walk this earth—from so small an act as our hygienic sexual unions seemed somehow appropriate. But Monique wanted to continue to devote herself to larger causes, she told me, and with a rather severe air, rejected my proposal.

One day Monique announced to me that she had received a letter. "A very odd, abstract letter," she said coldly. "It's from a woman who claims that you are in debt to her, and also that she owes you something."

"The postmark of the letter?" I asked, nervously.

"Why, here. In the city," she replied. "Who is she?" When

I didn't answer, she pouted, "Is there someone else?" she cried. "Are you trifling with my affections? It isn't fair!"

There could be no point in explaining to Monique, if the woman was who I thought she was. I asked to see the letter, which read as follows:

"My dear young woman," it began. "You are at present engaged in a liaison with a young friend and protégé of mine, who is considerably in my debt for my patronage and my love. But I too am in debt to him, which he will understand when you tell him of this letter. You must understand that I don't write him directly because I would not interfere with the love he feels for you. Love is all we women have. But I appeal to you to ask him to see me for an hour. I have something to show him, myself." Then followed an address in the city, a time the following evening for the proposed appointment, and the signature, "A Ghost."

I trembled, I must confess, at this missive, and at the sight of that familiar yet distorted handwriting; it was an unconvincing scrawl, like the look of distress on a face stiff with powder, rouge, and mascara; the same handwriting as in the letter to Lucrezia. I cannot bear scenes or reproaches. But I consoled myself that the letter was mild in tone, and by degrees brought myself to look forward to the appointment.

Close to midnight the next evening I presented myself at the address in the letter, a dingy wooden house near a railway station on the outskirts of the city. A woman opened the door, wearing a loose-fitting greyish Arab garment which covered her completely, except for the familiar large brown eyes with their alternately docile and imperious expression.

"Come in, my knight of the sad countenance," she said.

"Don't mock me," I said resentfully. "Tell me how you are, and what I may do for you."

"Would you like to see me?" she asked.

"That was always a pleasure," I replied, the wish to conciliate getting the better of my usual candor.

She turned her back on me and walked to the other side of the room, did something to her garment, and then uncovered to my gaze a misshapen scarred arm. "Did you notice my handwriting?" I nodded, without speaking. "There's more," she said, and opened the front of her clothes to let me see, briefly, the scars and ravagements of her torso. "And more." She took off the hood, and I saw that one half of her face was slanted in a painful derisive grin.

"What can I say?" I murmured. "Were you ever happy, before these calamities befell you?"

"Why yes," she replied, adjusting her garments, "I was. The man to whom you abandoned me was a gentle lover. He used to visit me three times a week between two and four in the afternoon before leaving for the mosque. I was confined in a small room, and not allowed to talk with anyone else in the house. I was terribly afraid of him. But when finally my fear gave way to pleasure, he tired of me and sold me to a trader who carried me into the desert. It was there that I was chastised in so visible a manner for my uncooperativeness, and my unfitness to survive."

"Tell me what I must do," I said. "Now it's your turn to command, mine to obey."

"Why, do with me what you will," she cried sternly. "Only remember that I am yours, yours to dispose of. I warn you, I shall be rather hard to dispose of. Women are quite durable, you know."

"What would be fair?" I said half to myself.

"Fair?" she exclaimed. "I've never heard you talk like that!"

I explained that it was perhaps the influence of the young woman who was my companion at the moment, and was gently, if coarsely, guiding me towards normalcy.

"I don't believe you will do anything that is fair," she said.

"In fact, I am counting on that. But I expect you to do something poetic, gorgeous, my Hippolyte. Surprise me, confound me, stir my senses." The seductive look in her eyes at that moment alarmed me, for I thought of the face beneath.

"I can't think so quickly," I said finally. "Give me forty-eight hours, and I will give you my decision." She started to entreat me to stay, but I would not listen.

"Remember me," she said sadly as I went out the door.

I did not go back to Monique afterwards, for I knew she would be of no help with my problem. Returning to my own apartment, I spent a sleepless dreamless night; and the next afternoon sought out Jean-Jacques in his usual café.

"I have a problem," I said.

"Impossible!" he said sarcastically. "How can you ever have problems, Hippolyte? Everything you do, you think you are bound to do—because you draw your motives from your dreams."

"Be serious," I answered. "Suppose you have a friend—"

"A friend," he echoed.

"Listen to me!" I said, in exasperation. "You have a friend who has the possibility of living several lives. I mean consecutively. Not side by side, the day and the night, as you do."

"A friend," he repeated.

"And this friend," I continued, deciding to ignore the way he was baiting me, "asks you to inaugurate a new life for her, because you have brought to a close the old one. Would you do it? Or would you consider her as dead?"

"Be careful of Frau Anders," said Jean-Jacques. "You'll have a hard time settling with her."

"Have you no more to say to me than that?" I replied, disappointed in him. "I did not mention her name, deliberately. Not because I wished to conceal her identity from you, but because I wished you to treat my problem seriously, generically."

"I have just told you what you don't know, which is the only advice of value."

"What don't I know?"

"That you won't get rid of her," he shouted.

There was a moment of silence. Then I remarked, "There is someone who shouts at me in my dreams. And to him I said, shouting has never made me understand anything."

We did not, understandably, part that day as friends. I had learned that I was truly alone in this problem, alone except for the counsel of my dreams. In this city what life could Frau Anders possibly live, with her damaged body and used-up past? Yet I could hardly order her to return to the Arabs, to suffer more. Luckily, that night, a dream came to my aid. For you must know that, by this time, I had learned to place great confidence in my dreams.

I was walking on a snowy plain, in the company of a bearded monk. I asked him to teach me how to bear the cold without feeling it.

"That is no art," he replied. "You must learn to feel the cold without bearing it."

He grabbed my sex with his hand. I pulled away indignantly, and told him it was my feet which were cold.

"Did you feel that?" he asked. I realized that he had no intention of helping me, and asked him to take me to the head of the monastery. He was wearing white boots. I thought of this as explaining why he had not been able to teach my feet not to be cold. But on looking closer I saw they were not boots, but thick bandages. Then I was surprised he did not limp.

He brought me to the entrance of a building made of blocks of snow, like the dwellings of the Eskimos. There was a woman there, dressed entirely in white, whom he addressed as Mother Superior.

I seem to have been taken to some room of my own, for I remember being brought a meal on a tray. I remember, too, thinking that I should begin to meditate, but I could not help looking out the window high on the wall of the room and wanting to get out.

Next I was in a sort of park behind the house. It was warm and sunny. The Mother Superior was there, seated at a grand piano under a cypress tree. She was conducting a music class. We were each to come to the piano and play for a few moments. I said I didn't know how to play, and others said the same, but she insisted that that did not matter. Then someone came forward to take his turn, with great reluctance and embarrassment, and picked out the national anthem with the index finger of his right hand. A second volunteer shyly played a hymn that was all chords. I thought these performances singularly inept, but I was beginning to understand that here ineptness was a talent. Then it was my turn. I knew I could not play a march or a hymn or a lullaby, even badly, so I just stood before the piano, and struck several groups of keys with my fists. Then I kicked the piano, turned, bowed, and returned to where I had been sitting on the grass.

"Now," the Mother Superior said, pointing in my direction in a way that disconcerted me, "you have learned the first lesson. And what is that?"

"That everything is good?" I murmured.

"Right," she said.

In the next part of the dream I was alone in the park. Snow had begun to fall on the green lawn; I found this peculiar, and tried to remember if it were winter or summer. I was hoping to encounter the Mother Superior again, for I was displeased with my own forwardness and troubled that I had not expressed my real feelings. I knew I had not been, consciously, insincere. I had believed what I had impulsively declared to her. But now I no longer believed it. The statement "Everything is good" did not seem right. I tried "Nothing is good." That seemed a little better, but still not right. Then I thought of "Some things are good." But this was even worse, in fact, impossible.

The snow was so deep now that my foot sank into it up to the ankle. The others had taken shelter on the verandah of the house, and I decided to go indoors myself. I came upon them jumping from foot to foot to shake the moisture out of their clothing. It looked like a sort of dance. I was also aware of a certain smell, besides the sour odor of wet woolen clothing, something like the mixed odor of antiseptic and disinfectant that one finds in the corridors of public hospitals.

Amidst the din the Mother Superior reconvened the class and called for the next performer. I took another turn, though I had already had one. To be more like my dancing fellow-students, I hopped and stamped and shook as I moved to the piano. But once there, I did not know what to do, so I climbed into the piano, pulled the stick that supports the lid, and closed myself inside.

"We are now in a position to use the full resources of the piano," I heard the Mother Superior say as I groped in the dark for a comfortable position among the wires and felt pads. I heard her giving instructions to someone else, telling him to use the right and the left and the center of the piano, all at the same time. Her voice became fainter, as I crawled further into the piano. Then I saw, crouching in a corner, a pale young man with a tiny moustache who asked me what day it was. When I told him it was Sunday, he began to cry. "All right, let it be any day you like," I said. And attempting to cajole him, as one would a child, I showed him a hole in the floor of the box, and urged him to explore it with me.

He told me he was too afraid. Then there was a tremendous barrage of noise about us: all the pupils, having climbed on top of the piano, were playing it with their feet. Frightened, I tried to push him down the hole. But he could not be budged, just whimpered and kicked at me whatever I did.

There were several more bangs, and the sound of splintering wood. I could not believe that the teacher would allow it, yet when I saw the rim of an axe blade appear above my head, there could be no doubt my shelter was being attacked. Furious, I resolved to make a stand here, instead of retreating into the hole. Revolver in hand, I settled in a corner and waited for the first face.

The banging and splintering sounds continued, but the piano did not give way. This gift of time inspired me to construct some defenses. With one sweep of my hand I wrenched away the piano wires and clasped them to my body as a kind of armor. Now I could almost stand in the box. I decided to fire one shot, as a warning that I intended to defend myself. The pistol shot sounded muffled and low, like a cannon.

"Bravo!" I heard the Mother Superior's voice. "Five tones lower than the lowest note on the keyboard. The most beautiful sound of all." Then there was silence.

The next moment I was out of the piano. She was angry. "Where is he?" she demanded. "He is hiding. He must be punished." I pretended not to know whom she meant, for fear she intended to send me back into the piano to retrieve my companion. But it turned out that she had given orders to the maid that the piano be bandaged. "Now he won't get out!" she said nastily.

I felt sorry for my frightened companion, who would surely suffocate. But despite my protests, the piano was bandaged and carried away. I started to run after it, when I had an idea. I would kill this despotic woman. She was standing with her back to me, conversing with some students. Holding the gun with both hands, for I feared that now it would not go off, I aimed at her back with care, and pressed the trigger.

"Bravo," said one of the students, and smiled at me approvingly. I shot him, too. Pulling the trigger was so easy that I shot them all. Knowing they were all on her side, I congratulated myself on my perspicacity and wondered why such a solution had not occurred to me before.

The next thing I remember is being in a tree. I'm not sure whether I was hiding, or celebrating my daring crime; or perhaps, this part of the dream had nothing to do with what went before.

"Come down," called the man in the black bathing suit. He was standing on the ground, and seized my arm without pulling it.

I protested that it was too high, but he insisted that I jump. When I told him that I would hurt myself, once more he ordered me to jump.

"All right, all right," I said. "But don't make me." I realized that I would have to jump, but wanted to do it myself. What I didn't want was to be coerced.

"Jump!" he cried angrily.

"Let me do it my way," I pleaded. "Look, I'm about to jump."

"Jump!"

I made no answer though, knowing I had to comply, I was genuinely readying my body for the jump. But the next moment he pulled on the arm which he had been holding firmly all the time, and tumbled me toward the ground. I would have jumped myself. Bitter were my feelings as I fell.

The day following the advent of a new dream had become a sort of holiday for me, in which I cancelled all regular obligations to give myself fully to reflecting on my new acquisition. How welcome this dream sabbath was to me now, after my "dream of the piano lesson," when I was faced with a pressing personal problem as well, the disposal of Frau Anders. My former mistress would be expecting me in less than twenty-four hours.

But it took a while to extract the sense of the dream. At first what preoccupied me was the way in which this dream was like the others. Again, confinement. Again, someone tried to teach me something. Again, the exacting presence of the man in the black bathing suit. And once again, the familiar emotions. Surprise, the sense of humiliation, and the desire to please are three emotions which occurred continually in my dreams; while in my daytime life I am much more independent. To my dismay I discovered myself in this dream again deferring to the opinions of other people. I refer to the moment when I told the Mother Superior that "Everything is good."

Yet this dream was not simply like the others. I wondered if the piano lesson might be interpreted as a gloss to the ancient heresies espoused by Professor Bulgaraux. To say that everything is good is one way of freeing the spirit from what makes it heavy. But perhaps I take too seriously the utterances in the dream. The doctrine "Everything is good" may possess a certain therapeutic value, but no greater than the doctrine "Nothing is good." All acts of disburdenment are equivalent, including the dreams themselves.

And later that morning I realized that I had underestimated the rebelliousness I had displayed in the dream. To be sure, I had deferred to the Mother Superior. But then I had killed her. I had killed them all. If one believes that "Everything is good," that, too, must be thought of as good.

I must add that the Mother Superior somewhat resembled in size and coloring Frau Anders, though the figure in the dream lacked my former mistress' regrettable disfigurements. However, as befitting a nun, and as Frau Anders had been the day before, she was almost completely hidden in her garments. And had not Herr Anders been under the impression that his wife was in a nunnery? I concluded that this was a dream about Frau Anders and about the fate which I was to provide for her.

But you must understand that in the events of the next twenty-four hours, though I acted on my dream, it was not in the same spirit as I had acted in the dream. I was not resentful, I did not feel oppressed. It was a decision ratified by thought, though prompted by the teaching of the dream. I put it to myself in this way: Frau Anders wanted a new life—even as I, with my earnest liaison with Monique, was searching for a new life. For some perverse reason, she had come to me as her arbiter. I was indeed, as Herr Anders had said, though I had not understood it at the time, her trustee in the world, the executor of her mundane estate. Well, so be it. I would not shirk my responsibility, though I did wish she had simply left me alone. I had to act, for having acted once—having sold her into slavery—I had become bound to the unknown consequences of this act. Frau Anders' demanding reappearance was this unforseen consequence which I now had to face. I would have to be bold, I knew. A new life? What life could Frau Anders possibly live with her abused body? There seemed only one solution: to end this life which had already ended, and wished greedily to prolong itself.

That afternoon I busied myself with careful preparations. I bought several litres of kerosene and some bundles of old rags. At midnight, exactly forty-eight hours after I had seen Frau Anders, I arrived again at her house. I counted on her being at home, awaiting my arrival; for she knew that I was punctual and always demanded punctuality herself. Along the base of the small dwelling I laid a thick rope of rags which I drenched with kerosene and then ignited at one spot; the flames travelled like a spark along a fuse and encircled the house with fire. I watched at some distance from the house while neighbors ran into the street, and the firemen were summoned.

The firemen entered the building several times, after consulting with neighbors and bystanders, including myself, as to whether anyone was inside. A distraught woman, who said she owned the property, reported that a foreign woman had moved in there a few weeks ago; and that the new tenant rarely went out, and had had only one visitor, two days before, whom she had glimpsed entering and leaving but had not really seen. There were no anguished faces at charred windows or screams of distress. The firemen could find no survivors before the building collapsed. I went home feeling assured that Frau Anders had perished in the flames.

TEN

Imagine to yourself, reader, that you are a murderer. What is it that makes a murderer? Is it the bloodstained weapon, the scratches inflicted on one's face by the struggling victim, the guilty heart, the inexorable police inspector, the bad dreams? No, it is not necessarily any of these. All these conditions can be absent. The murder may be colorless, bloodless, conscience-less, unpunished. All that is needed is that one has committed the act of murder. It is nothing in the present, only something in the past that makes one a murderer.

Still, I looked for consequences; for how else can we assure ourselves of the reality of the past. Upon awakening, I examined my sleep for a dream. I scanned the morning paper, and found a paragraph on page eleven reporting the fire. But there was no mention of Frau Anders, and of course no obituary. I wondered if there were someone who would come to apprehend me. No one appeared.

You must not imagine that I felt guilty, or craved punishment. But I should have liked some token from my life to register this act. I considered a confession, but felt it would surely lack credibility. What could I say? That I had murdered a woman that I had two years before abandoned into slavery, who had returned to the city clandestinely, who had been recognized by no one? How would I convince anyone that Frau Anders had returned at all? The only person who had any evidence of her presence was Monique. Would I say: I have set fire to the house and thereby to the woman who sent you that letter? Would we visit the ruins of the house and poke among the ashes? Would Monique demand that I surrender myself to the police? Perhaps she would merely admonish me that I had been unfair.

When I returned to Monique's arms the following evening, I averted my face, my gaze was troubled. I did not know if I embraced my confessor, my judge, or my next victim.

"Did you keep your rendezvous?" she inquired icily.

"I did."

"Is this woman very important to you? You don't have to tell me if you don't want to."

"She is my shadow. Or else, I am hers. It doesn't matter. In either case, one of us doesn't really exist."

"Don't you think you ought to find out which one of you it is that exists?"

"That's exactly what I have done," I replied. "You are embracing the victor at this moment."

"God be praised for that," she said sarcastically. "Are you sure?"

"I have made sure, quite sure." I put my arms around her and pressed her to me more closely. Desire, mixed with an obscure resentment, moved me. Monique sighed and lay still, her head in the hollow of my shoulder.

"You don't want to see her again?" she murmured.

"No."

"Then we can be happy. I feel it. Don't you?" I shook my head. She sat upright suddenly, looked at me sharply, and then buried her face in her hands.

I stroked her back, and spoke as gently as I could. "Don't suffer, my dear one. I cannot yet be reconciled to happiness. A fierce irony has me by the throat. It invades my dreams. It drives me to terrible, useless acts. It makes me take myself too seriously, and ends by preventing me from taking anyone else seriously—except the accomplices and mentors of my dreams."

"That woman—" she sobbed. "Is she one of your . . . accomplices?"

"Yes."

"Then I am even less real to you than her?" she cried. Her eyes became wide and unseeing. I saw the dull look of fantasy capture her features. "And if I took a lover? If I made you jealous?" By this time she was on her feet, and pacing before the foot of the bed. "I hate you," she said finally, drying her eyes. "I want you to leave me."

Obediently I rose and dressed. I had never felt more warmly toward my poor red-eyed mistress, more willing to please her; yet I was incapable of doing so. When I tried to embrace her, she pushed me away.

"Perhaps you're doing the right thing," I said sadly. "Would it console you to learn that the lover you are rejecting is a murderer?"

"I don't believe you. Just get out."

"How do you know I'm not a murderer? I know it doesn't show, but I assure you—"

"How do I know?" Her look hardened. "If you mean that you have killed my love for you, you're right . . ."

"No, I don't mean that. I mean real murder. The opposite of procreation. The coming together of two people, with the result that there is one left, not three."

"Get out," she said again, sullenly.

I had no choice but to leave, and return to my own apartment. The next evening, when I called on Monique, she refused to let me in, but slipped a note under the door informing me that we needed a separation of some time. I was to return only when I had changed. This proposal did not give me hope, for I doubted if there would ever be any greater change than had already taken place. A few days before I was not a murderer, now I was. What greater difference in myself than that could I ever aspire to?

Still, I persisted. For several weeks I visited Monique daily. Sometimes she let me in, but she never allowed our quarrels to have their natural terminus in bed. Sometimes she even forgave me, but with the same acrimony that she condemned me for my heartlessness. I know I should not have let things come to this pass. But, I was under the impression that love was necessary, and if not love, then at least the appearance of it. Why else would it be that all the time I spent with Monique— or with anyone else—I had to look at her and she at me, and neither of us could look at ourselves. Since this was the case, our eyes not being planted on the near side of a screen projecting from our foreheads so that we could gaze at our own faces, but instead set in our heads so that we were condemned to look outwards—from this anatomical fact, I concluded that human beings were designed for love. The only exception to this design is dreaming. In a dream we do look at ourselves, we project ourselves on our own screen; we are actor, director, and spectator all at once. But of this privileged exception, I did not inform Monique.

Perhaps this is why our affair failed, and why we did not become reconciled. I had never dreamt of Monique, and I had never told her about my dreams. Neither could I bring myself to tell her of that act of murder, which seemed more and more like a dream—all throbbing image, no consequences.

This brief period of renewed solitude was interspersed with variations of my "dream of the piano lesson" in which some-times, to my confusion and dismay, I did not kill the Mother

Superior; and a new interest in the game of chess. I tried not to question the means by which I had dismantled the dream—acting it out.

I thought then that I knew what my dreams were about.

Rather, the problem of interpreting my dreams had been replaced with another topic—why I was preoccupied with them. I concluded that the dreams were perhaps a pretext for my attention. Very well, then, the more enigmatic the better.

I became interested in the form of my attention, and in attention itself.

Why not take the dreams at face value? Perhaps I did not need to "interpret" my dreams at all. As it had become obvious to me in this most recent dream that, in order to profit from the Mother Superior's instructions, it was better never to have learned to play the piano, so it occurred to me that in order to extract the most from my dreams, it was better never to have learned to interpret them. I wanted to enact my dreams, not simply observe them. And that was what I had done.

A total attention was all that was required. In a state of total attention, there are no dark corners, no sensations or shapes that repel, nothing that seems soiled. In a state of total attention, there is no place for interpretation or self-justification or propaganda on behalf of the self and its revolutions. In a state of total attention, there is no need to convince anyone of anything. There is no need to share, to persuade, or to claim. In a state of total attention, there is silence. And, sometimes, murder.

Jean-Jacques said to me one day, "To be an individual, that's the only task."

There was no one in whom I could confide now, not even Jean-Jacques. I could tell him only in the most indirect ways about myself. Still, our conversations held great interest for me.

"To be an individual," he repeated. "But do you know,

Hippolyte, you've made me realize that there are two entirely opposite ways of becoming an individual?"

I asked him to explain.

"One way," he said, "is through accretion, composition, fabrication, creation. The other way—your way—is through dissolution, unravelling, interment."

I think I understood. "And you think your way," I said, "is the way of the artist?"

"I'll say yes. Then what?"

"To be an individual," I replied, "does not interest me. I am not in your sense interested in a distinguished or artful life."

"Neither am I," he protested. "What do you take me for?"

"You spend so much time, Jean-Jacques," I said, warming myself to my argument, "protesting against banality. Your life is a museum of counter-banalities. But what's so wrong with banality?"

"Really . . ."

"Look," I said, "do you grant me that art doesn't consist primarily in creation but in destruction?"

"If so, then . . .?"

"Then mine is the greater art, the more intense individuality, since I'm learning not what to collect but what to destroy."

"And what will be left of you?" he smiled.

"Your smile," I said. "If I have not offended you already."

"No, of course not, *mon vieux.*"

"Your smile. And my peace."

He smiled again.

"Let me tell you something," I said, somewhat embarrassed as I recalled the incident but encouraged by his seriousness. "You asked me before how I've occupied myself this week. I'll tell you. I have been attending the national chess tournament which is being played at the Palais de ——. There I have seen the greatest artist in our country, a boy of only sixteen. His game is a revelation to me. He plays so relentlessly that his game seems—no, is—entirely mechanical and without thought. He marches the pawns over the board, the horse jumps to the attack, his bishops close in like pincers, his castles move like tractors, his queen is a bloodthirsty despot."

"What did you decide about your despotic queen?" asked Jean-Jacques.

"I am not talking about Frau Anders," I replied coldly. "I am not talking about the willfullness of justice, but about the mechanism of perfect play. I'm talking about the game of a champion."

My friend allowed his curiosity to be thwarted. "His game overwhelms you because you don't play chess as well as he," said Jean-Jacques.

"No," I exclaimed. "That's not important, for I understand the secret of his game, even though I can't anticipate his moves. The secret of his game is that he is entirely destructive. Each day I have gone to watch him, and only him."

"I'll go with you tomorrow," said Jean-Jacques.

"No. I am not going tomorrow."

"Why?"

"Because today he looked at me. Every day I have sat in the spectator's gallery and watched his pale, relaxed face. He never looks up, but today he did, he looked directly at me. I tried to hold my gaze, to answer his. But I couldn't. His look was too destructive, and I lowered my eyes in shame."

What did I read in the boy's eyes? Contempt as well as indifference, perfect attention, an energy which burned away all words. I had met my master in crime. But all this would have been exceedingly difficult to explain to Jean-Jacques who, I thought, would probably want to explain my fascination with the chess player as the heat of sexual attraction.

"Don't say it," I said to Jean-Jacques sharply.

"I won't!" He was annoyed at being the one whose mind was read. "You're sure?"

"Yes."

"It wasn't lust which you felt for this . . . champion?"

"No," I said. "Lust and awe are incompatible. I can only desire what I can imagine myself possessing, or at least imagine can be possessed."

"You know what you discovered in your chess player, Hippolyte?" Jean-Jacques sat far back in his chair. "Another blank soul. Rather, a mirror for your own blankness."

"And yesterday the mirror looked back," I mused somberly.

"Precisely. And that's against the rules of the game." He stared at me a moment, as if he understood something I was not telling him. It was a long, inquisitive stare, speckled with disbelief. Then he shook his head and grinned at me in the old teasing way. "But come, I'm being too cooperative. You don't need me to explain you to yourself. Let's play chess ourselves. Or we might pick up a shopgirl for you to dally with, unless you're being faithful to that dreary lady agitator of yours. I know! Have you seen that charming American film about the ape-man that's showing on the boulevard? You must see it."

Jean-Jacques was suddenly so boyish and ebullient in his little projects for amusement that I could not refuse him. I liked him better as a playmate than as a mentor. So we strolled along for an hour, with Jean-Jacques stopping many times to greet people and then amuse me with brutal gossip about them after we had passed on. Eventually we went to the film.

One day I received a letter from my father, which indicated that his health was failing and that he would like to see me while still in the full possession of his faculties. I made the trip home immediately, relieved to have an excuse for leaving the city. I had been waiting to flee, but no one pursued me. To be summoned away at least gave me a sense of activity. I left without telling my concierge or Jean-Jacques or Monique, so that I might enjoy the semblance of flight.

This was my first time home, since I left to take up residence in the capital a decade before. My father was not in bed, but he was confined in a wheelchair in which he moved himself about vigorously. His character had changed since his enforced retirement, I noticed. I remembered him as a robust, matter-of-fact, and jovial man; he was now querulous and easily distracted. His illness moved me to pity, and I agreed to a prolonged visit. My brother, busy with the new responsibilities of totally managing the factory, was happy not to have to spend so much time with the old man and account to him continually. His wife Amelie was plainly exasperated with the chores of nursing the invalid, preferring to devote herself to her children. They were delighted to turn him over to my custody.

At first I found the company of the old man tedious. I had little sympathy with his fear of dying, and did not understand what he had become. My duties were simple. For several hours a day I read to him, within the limits of his now highly specialized taste, for he liked only novels which took place in the future. I must have read him a dozen. I imagine that they gave him a taste of immortality—and, at the same time, comforted him by their grim prognostications: it would not be so bad a thing to miss that future which they described.

One afternoon, while I was reading from a novel about life in the thirtieth century, a time when according to this author cities will be built of glass and the people in them fashioned from plants by priest-artisans, he interrupted me. "Boy," he said, brandishing the walking stick which he kept on his knees, "what would you like to inherit from me?"

The question was painful to me, not because I found the idea of losing my father insupportable, but because I dreaded the railing against death which would inevitably follow my answer.

"If you would continue the support which you have given me, Father," I answered, "I would be more than pleased."

"I own some property in the capital, you know. A house."

I did not reply.

He then questioned me, as to how I had used my income, how I justified even this amount of support. I decided not to embellish my life in the capital with a false luster of activity, and explained the modest preoccupations which filled my day.

"And women?" he said, nudging me with his stick.

"There is a young woman, Father, who now refuses to see me, because I did not assure her we were happy."

"Give her up."

"She has given me up, Father."

"Then win her back, when you return to the city, and then give her up."

"I couldn't do that, Father. I bear her no malice, and her betrayal would not relieve me."

He made no answer to this, and motioned me to continue reading. After some more pages, which related how the dictator of Nova Europa orders all children between the ages of twelve and fourteen tattooed and sent to colonize an abandoned continent, it was I who interrupted. "Father, what is your opinion of murder?"

"Depends who you murder," he said. "Don't know whether I'd rather be murdered, or just get old and ill and die. Best thing would be to be murdered when you're already dying."

"What about being murdered when you're already dead?" I inquired cautiously, hoping I would not be asked to explain.

"Nonsense," he said. "Continue reading. I like the part where the moon pauses and Europe is submerged in water."

I read to him long after my voice was tired, for he insisted I finish the book. Then I took him in his wheelchair about the estate as I did every day at this hour. The garden was no longer unkempt and luxuriant as I remembered it from my childhood, but was strictly arranged so that he could check daily on the conscientiousness of the gardener's ministrations. "I like order, my boy," he said to me the first day we had made the tour. "I'd like to put order into everything in this house, but they won't let me. Outdoors I am master, though. You'll see what I've done to this—jungle." I saw indeed. The year before, when he first became ill, the whole garden had been replanted under his instructions. It was now an alphabetical garden, for him; though for me, it was still a chronology of my evacuated childhood. Nearest the house were the anemones, then came the buttercups, then the carnations; here I had spied on the maid and the butler embracing in the kitchen. Marching round the sides of the arbor were an equal number of rows of daffodils, eglantine, foxglove, and gardenias. Then came the hyacinths, irises—halted by the pagoda where I used to set up my lead soldiers. Then the jasmine, knotweed. There were lotuses in the old well, and on the far side of that, marigolds. In the little pond where I sailed my toy boats, narcissuses. Then came the orchids, and a small square bed of poppies. "Had to stop here," he muttered. "No flower that begins with the letter Q." I think that tears came to my eyes at this moment, on the first day. I do not know whether I wept for the failure of my father's absurd, endearing project, for the lack of flowers to complete the alphabet, or for the pangs of remembering my childhood in the company of my childish father.

Did I say that I found that his character had changed? Perhaps you will see that I have understated the matter. I discovered with a shock of pleasure that my father had become eccentric, willful in his sickness and old age. He waved the walking stick which he kept across his knees at his grandchildren as if he longed to maim them. He screamed at my brother and his wife that he was disinheriting them, spat out the food which was served to him, and dismissed all the servants each Sunday after they returned from mass. But he treated me affectionately. His behavior toward me when I was a child was tolerably severe. Now it was real affection which I received from him, and not just because I was his son, but because he liked me. If my older brother fulfilled my father's expectations when my father was mature, hale, and active, I was my father's heir in his old age. We had much in common now.

My father had two only sons. How delightful it was to be one's father's only son, however belatedly!

I stayed with my father three months, during which his physical condition remained unchanged. His illness seemed to be arrested and the doctors said he might live for several years, but he was sure he would die before the year was out. "Go away," he said to me, "I don't want you to see me die."

"I'll read you more novels," I replied.

"I don't want to hear any more."

"I'll go to the National Library, and find a flower that begins with Q. I'll send for a seedling, from no matter how far."

"Doesn't matter," he said. "Go back to your woman, and try to be happy."

I bid him a loving and painful farewell, and returned to the capital. As soon as I had unpacked, I went to Monique's apartment, eager to see her after our long separation. It was a weekday, and mid-afternoon, so I assumed she would be at work, but I was going to wait for her and then take her to dinner. I let myself in with my key, and discovered her there with a man in his underwear who was bent over a typewriter.

She was very calm, much calmer than I; and the man even calmer than she. He sat there during our halting tearful conversation, aimlessly fingering the typewriter keys. Occasionally he struck one by accident; then he cursed, took a typing eraser from one of the desk drawers, and neatly erased the errant letter from the first page and each of the carbons. He seemed anxious to resume the typing which I had interrupted. Monique ignored him, stricken with a shame which I did not attempt to relieve. I, I felt no shame at all for my intrusion, but a little embarrassment, yes.

Have I made it perfectly clear? Monique had married. The typist in his underwear was a translator from obscure Slavic languages, possessing the most admirable political sentiments. Together they would translate the whole world into their wholesome, hopeful idiom. I congratulated them. Monique kissed me on the mouth. The young husband rose gravely and shook my hand. I let myself quietly out of the apartment and waited on the next landing until I heard the sound of the typewriter again. I did not have to wait long.

I returned to my solitude, and to my dreams. Poor Hippolyte! I had been rejected in the circumstances in which rejection hurts most, thinking it would be I who would do the rejecting, lacking even the distractions of an unrequited love to console me. For the first time in my life, I felt painfully alone. All I had to do was what I had judged impossible for Frau Anders: to begin a new life. It was not so easy. Yet I believed my case was different. After all I was hale and fit, only a little past thirty. If one could not begin anew at my age, when was it possible?

Only, you see, I kept dreaming my "dream of the piano lesson." I kept dreaming of a commanding woman who ordered my life, and of a man in a black bathing suit who urged me to jump. I had killed the woman, I had jumped. But, as in the dream, bitter were my feelings as I fell.

The first time that Frau Anders had left my life, I had felt relieved of a great burden. Now there was only a space, the space further enlarged by the absence of my well-intentioned Monique. If this were a dream, I thought, I would summon Frau Anders back. I would explain to her why I had killed her. I might even ask her permission. A failure of nerve? Perhaps.

But as it turned out, all this was unnecessary. The murder of Frau Anders was not a dream, although for all purposes it might just as well have been. For one day she simply appeared. It was a dreary spring day, still cold with winter. I was sitting in a café, indoors and in back where it was warm, cupping a brandy with both hands, when I saw a face pressed against the window pane. I had just exchanged a few words with the waiter, who had gone away. And then there was this face, a strange ravaged face that seemed all a blur to me because of the pane of glass and the dim interior of the café that separated us. It was a face I remembered, and it was all faces that peer and scrutinize and judge. I picked up my newspaper, and put that between us as well. Then I looked again. The face was still there. It was smiling, or making a spiteful expression; but the expression was either not well defined or unsuccessful. Then a hand reached up to rub the pane of glass where the face's breath had clouded it. The face was clearer then, but still not clear.

When you want to determine whether or not someone is dead, I know, you put a mirror or any piece of glass to the mouth, and see if the glass records a blotch of moisture from the breath. To breathe on glass is the signature of life, in the appearance of death. Then I knew. It was a resurrection. It was Frau Anders.

She entered the café and walked determinedly to my table. I had a moment's impulse to call for the waiter or to fling myself under the table.

"Don't run," she said sternly, seating herself. "I want to talk to you."

"It's a dream," I whispered to her.

"Don't be an ass, Hippolyte! No one is more real than I."

"That's true," I said, in bewilderment. "How indestructible you are."

"No thanks to you! I suspected you'd do something like that.

I was watching you all the time, and slipped out the back door, stepping right over your clumsy bundles of kerosene-soaked rags, while you were busily touching a match to the front of the house. My dear, you're no better as a murderer than as a white-slaver."

"What have you been doing all this while?" I murmured.

"I'm not answering any more of your questions. I'm here simply to inspire remorse in you. But you may tell me what you are doing. What, for example, were you doing the very moment I caught sight of you?"

"I'm waiting for my father to die," I said, sadly.

"I hope you are not helping him in this final project of his," she said, in a tone of severity.

"What do you take me for, a parricide?" I replied indignantly. And I told her briefly about the three months which I had spent nursing the old man.

"Well," she said. "I shan't ask you to nurse me. I'm doing very well, thank you."

"But your wounds," I exclaimed.

"Look to your own. I can take care of mine."

"And where do you live?" I asked, humbly. She paused, and looked into my face. "I'm not asking you to tell me your address," I added quickly.

"If you must know, I rent a portion of the apartment of an impecunious titled lady. I have the ballroom and several antechambers. There are many mirrors in these rooms, but I don't mind. I am learning to be brave."

"Do you see other people?"

"Why do you ask me so many questions? Haven't you asked enough? . . . I see mainly doctors. At a certain clinic I am recovering the use of my right arm."

"And Lucrezia? Do you see her?"

"That frivolous child? Never! She would despise me."

"Don't be afraid," I said gently. "I'll help you. I promise.

I'll devote myself entirely to your welfare, without imposing on you in the least." She regarded me suspiciously. "It will take a little planning, but when I am finished, I shall present you with a great surprise." A marvellous idea had occurred to me. I began to talk more rapidly. "Within a year, after certain things have happened which will free me to pursue your welfare and give me the means to do it, I shall be able to present you with something that you will have for your whole life. A life," I concluded, "which I shall do everything in my power to make as long as possible."

"You're going to give me something?"

"Yes."

"Something I want? Something I will have by my side, something I can keep all my life?"

"Yes. You will keep it, and it will keep you."

She smiled. "I think I know what it is."

"Do you? I wonder how. I myself just thought of this solution."

"Women are very intuitive, you know," she said archly. "How long must I wait?"

"Oh, it might be a year or more. It partly depends on my raising a certain sum of money."

"I have money," she said eagerly. "That needn't stand in our way."

"No," I replied firmly. "It must be my money. You believe that women have a monopoly of intuitiveness. Surely you will accede to the equally conventional pride that a man feels in being the one who dispenses the money." She sighed. "Will you wait?" I asked.

She nodded. But then she added, "I'm a trifle afraid of you."

"And I of you," I said. "But in this meeting of fears, I also love you."

"How strange," she murmured. "When I came in the door of this café, I hated you so much. No, it was worse than hatred.

I felt contempt for you. And now your imperturbability quite seduces me. I think you do love me, in your own impossible way."

"To be entirely candid," I replied, "I may be simply mistaking fear for love. This is an error I often make in my dreams."

"Why should you be afraid of me?"

"Because you are there," I answered curtly.

You may wonder what present I had in mind for Frau Anders. It was this. As she had been sitting across from me in the café I reflected that I had twice over made her homeless —first, by being the agency of her leaving her husband and daughter; and second, by burning down the poor house in which she recently lived. What better recompense could I offer than a house in which she could live undisturbed by me or anyone else. All that I needed was the means which I would acquire upon my father's death.

The painful news came the following January when I had just turned thirty-one: my father died, and I came into my inheritance. Not wishing to be encumbered by the things I might be tempted to buy, I arranged to dispose of the cash and negotiable securities. My father's lawyers were instructed to divide the sum between two persons who were to remain ignorant of the identity of the donor. Half was to go to Jean-Jacques; the other half to a young poet just done with his military service whose first book I had read and admired greatly. Why did I give the money anonymously? Because, with Jean-Jacques, I did not want our friendship to be disfigured by either gratitude or resentment; and, with the ex-soldier whom I had never met, I felt it would be inauspicious to begin an acquaintanceship with an act of benefaction. You must understand, the giving away of my legacy was no great sacrifice. I still had the monthly income from shares in the family business on which I had lived ever since I came of age and left home. What mattered to me in my inheritance was the house my father bequeathed to me, as he had promised. He had acquired it some years before with the intention, never carried out, of having a residence in the capital several months during the year.

I did not immediately install Frau Anders in the house, for I intended to remodel it and furnish it for her use. I have always had an interest in architecture that expresses the most intimate longings of its inhabitants. While I vowed to keep my fancies within bounds, I could not resist an almost voluptuous feeling of anticipation when I had determined on this project. Such were the pleasures of my idle life, and the ease with which I assuaged my guilt.

I remember the building project which hitherto had given me the most pleasure, although I had nothing to do with it. There lived, year round, on the island where Frau Anders and I had stayed for the winter on our trip south, an elderly English spinster. She had a small immaculate white house, just outside town overlooking the sea. One day, as she was walking the stony road into town, she saw a woodcutter ferociously beating his horse which was lying prostrate on the ground. The old lady attacked him with the grey silk parasol which she always carried. Imagine her horror when she learned that the flogging was only preparatory to shooting the horse, which had stumbled and broken two of its legs. The old lady, not in the least inured to the cruelty with which the islanders habitually treat their animals, immediately offered to buy the horse. Too astonished by the absurdity of such a transaction to be in form for protracted bargaining, the woodcutter settled quickly for a price twice what he had paid for the horse, and went away, hauling his cart himself, to get drunk in the port and relate the story to his friends.

The old woman had the horse carried to her house. She sent for the local veterinarian, who bound the animal's legs in splints and prescribed some medicines for its fever. Not content with these ministrations, she then called a veterinarian from the mainland, who pronounced the animal a hopeless cripple.

Now comes the part of the story which I like best. The horse was quartered in a small wooden shed behind the house. The old lady fed it every day herself, massaged its legs, and gave it its medicines. Gradually its fever subsided, and it began to stagger about in a determined but helpless way. The old lady had no thought of challenging the doctor's prognosis. She was delighted that the horse could walk in any fashion at all, and she now set about to construct a permanent residence for her companion. The bare rectangular shed in which he lived did not seem a happy enough place for a horse who would forever be deprived of the pleasures of walking, cantering, and pulling a woodcutter's cart. "Horses like views," she told the people in town, who had nothing to reply to such a singular assertion. She then proceeded to hire masons and bricklayers, and had built a small tower, about six meters in height on the other side of the garden. Around the tower was a spiral ramp which led to a comfortably-sized room at the top. The horse went to live in this room. In the morning she would bring it down, and tie it to the fence; in the heat of the mid-day sun she would return it to the tower; and at tea time she would lead it down again to stand or lie beside her while she rested in her hammock in the garden. Soon the horse's way of dragging itself about became stronger and more surefooted, so that it could negotiate the ramp by itself. It would clamber up and down from its tower at all hours, without ever straying from the old lady's property.

After some months of life in the tower, watching the blue sea, the horse's wretched gait could actually be described as a walk, albeit with a severe limp, and the old lady began to lead it by the bridle back and forth with her into town when she went to market. Everyone laughed at her amiable folly, and no one noticed that the horse's limp was steadily diminishing. One day, an occasion which I was lucky enough to witness, she made an appearance in town riding sidesaddle. The horse bore her calmly through the port streets without the trace of a limp. Whether it was the fine view of the sea which was its privilege, or its gratitude to the old lady, the truth was that the horse was entirely cured. In fact, both the foreign residents and the islanders said its legs had never been so slim and straight in its previous existence as a woodcutter's drayhorse. Such are the curative powers of the right dwelling, with the appropriate architecture.

I thought a great deal about this story, when I undertook the architectural commission for Frau Anders. I believe I was undertaking to build her a house in the same spirit as the old lady built a tower for the horse. I thought how this house might open new vistas for Frau Anders. Why, she might recover her health entirely, find love and happiness, abandon her rights to beauty, prosperity and acclaim, under the impulse of a novel architecture. Thus, far more acutely than when I plotted to murder her, I experienced the sensation of power—such as a magician must feel when he is beginning his exorcism, or a doctor when he starts a delicate operation, or an artist when he faces the nude canvas. I imagined the house enclosing Frau Anders, transforming her, allowing her to enact her secret fancies, whatever they might be.

You see my weakness, my vice, of that period (I freely confess it): I could not help wanting to aid others, but I know it appeared as an outrageous tampering with their lives. Others saw this more clearly than I did. I remember, for instance, Jean-Jacques' reaction when I told him of this new project, without mentioning the double injury which I had caused to Frau Anders of which the house was the merest gesture of restitution. I did, however, tell him that Frau Anders was not well, and that I hoped the house would cheer, perhaps heal, and, at the very least, shield her. I also related the story of the old lady, the horse, and the tower. At first he laughed, I thought approvingly, but then he said, "Hippolyte, you are laboring under the friendliest but least plausible of all delusions, that everybody is like you."

"No," I replied firmly.

"Now I understand," he continued. "This is why you don't suffer."

I don't know what I said to him in reply, but I remember that I thought: It's not true. I don't consider anyone like myself. Neither you, Jean-Jacques, nor Frau Anders, nor my father and brother, nor Monique. I want to let them be what they want to be. How could Jean-Jacques be right? Why, I don't even think I am like myself, much less do I think other people are like me. Though I try to be like myself—and for this reason pay so much attention to my dreams.

ELEVEN

During the time of my work on the house, Frau Anders and I met once a week, usually at the Zoological Gardens. My old friend was extremely changeable in mood, sometimes reproachful, sometimes quite gay and charming. The worst moments followed greater intervals in our meetings, when I had not seen her for perhaps a month, which meant that she had been in the clinic and had undergone some plastic surgery. Even at her most fretful, though, the sight of the caged animals never failed to soothe her.

"I feel at peace with the animals," she confided to me one afternoon. I had noted that her preferences were for the larger animals: the lion, the elephant, the gorilla. "I never appreciated them," she continued, "until—you know." How could I reply? For I understood that she was referring to her own captivity.

My own feelings toward her were tender but timid. I suspected her warmth toward me; I could not understand why she was not more angry. I dreaded this anger, which I always expected to break forth. Yet I would have preferred it to this inexplicable mildness and serenity. When the animals were pacing or scratching themselves or being fed through the bars, she was most affectionate. She would slip her good arm in mine, and we would silently promenade before the cages. That was when I felt most uneasy, when I felt—dare I confess it?—that she was courting me.

It was on one of these walks that I tried to break the silence that bound me closer and closer to Frau Anders, seeking to say something that would define our relationship. Her forgiveness, her mood of expectancy, was strangling me.

"You know my father has died," I began.

"I know."

"Do you remember I promised you something after his death?"

"I am waiting," she said.

"Well, I can't tell you all that I plan, for I want you to be surprised, but I will tell you this much. My father has left me a splendid house here in the city, which I want you to occupy when I have prepared it for you."

She made a crooked smile with her face, but said nothing. "It's to replace the house which I burned down," I added.

"And more than that, I hope," she said.

"Much more," I replied reassuringly. I was thinking of the wonderful plans I had for this house, which would not be just an ordinary dwelling but a gift of my imagination—a palace of seclusion and rehabilitation.

Work on the house was already well underway at the time of this conversation. The site was in a quiet neighborhood near the large river which bisects the city; the house was an old three-storied *hôtel particulier*. For a while I thought of demolishing the building and erecting something entirely new in its place, but after examining the house carefully I decided that, with some few structural changes, it could be preserved. It was essential to my idea of it that it have a marked and very special unity. But I determined that this unity would not come from a dominant room, such as a ballroom or library. Neither, since I was working with an old and complex structure, would I impose on it my fondness for a given material, such as brick or glass or wood or marble. The house was to be unified only by its purpose. That was what I had to supply. What would Frau Anders want with this house? Privacy was my answer. Privacy from her old life to conceal the ravages of the new. Privacy from the life from which she had escaped. Privacy from me: her shadow, judge, accomplice, master of ceremonies, and victim. Privacy from her body, cruelly ravaged, to educate her soul.

My problem was how to impose this requirement of privacy upon a building which already had a certain traditional structure. The house which I had inherited was symmetrical and almost two hundred years old. It consisted of a court which faced, but was screened off by an iron fence from, the street; two small wings, on the right and the left, formerly offices and stables; the principal part of the house at the back; and in the rear a small garden. My first alteration was with the court, which I did not want thus exposed to the street. In place of the iron fence I had a wall built which joined the two wings and enclosed the courtyard, thus making the structure entirely rectangular. So that from the street view the house would present a wholly conventional appearance, as if this brick wall actually gave on to a set of rooms, I had wooden shutters affixed to the wall in the places where passers-by would expect windows. The second alteration was to cut the two wings off from access to the main part of the house. The basement and ground floor of the *corps de logis* were left intact, except that I converted several ante-chambers and closets into secret rooms by disguising the doors.

In the old house there were two more stories, but I had the second story demolished. The first story, whose alterations were more extensive than on the ground floor, was divided into four large rooms, each surrounded on all sides by corridor. These rooms on the first floor were windowless and, to secure the maximum amount of privacy, they could be reached by an outside staircase from the garden at the back of the house.

When the work of remodelling was nearing completion (I went every day to oversee the labor of the construction company I had engaged), I turned my attention to the furnishings. This was in many ways the more important task, since a house is truly unified not by its exterior but by what it contains. I asked Jean-Jacques to assist me, since I am not a collector or a browser. You will recall that I had for some years lived with a minimum of furniture and possessions. Naturally, I did not aim at imposing my own sparse tastes on Frau Anders, who had been used to a comfortable life before she left the capital. Neither did I want to share with her any of the images of dwellings which were presented to me in my dreams. Thus I worried that there was some resemblance between this house and the mansion of the tobacco millionaire R. in my "dream of an elderly patron," but I could detect none except the size and luxurious scale of both houses. And one of the purposes served by my enlisting the aid of Jean-Jacques was that I could be sure that no two rooms would be furnished exactly alike, as in my first dream, "the dream of the two rooms."

Together, Jean-Jacques and I spent a month in shopping forays. We did not neglect the newest and most vulgar department stores of the city. But we found more of what I wanted in used furniture stores and on the grounds of the Marché aux P——, treasurehouse of old jewelry, armor, antique furniture, hardware, discarded clothes, and musical instruments. Here, even before we selected one item for the house, Jean-Jacques made some purchases for himself: a ring made of three coral roses set in gold leaves, and a sailor's uniform.

I must explain to you how I proposed to furnish the house,

so that you will understand how my sombre ideas of Frau Anders' rehabilitation and Jean-Jacques' precious and perverse taste could, in this one instance, work in tandem.

One room, where Frau Anders could re-enact her captivity, was to be furnished in the Moorish style. There was to be sand on the floor, the odor of camel dung, a potted palm, a portrait of the Prophet, a divan, a deck of cards.

Another room was walled entirely with mirrors, even on the ceiling, though there were no mirrors elsewhere in the house. Here Frau Anders could survey the ruins of her beauty. In this room, furnished with special gusto by Jean-Jacques, was a dressing table, cosmetics, fans, a wardrobe of elegant clothes— all the appurtenances of vanity. It was a room such as I imagined might have been occupied by one of those dissolute ladies of society in eighteenth-century novels who are punished for their profligacy by smallpox, and spend the rest of their lives cloistered and pining for their sins.

One of the rooms on the first floor was a chapel, which I planned to have consecrated. Besides the usual altar and crucifix, it was decorated with various paintings of martyr saints: the boy transfixed with arrows, the woman bearing her breasts on a plate, the man (the patron saint of the capital) carrying his head in his arm. The odor of incense in this room would provide a welcome refreshment from the desert smells of the Moorish room.

There was also a room on this floor for the expression of strong emotions. This room contained photographs of Frau Anders' husband, her daughter, and me; darts; a swing; a tool chest with hammers, saws, scissors, and the like; a chest of counterfeit money; and a good deal of ornate furniture which I imagined it would be a pleasure to abuse.

Another room upstairs was for sexual purposes. I installed in it a sunken bath tub in the center of the floor, a comfortable rocking chair, a fur rug, candles, chains on the wall, obscene books and pictures, and a metronome.

Another room, on the ground floor, was a salon in the style of two centuries ago, furnished in the taste which Frau Anders' former house had lacked. Her old reception room was disfigured with abstract paintings, indirect lighting, and a white telephone. This room had slim chairs, tapestries, snuffboxes, and candelabra. There were two or three more rooms on the ground floor, which I furnished according to my fancy. . . . I know the house was large for one person, and that there appears no sequence between the rooms. But I felt, at the time, that a house is either one room or an indefinite number of rooms. It is either a single cell or one of those organisms to which chambers can be added indefinitely, as long as one has something to put in them—like a brothel or a museum. This house for Frau Anders was to have the latter character. It was to be both a museum of her past and the whorehouse from which she could select the pleasures of her future.

In furnishing the rooms in this way, I tried as far as possible to blend the imaginative with the obvious, in order to accommodate to Frau Anders' limited vision. I had even decided not to tell her what the rooms were for, hoping she might discover their uses for herself. Yet, even with these precautions I worried that I was allowing my fancy too free a play. After all, I had no access to Frau Anders' dreams. Nor could I imagine that she was capable of taking her dreams seriously. (Her fantasies, her day-dreams, yes; but not the disgraceful, unflattering scenes that were thrust upon her, unbidden, in her defenceless sleep.) I hoped, since Frau Anders considered herself a lady of the modern school, she might accept what I had selected for her out of gratitude that I conceived her taste to be so advanced. But I could not be sure of this. For all I knew, she might be displeased with what I had done, and I still dreaded the outbreak of her violent temper. Thus I was not entirely reassured when I described to her, one day when we met in a secluded corner of the Zoological Gardens, the progress of the house, and she replied that she hoped to be satisfied with whatever I might do.

In early November, not far behind schedule, the house was more or less completed. I sent an invitation to Frau Anders, requesting her to come and view it the following day.

That evening, I sought out Jean-Jacques in the cafés and on the *quais* but, as sometimes happened, my search was unsuccessful. Actually I was pleased when I didn't find him. I had intended to tell him of Frau Anders' visit, and to invite him to be present. But although Jean-Jacques had expressed great eagerness to see Frau Anders again and to witness her initial reaction to the house, I did not look forward to their meeting. It was not that I wished to deny a colleague his share of the credit. But I was afraid that Frau Anders, in her present unfortunate condition, might not understand Jean-Jacques' style of perpetual levity and think, mistakenly, that she was being mocked.

The next morning Frau Anders arrived in a chauffeured car in the company of a youthful red-haired woman whom I immediately recognized as the celebrated music-hall actress Genevieve. My former mistress was heavily veiled and wore only black but was more expensively dressed than the other times I had seen her since her return. "I am happy to see that you are prospering," I ventured to say after the introductions were made.

"This estimable lady has befriended me," said Frau Anders solemnly. At that moment the actress turned away to remark on some feature of the house, and Frau Anders cast a broad, somewhat lewd wink in my direction. I was so startled that, quite involuntarily, I brought my index finger to my lips.

"I have always a need for protégés," Frau Anders continued, heedless of my warning and of whether she was overheard by her new friend. "At least in the absence of someone to protect me." I bowed my head at this mild and thoroughly deserved reproach. "I am giving her the benefit of my incomparable and edifying experiences with the treachery of men and the brevity of beauty," she concluded.

"Shall we see the house?" I said.

The two ladies followed me about for an hour, as I escorted them through all the rooms and explained something of the origin and meaning of my purchases. "What a magnificent gift," Genevieve exclaimed several times. She appeared charmed with the house and complimented me profusely. But Frau Anders' reaction, as I showed them about, was more non-committal than I had expected.

"Most imaginative, Hippolyte," Frau Anders said finally as we stood in the large basement kitchen, the last stage of our tour. "I am flattered that you think I would appreciate the uses of. . . ."

"Of so honest and articulated a building," I finished the sentence for her.

"Well, yes. But why did you imagine that I would accept—"

Again I interrupted. "Reparation is a delicate matter," I said. "Therefore it's imperative that you not think of this house as—I trust I may speak freely before your friend—in any sense reparation for the wrongs I have done you. It is simply a gift, more accurately, an act of homage to your good nature and your indestructibility. I do not dare to hope to settle any debts between us in this way. All accounts are left open, whether or not you live in this house."

"Surely they are," Frau Anders replied, with a trace more malice in her voice than I thought called for in the circumstances.

"Will you accept the house?" I asked, steeling myself for a refusal.

"Do take it," said Genevieve gaily. "You don't need to use all the rooms, darling. I'll invite Bernard and Jean-Marc and everyone from the theatre, and you'll have wonderful, wonderful parties."

"I should like that," Frau Anders murmured.

"Don't refuse," I said hopefully.

Frau Anders looked at both of us. I sensed the fretful, bewildered expression even through the heavy veil. "I don't think I would like to live here alone," she said.

"Alone?" I said. "But you won't be alone. You have new friends, you have Mlle. Genevieve, you have me. You'll have constant visitors. Did I tell you that Jean-Jacques wishes to pay his respects? He would have been here today, if I had found him in time to let him know when you were coming."

"I don't mean visitors," Frau Anders continued obstinately. "I mean a husband. I want to marry again."

Neither Genevieve nor myself replied to this.

Frau Anders went on, searching both our faces. "I'm not young any more, but I have a great deal to offer. I'm kind, forgiving, gay." She paused, as if waiting for an answer. "I'm not as foolish or naive as I used to be—don't demur, Hippolyte —and, look," she said, removing her veil, "I've passed not only the summit of beauty but the peak of ugliness as well." It was true. The treatments and surgery which I knew Frau Anders to be undergoing in the past year had worked wonders on her face. The large rectangular burn mark on her left cheek was barely detectible now, just a slight shadow, and the muscles around her left eye and mouth had been tightened so that only the faintest asymmetry remained.

"Why do you remain veiled, my dear?" I cried, delighted at this happy restoration.

"My husband shall unveil me," she said.

This urge for domesticity somewhat dismayed me. It was not this which I had envisaged for Frau Anders in the house which I had furnished for her rehabilitation—any more than I had anticipated parties with her new theatrical friends. But I could not object. All that mattered now was that she accept the house, and not render waste and void the effort I had put into it. I trusted its proper uses and benefits would be revealed to her after she had lived in it a while.

"Will you accept the house?" I repeated.

We walked upstairs and out to the car.

"I will try," she said simply. They offered to drive me wherever I liked, but I wanted them to be alone in the hope that Genevieve might assuage Frau Anders' timidity about the house.

"I will meet you tomorrow at four o'clock at the gorilla cage," she said after we had embraced and Genevieve was already in the car.

"You can wait for a husband in the house," I called after her as the car pulled away from the curb.

I went to report to Jean-Jacques the results of this inconclusive interview. I was not discouraged, even when Jean-Jacques said, "I didn't think she would like it. Did you expect otherwise?"

"But I did expect otherwise," I protested. "I think I may have made a mistake in actually furnishing the house before she had learned to appreciate its use. Perhaps at this moment labelling the rooms and giving an itemized list of the proposed contents would have been enough. The rooms with their real furnishings do not allow Frau Anders the exercise of her own imagination."

"My friend," Jean-Jacques replied, "Frau Anders could never imagine this house unless you set it before her in its completed form. Our former patronness is a woman of strong appetite and will, but she is also obstinate, literal-minded, and incapable of imagining anything. Such people can only be shocked, which is the dullard's substitute for the pleasures of the imagination."

I told Jean-Jacques that I thought he underestimated Frau Anders' spiritual capacities, but otherwise his answer pleased

me. I would try not to be too disappointed if Frau Anders refused to occupy the house. I had no desire to force anything
on her.

The next day we met, she and I, at the gorilla's cage.

"I will wait for a while in your house," she said gravely.
"Don't think I am ungrateful—if I want more."

"Oh, my dear friend," I cried, deeply moved, and seized
her trembling hands with mine.

"Don't fail me," she said tearfully.

"I will always serve and honor you," I replied.

Shortly after, Frau Anders moved into the house. When I
went to call on her the first time, she seemed happy. While she
chided me a little about the expenses I had incurred in remodelling and furnishing the house, I could see that she was
not displeased at my extravagance since, like many rich or
formerly rich people, she thought that caprice and waste were a
necessary ornament to wealth.

You may be sure that I was not unaware of Frau Anders'
further demands on me. I tried not to think of them, but
gradually I could not put the idea out of my mind. There
was really no gift I could make to repair the injury I had
done her except the gift of myself which, as willing as I
was to make reparation, I was unwilling to give. Why she
should have wanted me, I cannot tell. But her hints were unmistakable, her persistence—whenever I came to call on her—
unflagging.

Finally I decided that there was only one way to put an
end to Frau Anders' embarrassing hopes, and that would be to
marry as quickly as possible. I believe this idea might have occurred to me even without Frau Anders' prompting, for furnishing a house—albeit for a woman who, I presumed, would live
in it alone—made me think of those who usually occupy
houses: of the family, and the whole sanctified order of do-

mestic relations. I thought, too, of my brother, whom I had always respected for marrying early and decisively. Most people remain unmarried in order to wait for the choicest mate. But I had stayed a bachelor out of apathy. I decided to exert myself and to marry.

While looking about for someone suitable, I tried to clear my mind of any fixed or preconceived ideas of whom I would like—either in age, station, or personal appearance. It would not matter whether she was older or younger than myself; whether beautiful or ugly, according to the world's standards; whether virgin or twice widowed; whether whore or aristocrat or matron or shopgirl. My only requirement was that the woman I marry should arouse in me a strong and positive emotion, and that I should do the same in her.

How would I recognize this feeling? Since I did not want to waste any time choosing a wife, it was important that I have some idea of what I should feel when I met her. In other words, I had to decide in advance what feelings on first acquaintance would be sufficient token that this woman was worth considering as a wife. I reviewed the various feelings I have had with women and decided that sexual attraction was not the one I should allow as decisive, since I have been attracted sexually to many women. For the same reason I ruled out intellectual attraction: I have been attracted to several women in my life for their skills in conversation and discussion, most recently to Frau Anders' daughter, Lucrezia. The feeling I was looking for was to be one I had not experienced before and this was only logical, since I had never before thought of marrying.

With this resolve, I renewed my relationship with several acquaintances from my student days, in the hope that they might have eligible sisters. While I found it interesting to learn the successes and failures of my ambitious comrades of a decade before, I did not find in these circles any woman who roused the nameless feeling which I was awaiting. At the same time, I took care not to neglect the daughter of the horse butcher at the corner, nor the concierge's niece, nor any of my unmarried female neighbors, however harsh their voices. But in all these encounters I felt nothing that was distinctive.

After several months I began to fear that, proceeding on this basis, I should never find a wife. Discouraged, I began to relapse into my unsociable bachelor habits. I had almost abandoned this worthy project when, one evening, something happened which accelerated my search. I had spent the afternoon with an old schoolfriend; I was still in a half-hearted way continuing my perfunctory search, for this friend had a divorced cousin. I came up the staircase in a meditative mood, thinking how difficult it was to accomplish anything, when I saw a dark figure, a woman with a black scarf around her head, seated on a little collapsible canvas stool in front of my door. Only one woman could be so silent, and so persistent; so I addressed her by name.

"Yes, it is I," replied Frau Anders. "May I visit you in your house?"

"There is nothing here," I said, as I unlocked the door and beckoned her to come in.

"I have a plan for you. No, for us. It will solve the problem which I posed for you last year when I returned to the city—the problem you solved for me in such a rude, but unsuccessful manner."

"Your murder," I said.

"Yes. My dearest Hippolyte, you have proved yourself a bungler in crime. Your talents are adequate neither to enslavement nor to murder."

I bowed my head. It is bad enough to be belittled by one's own conscience, but imagine the distastefulness of being condescended to by one's intended victim. "What do you think I am suited for?" I asked.

"You might make a good husband."

"Oh, my dear," I replied ruefully. "It's strange that you speak of that. Ever since I built that house for you my thoughts have turned, strenuously, toward domesticity. But if I may judge from the fruitlessness of my attempts to find a wife, I believe I should be less successful as a husband than as a slaver or a murderer."

"What of that benevolent young woman whom you were seeing when I returned?"

"Married."

"And the others you have considered?"

"I feel nothing."

"Well," she said, "I have a candidate for you—a woman older than yourself, and in somewhat damaged physical condition. But, these liabilities aside, she is bound to you by ties of lengthy friendship and many joint spiritual ventures, and by an abiding affection for you."

"My dear friend!"

"What obstacles are there to prevent our happy union?" she went on. "My husband has remarried. My daughter cares nothing for me, nor would I wish to mar her pursuit of pleasure with my ruined visage and insatiable longings."

"My dear friend," I said more firmly. "What you propose is entirely out of the question. We know each other too well. Neither one could bring felicity to the other."

"I thought. . . ." she trailed off.

"I know, I know. But I can't be other than I am."

I took Frau Anders home in a taxi. You might think that I was relieved that the issue had been brought into the open, and I had been direct with her. But I had every reason to feel that Frau Anders would not give up so easily. I redoubled my efforts at sociability, and was hardly ever at home.

A week later, I was to spend the evening with my former mistress. I had been at another unrewarding reception, and arrived at the house in a mood of discouragement. Frau Anders came to the door. She was looking better, more vigorous that evening, and I told her so. She did not reply to my compliments and preceded me silently into the house. I realized something was wrong when she did not go to the salon, where we usually sat, but instead led me up the stairs to the room with the pictures, tools, and play equipment which I had designed for the expression of strong emotions.

"I'd rather not go in here this evening," I said. "I'm tired. I've had a discouraging day."

"I'd rather you did come in," she replied. "I have a strong emotion to express, and I intend to do it with the means you have supplied. Have you the right to refuse me?"

"No," I murmured wearily. "Only the desire."

"Insufficient," she said. "Enter."

We entered the room, which looked much used. I noted an ominous sign: my torn photograph lay scattered in several pieces on the floor.

"Now," she said, seating herself on a swing which hung from the ceiling. She began to pump herself on the swing. "I want to tell you that I hate you. You have broken my life, as a naughty child hurls a clock to the floor, and I cannot repair it."

What could I answer to these words? I waited a moment in suspense.

"Repair me," she said imperiously.

When I didn't move, she repeated her command. I had to do something, so I went to the tool chest, picked out hammer, saw, and nails, and advanced toward her. But I couldn't approach closely, for fear of being hit by the swing or by her feet which repeatedly lunged at and then withdrew from my face.

"Not those," she laughed, as she rode past me. Then she brought the swing to a halt, and stood up. "Like this. Put your arms around me." She put her arms around me. I dropped the saw with a clatter, but I still held the hammer clenched in my left hand. "Drop the hammer," she said. I obeyed, either out of fear or deference. She parted her veil and whispered, "Kiss me."

I don't know what possessed me then. I was seized by an erotic fury such as I had never experienced. The room swayed in my vision. I clawed at Frau Anders' garments. There seemed to be so many layers of clothing, I think I half expected not to find a body underneath. Layer after layer I stripped off and flung on the floor, until she stood there naked and more desirable to my eyes than ever.

"The house has healed you," I cried in delight. It was not only her face, the remarkable restoration of which she had already revealed to me, and which was none of my doing or the house's. Her body as I saw it at that moment was intact, without blemish, the same smooth over-ripe body I had known in the past, before my inexplicable crimes had separated us. I seemed to recall that she said something about make-up, cosmetics, a disguise to win my pity. Is it possible? I was certainly not in my right mind, and I know that I became utterly incoherent. "My horse," I called her, caressing her robust thighs. "My little lame horse." I called her my swan, my queen, my angel, muse of my dreams. At that moment she slipped from my grasp—we were already rolling and grappling on the floor—and ran into the corridor. I followed her, calling "my queen" and "eternal tenant of my heart," and saw her disappear into the room which I had thought would be set aside for sexual purposes. I flung myself at the door, and found it locked.

"Marry me," she called from the inside, laughing.

I banged in fury on the door.

"I'm in the bath tub, Hippolyte. Waiting for you," she called out. I banged harder, and yelled at her to open. "No," she shouted, "I am at the wall—remember your dream?—my wrists are encircled with chains. The metronome is marking the rhythm of my desire for you."

"How can I?" I groaned. "I can't marry you, my queen."

"In the chapel," she called back. "You can marry me in the chapel down the hall." I had forgotten about the chapel. Why had I installed a chapel in the first place?

"No priest," I shouted back. There was silence. I leaned my head against the wall; tears of rage and frustration came to my eyes. She opened the door and peeped out.

"Are you ready, my dear?" she said sweetly.

I nodded dumbly. She emerged, wearing a white bathrobe, and took my arm. We went into the chapel and knelt before the altar. She muttered some words to herself, then said to me, "In the eyes of God, you have always been mine. Since I first saw you, a shy young student with your head full of books and dreams—"

"The dreams came after," I interrupted.

"Oh, those dreams. But didn't they begin after you knew me, and desired me?" she inquired triumphantly.

"No," I answered, "the dreams have nothing to do with you. I should never have told you about them."

The thought of my dreams gave me courage, and seemed to restore me to myself. What was I doing with this insatiable woman, kneeling on the floor before an altar? I feared her sufferings had unhinged her mind. Certainly they had affected me only a few moments earlier, when I'd been under the delusion that I desired her.

"You must pardon me," I said as I rose to my feet. "I can't marry you. I have told you so before. I am resolved to marry someone else, whoever that might be."

"But I've been waiting for you," she sobbed. "I and the house are waiting. You made us what we are. Without you we are empty."

"No, no," I cried, backing away. "You must be in peace. You musn't pursue me any longer. I can't help you."

"Don't go," she said. Strange that until then, I had not thought of going, had not thought myself capable of it. Then at that instant I realized that I could go, that I was free—free to move, as long as I acknowledge to myself that I was in flight.

Do we only move when someone pursues us? Is all motion running away? It seemed to me that I had never run, never even walked before in my life until that moment, when I fled the house which I had given Frau Anders, and the angry woman within.

TWELVE

Fearing that Frau Anders would follow me to my apartment, I took a room in a hotel in another quarter of the city, where I stayed for a week. At last I was in hiding for my murder, though pursued not by the police but only by my victim. And she wanted not to kill me in return, but to marry me. Of course, one solution to my problem was to kill her again, this time successfully. But I preferred to go on with the solution I had already chosen—to marry someone else.

I had only to determine the means, for on the basis of my recent efforts I feared I should never find a wife. It is difficult to make a choice without standards for choosing. But now there was a new urgency to my search for a wife, the urgency of terror, and to my aid came a visitation: not the knock on the door which betokened the dreaded arrival of Frau Anders, but the soundless visitation, during a restless nap, of a terrifying but fortunate dream.

I was in the luxurious private ballroom of a chateau, a room that I had never seen before though I knew in the dream exactly where I was and felt no surprise at being there. It was a

large long room, furnished with velvet curtains, crystal chande-
liers, gilt chairs, ancestral portraits, and a tall mirror.

The first thing I remember is just standing in the middle of
the room with my eyes tightly closed, trying to recall a name
which I had forgotten. Whatever it was, I couldn't remember
it, so I relaxed my efforts of concentration and opened my eyes.
I then thought that the most emphatic way of opening my
eyes would be to go to the mirror and look at myself. I did
this, and found there my own reflection which I began to study,
as if it were a portrait whose authenticity I was examining. At
moments it was a portrait of me and not a mirror. And when it
was a mirror, the substance of it kept altering; at one moment,
it was glass, at another moment, it had the look of polished
metal, at another moment, of silvered wood. Besides all this,
there was something odd about my reflection which, while it
was no doubt mine, was, in some detail which I could not
discriminate, unfamiliar to me.

Then it occurred to me how to determine whether this really
was a mirror, and my own reflection. I would remove the tuxedo
I was wearing. I reasoned that the surface could not reflect my
naked body if it were not truly a mirror, and further that I
should be able to identify myself with certainty if I were
naked—and in this way solve both problems. I undressed and
placed my clothes on a chair beside the mirror. But when I
saw myself naked, I still felt puzzled. "This is your only body,"
I said aloud to myself.

There was someone else near the mirror, a footman in livery.
He was standing behind the mirror polishing the frame. Although I knew he could see me, I felt no embarrassment at my
nakedness. Yet, having spoken aloud, I felt I owed him an
explanation.

"This is a naked mirror," I said.

He shook his head. "It's you who are naked."

Upset by his failure to understand, I explained that it was

of no importance that I looked at myself in this way. "This isn't vanity," I said. "You must understand that I have always regarded my body as if I were a potential amputee."

The clarity of this explanation pleased me, but he still looked at me with indifference, so with the idea of giving him further proof of my point, I took hold of my left leg with my hands, and broke it off.

Immediately I was horrified at my recklessness. I knew I'd gone too far, that I could never grow another leg again. My eyes filled with tears.

"There's only one cure for you now," the footman said. He left his post behind the mirror and crossed the room. I followed. While my walk was hobbled, I could almost keep up with him. I was surprised that it was not more difficult to walk with only one leg, but I took the absence of pain for granted.

"Please don't help me," I said, mustering all the bravery at my command. I wanted to go where he was leading me, but I didn't want his company.

"I want to watch," he said. "I love operations." I implored him to remain behind. I became angry and wanted to stamp my foot, but this gesture was out of the question.

Then we were standing outside a large auditorium. Before the door a functionary was collecting tickets. Having no ticket myself, I despaired of being allowed to enter, and hoped the footman might have two. At that moment I felt myself being shoved from the rear by others seeking admission, and in the confusion entered the auditorium alone, where I took the center aisle seat in the last row.

The people seated near me were as dejected and restless as condemned prisoners. I don't know whether I overheard this, or the idea simply occurred to me, but I suddenly knew that those gathered in this place were volunteers in a scientific experiment, who had agreed to allow their eyes to be put out. It seemed that, although everyone was here of his own free will, the management was aware that the volunteers might lose heart at the last moment, for, behind me, I could see the doors of the auditorium being shut, and an armed guard taking his station.

I felt doubly tricked. I had come here with the idea that I would recover the leg which I had so imprudently sacrificed. Instead I found that I would lose something more, my sight. I signalled to an usher who was standing in the aisle, explained my mistake to him, and asked his permission to leave. He told me curtly that I could not leave until "after."

I could scarcely believe my ill fortune, even when I saw the uniformed ushers with long knitting needles begin to move among those seated in the first row. The people submitted obediently, each making only a faint cry as his turn came. The ushers advanced inexorably, a row at a time. My possibilities of escape seemed nil. With my leg in this condition I could not run away; besides, the exit was guarded. Neither could I convince anyone that I was not one of the volunteers. The only chance I had, I reasoned, was to make an offer of myself even more generous than that of the others. I resolved to approach the man standing on the stage and try to strike a bargain with him. I would propose to donate my entire body, if he would return my leg and not blind me.

Most of the people in the auditorium had now been operated on by the ushers with the needles. I left my seat and hobbled down the aisle. On the stage I saw the man in the black bathing suit who was shaking hands with a line of already blinded people who filed before him. I felt discouraged, for I thought I would have better luck with a stranger. Nevertheless, I took my place in the line and when my turn came, put out my hand, too.

"Here he is again," said the man in the black bathing suit.

"Just once more," I said bashfully. "Don't be angry."

"Why should I be angry?" he replied.

I cannot begin to describe the immense sensation of relief

which I felt. All my ingenious proposals seemed unnecessary and irrevelant. I thought of how I might repay the bather for his kindness. "I will give you all my money, all that I possess," I said. "You shall tell me what to do. I will obey you in everything. I will be your slave."

"He runs," said the bather. "This is his first command."

Glad to be able to obey him at last, I jumped off the stage and ran down the aisle as fast as I could. As I ran, I imagined how pleased he must be at how rapidly I obeyed him. When, leaving the auditorium, I tripped and fell, I didn't mind the burning sensation in my face. I only thought that he would be further impressed that I had even incurred pain in his service.

After a while, though, I stopped running. I would have liked to return to the auditorium for further instructions, but I supposed the man in the bathing suit would prefer if I could manage alone. I did not altogether trust my good luck, either. If I went back I might not get out again so easily.

The streets where I walked were the familiar peaceful streets of my childhood. I saw a bright light in the distance. As I approached the light, I saw that it was a burning house. The building had certain features of the house of Frau Anders I had set fire to. Servants were scurrying back and forth carrying out furniture and portraits. Then I saw that it was my house. I knew I had promised all my possessions to my master, the bather. What would he do to me if all my goods were destroyed?

In spite of the warning shouts of the neighbors, I ran into the building and mounted the steps more flying than running. But when I gained my room, I stood still for some moments. There was so much to take: my clothes, my bed, my maps, my desk, my books, my ivory chessmen, my collection of butterflies. How could I choose even among the smaller objects I could carry? I paused a moment longer, then took from the shelves a book of ancient history; from the drawer I snatched my journal; and from the table I took a tray of tiny cups and saucers which were exceedingly hard to balance. Though tormented by the thought of all that I could not save, I knew I had to leave before the flames reached me. The air was dark with smoke and I could scarcely see.

In the street, I met my father. Knowing he was dead, I wondered what I might say to console him. But as he stepped toward me, I realized he meant to console me—about the fire. He told me I'd made a good choice and that with the things I had salvaged, I could begin a new life.

"But think of all that I left, all that I couldn't carry," I replied sadly.

At that moment he brushed against the tray of little dishes. One of them fell to the ground, and broke. I was enraged at his clumsiness. "How could you do that!"

"It broke," he said.

My anger subsided. "Perhaps you didn't mean to do it," I said.

He told me the cups and saucers were a wedding present, then asked me what I had decided to call my wife. We were walking away from the blackened house, chatting amiably. I explained that I was considering many names, but that I would like to choose one that was not unusual and would not excite ridicule.

"Why don't you call her Marie?"

"That's still too uncommon," I said.

I awoke from this dream with a distinct sense of relief. A fresh dream, instead of the exhaustive repetitions of the old ones, was particularly welcome to me at this moment. And then, I felt this dream marked a definite progress in my career as a dreamer. The dream had, it is true, more the character of a nightmare than previous dreams. The terror I had felt at the loss of my leg and when facing the punishment in the auditorium was acute. Yet, I estimated my emotions in the dream to be more straightforward and closer to the way I should like them to be. For it had become very important to me that my character in my daytime life and my character in the dreams should accord as closely as possible. I was prepared to make as many concessions on either side as were necessary to bring them together.

You may ask how this might be done. The problem of changing my life to fit my dreams was not insuperable—easier than changing my dreams to fit my life. But in neither case would an effort of will alone be sufficient. I believe this latest dream gave me a clue to the proper method. The dreams, all of them, were a mirror before which my daytime life presented itself, and which gave back to me an unfamiliar but not unintelligible image. With perseverance and attentive inactivity, the two would come together—even though it might be necessary to spend my life before a mirror. This is the destiny of mirrors, and of that which is mirrored.

As I thought about it that morning in my hotel room, I saw also that the new "dream of the mirror" furnished me with substantial help in my current project of marrying. No wonder I had been discouraged! I had neither understood my project, nor the reasons which justified it. Foolishly, I had believed that one could simply venture into the world to find a wife, without advance demands and expectations. I now realized that the only way I would find a wife—and you must remember the urgency of my search, with Frau Anders pressing close behind me—was to conceive very clearly what would suit me, as one chooses a name for a child. I would no longer cast about aimlessly, in effect waiting for my future wife to appear before me, but would seek her out myself in the most likely place. What marriage would repel the unwanted advances of Frau Anders more surely than a union which was entirely fitting and respectable? It had been absurd of me to imagine that I could repudiate the eccentric marriage which Frau Anders offered me with an equally eccentric marriage to someone outside my own class, whether a prostitute, a shopgirl, or the niece of my concierge.

I decided to return home to look for a wife, for it is, after all, where we are born and reared that we learn whatever sense of the fitting and of the improper we possess throughout our lives. Certainly, there are many activities which I pursued in the capital, such as my excursions with Jean-Jacques or my liaison with Frau Anders, which I would not have thought of doing in my native city. I would not have done them not because I feared discovery and censure by my family, but out of respect. In one's native city, there are many things which it simply does not occur to one to do.

I spent a few more fearful days and nights in the hotel, consulting the inclinations and strategies suggested by the dream. As usual, the dream began to repeat itself but with a number of variations. The following night, the mirror fell on me; it was in that way that I was injured. The night after that, I returned to the auditorium to confer my possessions on the bather and was trapped inside. The third night, my father forbade me to marry. The morning after this last version I decided not to delay any longer, lest I be shaken in my new resolutions on how to marry. What better place should I look for a congenial wife than in my native city, among the women of my own class? I wired my family that I was about to pay them a visit and checked out of the hotel.

My older brother was off on a business trip when I arrived home. I was glad of his absence because I thought that such matters would be better handled by the women. For while my brother was a typical man of business and a respected husband and father, the women in my family were more conventional still. The way in which my brother fell short of being able to make an entirely conventional choice for me had nothing to do with the fact that he maintained a mistress in another part of town; at least in this country, it is the exceptional middle-aged husband who does not have an extra-marital arrangement. But I had had some conversations with my brother—while our father was dying—and I suspected that he had certain ideas about my character and my independent way of life which would compromise his judgment, were it he to whom I entrusted the delicate task of helping me to find a wife. While I knew that he would recommend to me only certified ladies of our family's social circle, he might at the same time favor those few who were in some respects a trifle interesting. In short, he might try to satisfy me—which was just what I did not want.

I had seen much less of my brother's wife, Amelie; she had been too busy with her children. She knew little of me, I was sure, and never thought of me. There was also my older sister, now a widow, who had recently returned to the town after many years' residence abroad. And there were several aunts, married and unmarried, whom I had barely seen (except at my father's funeral) since I left home as a young man twelve years before. It was to these ladies that I put my problem, with confidence in the simplicity and certitude of their judgment.

I explained my mission to my sister-in-law and sister, and entrusted them to reintroduce to me to the society of the town. In no time I was invited to teas, dances, and Thursdays at home, and out of several eligible prospects I selected a young girl of plain appearance and modest character who seemed genuinely pleased at my attentions. She was the daughter of an army officer, convent-educated, fond of children, and of irreproachable reputation. My relatives thought her an excellent choice.

After several visits to her family's house in which I listened respectfully to her father's boasts of how our country would revenge herself against her ancient enemy in the coming war and played duets with the daughter, and after a final conference with my relatives, I spoke to the old colonel, received his permission to propose to the girl, proposed, and was accepted. The wedding took place when my brother came back from his trip, looking tanned and younger than when I had last seen him. Shortly after, my bride and I returned to the capital to begin our new lives.

THIRTEEN

"So you have married, little Hippolyte," Jean-Jacques said to me.

I didn't think it right for my wife to meet or talk with Jean-Jacques, but he had heard the news from me, along with an account of my reasons for marrying and my mode of choice. He agreed with me that this was the one way in which my family could have been useful to me but found the act itself a questionable one.

"I disapprove of your acting in this stale way, acting out of a conviction."

"What conviction?" I asked.

"Why, this conviction you have just expressed to me of the propriety of marriage."

"That's no conviction," I said. "It's a need which I discovered with the aid of my dreams. You know, Jean-Jacques, how I relish solitude. Solitude, if anything, is my only conviction. But there is no contradiction between my solitude and my marriage. Never have I done anything merely for the sake of order. Nor—as you do—for the sake of disorder, either."

"Haven't you married for the sake of order?"

"No," I replied. "If my life expresses a faith in order, it is my nature, that's all. The proof of this is that to others this order will appear as disorder, even flight."

"And your convictions?"

"I don't want to have any convictions," I said. "If I am or believe something, I want to discover it through my acts. I don't want to act in the way I do because it accords with what I am or believe."

"It was I who told you that once, remember?"

"You were right," I said. "Don't I always believe you when you are right? I want to follow my acts. I don't want my acts to follow me."

"But you put a special interpretation on my idea. For you, it seems, the fewer acts the better."

"Yes," I said, "only those which are necessary, those which define, those which destroy."

"And your marriage, Hippolyte? Is that an act which defines and destroys?"

I was prepared for this question, and could answer quickly, "Yes."

After the turbulence of my pursuit and near-seduction by Frau Anders, being with my wife was a paradise of quiet and ease. But do not imagine that my marriage was only a haven, a refuge for the guilty benefactor. I had much pleasure in my marriage, and learned to love and admire my wife. What I liked best about her was her capacity for respect. She respected flowers and children; she respected uniforms, even the uniforms of the enemy soldiers who now occupied the capital; she respected the effort of the youth who carried the coal up six flights of stairs each week to our apartment. She communicated to me some of this respect and gravity, which seemed beautiful next to the boredom and self-seeking that characterized many of my old friends, like Jean-Jacques and Lucrezia. I was tired of what is called sophistication.

I appreciated my wife's quietness, which left me all the time I wanted for myself and my thoughts. Her devotion to me was of such a generous sort that I never felt in any way hampered. She disliked parties and cafés but I was entirely free to come and go as I liked—to walk by the river, to find Jean-Jacques in his café and converse with him, to go to the national film archives occasionally with Lucrezia. Also, enduring the austerities of wartime, the shortages of coal and food and clothing, was easier in the company of so undemanding a person.

We occupied the same apartment where I had lived the last two years, since I first knew Monique. Although in a working-class neighborhood, the rooms were pleasantly furnished and in good repair. I was concerned that the mode of living which I had invited my wife to share would compare too unfavorably with the comforts she had enjoyed at home. She reassured me in a charming way, telling me that this was a luxury compared with the convent where she had slept in a room with twenty other girls. Even as a child, she said, she had never had a room to herself but had always to share it with one of her sisters. I then suggested—it was a few weeks after our wedding—that she take a bedroom for herself, which she did with the greatest contentment.

Because my wife was not, as far as I could see, a sensual person and would consent to fulfill her conjugal duties only out of a sense of propriety, I saw no reason to bother her with them. She was very young, and I respected her youth. I wanted to do with her what I knew she genuinely liked. As a girl, she had learned how to make excellent preserves and marmalades, and was justifiably proud of her skill; I procured extra quantities of sugar on the black market for her. The promenade was another of her favorite pastimes. I remember walks in the public gardens, in which I felt the most delicate sensations of marital serenity—my wife, beaming, her arm in mine, wore a yellow straw hat which she had brought from home and which looked delightfully rustic and old-fashioned in the capital. She also liked me to read to her, which I did each night before she went to sleep. During the spell before my marriage in which I had kept my ailing father company, I had learned that there is an art to reading aloud, and that there is one kind of book which each person prefers above all others. To my wife I read children's stories and fables, but she liked even better the ones which I made up myself.

One that she was especially fond of, I called "The Invisible Husband." It goes as follows:

"Once upon a time, in a city near a forest, lived a beautiful princess. And far away, in the mountains called the Himalayas, lived a plain but hard-working young prince.

"It was always snowing where the prince lived, and to protect himself from the cold he wore a handsome suit of white leather and white leather boots. In this costume, too, he was almost invisible, and could move about the mountain without being menaced by any of the dangerous animals who lived there.

"One day the prince thought that he would like to have a companion on the mountain, a wife. He descended to the valley, crossed the forest, and arrived at the city. There he promptly asked to be directed to the royal palace. For, being a prince, he could only marry a princess.

"Now the princess of this city, although young and lovely, had very weak eyes. When the prince, dressed all in white, was presented at the court she could barely see him. But because, with the keenness of hearing which is often given to those with poor sight, she heard the deeper tones of his voice and found these attractive, she wanted to accept his proposal of marriage.

" 'What does he look like, Father?' she asked.

" 'There is no doubt that he is a prince,' the king replied. 'I have seen the records of his birth.'

" 'I will marry him,' she said. 'He will be a restful and melodious companion.'

"So the prince took the princess with him back to the mountain and guarded her in his house of snow. With his own hands he fed her milk and the raw meat of coconuts and rice and sugar and other delicacies.

"Though the princess' eyesight did not improve, since everything around her was white it did not matter that she could barely see her husband.

"But one day, while the princess was alone sewing a tablecloth, there appeared before her a black mountain bear. Ignorant that this was the most dangerous animal on the mountain, the princess was not frightened. But she was startled, because she was not accustomed to seeing anything so clearly.

" 'Who are you?' she inquired courteously.

" 'I am your husband,' said the bear. 'This suit of fur I found in a dark wet cave on the other side of the mountain.'

" 'But your voice is so hoarse,' she said. 'Have you caught a cold?'

" 'Undoubtedly,' said the bear.

"The bear spent the afternoon with the young princess. When he rose to go, she was sorry to see him leave. He explained to her that he had to return the black suit to the cave; its owner might, by this time, be looking for it.

" 'But can't you wear the suit again?' she pleaded.

" 'Perhaps I may find it again when I pass the cave. And then I will come home in the middle of the day to visit you.'

" 'Oh, yes,' she cried.

" 'But you must promise,' said the crafty bear, 'not to mention this black suit to anyone, not even to me. For I loathe dishonesty, or wearing anything which is not mine. I do not wish to be reminded of the sacrifice of my honor which I will be making for you if I don this suit again.'

"The princess had respected her husband's moral scruples, and she agreed. And so the bear sometimes came to visit her, but she never mentioned his visits in the evening when her husband returned. What she enjoyed about the bear was being able to see him, but she did not like the hoarseness which afflicted his voice each time when, as she supposed, he ventured for her sake into the wet cave.

"One day, she found his voice so unpleasant that she urged him to take some cough syrup.

"'I detest medicines,' said the bear. 'Perhaps it is better for me not to speak at all when I have a cold.'

"Reluctantly she agreed, but from that moment she began to find less pleasure in her husband dressed in black.

"'I would rather hear your voice,' she said one day to the bear, as he was embracing her roughly. 'In fact I no longer enjoy seeing you as much as I did.'

"Of course, the bear did not answer.

"When the bear went away in the mid-afternoon, she determined to speak to her husband upon his return in white that evening.

"But when he did return, she said nothing, not daring to break her promise to keep silent about the black suit. That night, however, she stole from the bed while her husband slept and went out on the mountain. Although it was black night, she could see no less well than in the white day.

"For three nights and days, she wandered about searching for the dark cave where she supposed her husband to have found the suit. It snowed most of the time and she was very cold. Eventually she touched with her finger tips an arch of stones and felt a space before her hands which could have been the entrance to a cave. She sighed with relief.

"'I will leave a note for the true owner of the suit,' she said, weary with cold and exhaustion but determined to complete her mission.

"She tore off a piece of her white dress, took a pin from her hair, pricked her white skin and, using the pin as a pen and her blood as ink, wrote the following message on the cloth: 'Do not leave your suit any more. Thank you.' She signed it, 'The Princess of the Mountain.'

"Then, feeling quite ill, she wandered for several more days and nights on the mountain until she found her way home.

"Naturally, the prince was overjoyed at the return of the princess and put her to bed immediately. He tended her faithfully, feeding her one teaspoon of sugar and a mug of cream each day. She was ill for some time, but she recovered. In the course of her illness, however, her eyesight failed even more. She was completely blind.

"But the princess was not distressed at this result. Now there was no problem of choosing between her husband in white and her husband in black.

" 'I am happy now,' she said to her husband.

"She heard her husband reply in his gentle voice, 'We have always been happy.'

"And they lived happily ever after."

My wife was above all obedient and uncomplaining. She was the sort of woman who would have enjoyed the mother-in-law which, alas, I could not supply her. Further, her nature was quick to generosity, to the point where she became careless of risk. When the Jewish family on the floor below was rounded up in the middle of the night by enemy soldiers to be deported to the concentration camps, she stood in the doorway and threw her bedroom slippers down the landing. Luckily I pulled her into the apartment before she was noticed by the soldiers and herself arrested. This will explain how it happened that one afternoon some weeks later, when a woman presented herself at the door while I was out, and told my wife that she was an old friend of mine, a Jew, although a convert, and in immediate danger of deportation, my wife invited her to come in and to remain with us. Within an hour the woman had brought her few bags and belongings to the apartment, and was installed in the back room. You understand, I would not want to have refused anyone who had knocked for such a reason in those dreadful times and begged for shelter. Yet I confess that when I returned home my heart sank with apprehension both for myself and my wife. For the woman was none other than Frau Anders.

My wife hurriedly explained her presence to me. I went into the back room where I found Frau Anders sitting on a wooden chair, fenced in by a few small valises at her feet.

"You know I wouldn't have come," she began in a resentful tone. "I have some pride."

"I know, I know," I said reassuringly. "A great disaster cancels all private quarrels. My house is yours."

She laughed bitterly. "All your houses, eh? Oh, never mind. . . . You must let me stay a while, Hippolyte. They're taking everyone away now. At first only a few, now everyone. No one they take ever comes back—I know it, I can feel it!"

"Don't explain, my dear," I said. "And calm yourself. Did you tell anyone you were coming here?"

"No one."

"Then stay as long as is necessary, or as long as you want to."

Frau Anders yawned and stretched. At least in the somewhat shapeless unfashionable woolen jacket she was wearing, I could detect no difference between her two arms. I did not think it the right moment, however, to ask how her cure had been proceeding in the two years since I had seen her. "I want to sleep now," she murmured.

I left her and returned to my wife, who was staring fixedly out her bedroom window at a military limousine filled with soldiers parked in the street. "We have to whisper now," she said in a low voice, looking up at me. "You're not angry with me?"

I implored her not to think that, ever.

"I'll take care of her," she said. As if she could have taken care of anyone! I was moved to the point of tears by her goodness. My wife thought nothing of the terrible penalties for us, should we be caught by the soldiers who were constantly searching houses for just such helpless fugitives as Frau Anders. And, you understand, she knew nothing of my past relations with Frau Anders: only that we had once known each other. My own motives were more pressing. Yet to call them generosity and courage would be flattering myself. I could hardly decline to risk my own life now, when I had previously put Frau Anders' life to the risk of enslavement and murder. And generosity seems out of the question to describe the aid given to a person to whom one has denied so much.

My former mistress stayed with us for several months, without once leaving the apartment. My wife spent most of the days and evenings in the back room with her. Frau Anders had not lost her old trait of being a congenial companion and a good listener. I used to sit in the parlor, straining to hear the sounds of their whispering together; occasionally I would hear my wife's youthful laughter. My wife, ordinarily so silent, seemed to flourish in this sad company; she was not, as I feared, depressed by Frau Anders' ambiguous scars and pitiful circumstances. Frau Anders, however, I never heard laugh; she had been rendered almost mute with fear.

Frau Anders' being in my apartment seemed so strange to me. I had, more or less successfully, escaped all her traps until this one. I had dared to think of myself as persecuted by her, until she arrived once again on my doorstep, this time with the official badge of her own persecution. The ghost which had genteelly but irrepressibly haunted me for so long now settled in my house with a permit of entry which I could not refuse.

Yet I avoided all opportunities to be alone with her. I could not anticipate what new demands, what new reproaches she would spring. Perhaps she would confront me as I was coming out of the W. C. with the proposal that I carry her on my back through the labyrinthine sewers of the city—to freedom. For all I knew, she might, one evening at dinner, ask me to assassinate the enemy commander of the city. Or she might direct me to summon her former husband, so that she could explain to him that she was despite all her efforts still a Jewess. None of these things happened, however. After the neighborhood had been searched several times in the middle of the night, and soldiers even entered our apartment and stood about, shouting, in the very room where Frau Anders was crouching in the linen chest, her terror overflowed the limits of our apartment, and she implored me to find her a better shelter. I did so, reluctantly —an ingenious hiding place, which I shall describe in a later chapter—and my wife and I were left alone.

For my wife's sake I was sorry to lose Frau Anders as a boarder. I worried sometimes that my wife must be lonely in the capital, where she had no relatives or friends. She had not seemed to be lonely. But when I saw how pleased she was in the company of Frau Anders, I knew she could be happier than she was. It occurred to me that she might want to have a child. But I didn't think she was old enough; she was still a child herself. Foolishly trusting in fate and the longevity of both of us, I thought there was plenty of time. Besides, I wished to prolong the peacefulness and purity of our relationship.

You may imagine that since I respected my wife's virgin nature, I still took care to satisfy myself outside the home. This was not the case. I wanted to be faithful to my wife, as I hoped she would be faithful to me. It was very convenient: in being faithful to my wife, I could at the same time be faithful to myself.

About this time I clarified my ideas on what constitutes proper self-love.

I beg the reader not to react disapprovingly. I do not believe there is the slightest vanity in the following reflections.

I reasoned thus: the one criterion of love upon which all can agree is intensity. Love raises the temperature of the spirit; it is a kind of fever. Men love in order to feel alive. And not only love. This is also why they go to war. If war did not satisfy an elementary desire—not the desire to destroy, which is superficial, but the desire to be in a state of strain, to feel more intensely—the practice of war would have been tried once and abandoned. Men rightly regard their own deaths as not too large a price to pay for feeling alive.

War does not fail. But love always does. Why? Because it is at bottom the desire for incorporation. The lover does not seek a beloved, only a bigger self. But thereby he adds to the weight of his own burden. He now carries the other person, too.

One possible solution to love is hate. In hating, we push the burden aside. But then we are left diminished, weighing half the amount we have become accustomed to.

The better solution is detachment—neither loving nor hating others, neither assuming burdens nor laying them down. The only proper object of both love and hate is oneself. Then we can be confident that we are not mistaken in paying the tribute of our feelings. We can be sure the object will not flee, or change, or die. Only in this way are we satisfied.

To this line of reasoning, I will append an anecdote.

One afternoon, some months after the departure of Frau Anders, my wife and I were sitting at a window of our apartment. Across the courtyard a neighbor was doing her laundry. We were entranced by the motions of her stout red arms plunging in and out of the tin tub.

When she had finished and pinned up her wash, she went in, without removing the tub. Then we saw the wash flutter as if the wind were moving it. From behind a large white sheet emerged a dark figure wearing a cap. It was the strapping adolescent boy who delivered our coal. He gazed up at our window. For a long time he stood there staring, and then began to move slowly backwards. He did not see the tub of suds behind him, bumped against it, lost his balance, and fell, knocking it over. My wife sighed and smiled.

The boy sat in a puddle of warm water, which had streaked the coaldust on his handsome face and work-clothes, and began to curse. Then he rose and leaned against the wall, half-sitting on the yellow bicycle propped up there which belonged to my wife. He picked his nose and gazed at our window. Once he went away, but came back shortly, chewing on something, and stood there in the twilight.

When it became dark, I told my wife to go out and invite him to have supper with us. She prepared a simple meal of bread, boiled potatoes, radishes, and cheese, which I ate heartily. The boy stared intently at my wife and she refused his glance by looking into her lap.

It was the coal delivery boy to whom I commended my wife, praising her charms not the least of which was her purity. Neither of them replied to my eloquence. I announced that I was going out for a walk, possibly to see a film, and invited him to stay for the evening. When I returned at midnight, the boy was gone, my wife in her bed asleep. The next morning, as she did not bring up the previous evening, neither did I; and I abstained from examining the sheets for traces of the coal-boy's water-streaked grime.

My second line of reasoning on the topic of self-love will be shorter than the first.

Every change of emotion we experience as a momentary invigoration. But this flush of feeling is deceptive. It is the prelude to a tapering off of vigor, which sets in when we realize the dependence of our feeling upon something or someone external to ourselves. True vigor results only from the knowledge of separateness.

Community, friendship, love are makeshift expedients, devised because men cannot bear to be separated. Above all, it is love which impedes our ability to remain separate. Yet love cannot be denied. How then reconcile love and separateness? Self-love.

To this second line of reasoning, I will append a second, shorter story.

One day I was standing before my mirror naked.

For some time, I had been schooling myself to remove my clothes during the day. For while clothed I am tranquil and undifferentiated, my mirror confronts me with the taste of myself which is sharp and saline.

When my wife entered the room, my first impulse was to cover my nakedness. But I conquered my sense of discomfort, for I was always entirely honest with her, and proceeded to touch my sex. She moved about the room, humming quietly to herself.

I thought of three things: the egg, the butterfly, and the rain.

When I reached the climax of my meditation, my wife came and dried me with a towel.

This was my third line of reasoning.

I think best when I think one thing, feel most deeply when I feel one thing. If I could redesign my body it would be celestially large, so that the cities of men would appear as a single speck to me. Or else I would make it so tiny, that I could only see a single blade of grass. How lovingly I would examine that blade of grass! I would caress its blunt fringe, peer into its dark crease, hurl myself against its green wall.

There are two great passions in my nature. I like to concentrate on some small problem, and I like to be surprised. But nobody is as small as I. And nobody surprises me as much as I do myself.

My third story:

Frau Anders had left. I was immensely, selfishly relieved that she had to hide but I was safe, that she was in flight, but not from me. I walked the streets boldly each afternoon and evening until curfew, glorying in the absence of something to hide.

Then, in the vacancy of my wit, I struck a passing beggar. He had done me no injury; I didn't know him. Whom did he resemble? I don't know.

The horse butcher, rushing from his shop, seized me by the ear. Curses fell like droppings from the golden horse's head. A crowd of shopkeepers and marketing housewives gathered. A policeman came with his stick.

Someone in the crowd offered me a revolver, and told me to run. But I did not wish the death of the world, or indeed of any person in it.

Therefore I went along with the policeman, was fingerprinted, interviewed, locked up for the night, and released the next morning.

My fourth and last line of reasoning follows:

Man strives to be good; being bad is just the name for some people's goodness. The essence of goodness is monotony. Note, please, that I say monotony—not consistency, which so many incorrectly hold to be the *sine qua non* of good character.

From monotony comes purity. This is why marriage to one

woman is better, purer than polygamy. But monogamy is polygamous, when matched against the purity of self-love.

What is more monotonous than the self?

A little story:

The night Frau Anders left I dreamed the same dream three times. In this dream I walked on a frozen sea.

FOURTEEN

In this fashion my wife and I lived without discord for several years. I had no particular desire to travel and, except for one trip to visit our families, we did not leave the capital. But then my felicity was brought to a swift and cruel end.

One day my wife told me that she had been feeling ill. I had already suspected something was wrong, by her drowsiness in recent weeks, and by the unusual pallor of her face and certain patches of white which had appeared on her arms and legs. She had always been an extraordinarily even-tempered person; cold and dull, some might say, though I did not find her so. But lately her habitual manner had taken on the unmistakable aspect of debility and sluggishness. Even in telling me how ill she felt, she minimized it—as if it were too great an effort for her to be alarmed. Despite her protests that it would be a waste of time and that any doctor would tell her she suffered from a liver complaint, I hastened to procure medical advice. She was of course justified in anticipating this diagnosis—which is the beneficent myth of the national medical profession, and has cured many patients by distracting their attention from real ailments to imaginary ones. Would that she could have been made well by such a diagnosis!

In disease, the imagination is everything. Proper appeal to it cures, though the imagination also kills. But the body's imagination is usually prosaic, even literal-minded. Dreams are the poetry, disease the prose of the imagination. I knew an incessant chatterer who died of a ailment which began in the ear, and a cousin of mine, a trial lawyer, given to very expressive arm gestures, who was stricken with paralysis. There are fashions in diseases, too. In simpler societies than our own, illness, like everything else, has a collective or communal character: the typical form of disease is the plague. In our society illness is a private matter; the modern diseases are not infectious. Disease attacks each man alone. It is individually elected, in the organ or part of the body that he has either unduly neglected or excessively cultivated. It is now an individual judgment, rather than a pollution. Therefore it must be endured with greater resignation, for it cannot be passed on to anyone else.

My wife's illness, as the doctor explained to me—for she was, alas, seriously ill—had this modern character. It was not communicable, so I was in no danger. And it was incurable. Already she was afflicted with a dropsical tendency, denoted by a phlegmatic condition of the body, known as leucophlegmacy, and an abnormal whitening of some parts of the body, leucosis. But these were only ornaments to the fatal complaint which was leukemia, an excess of white corpuscles in the blood.

My wife received the news from me bravely. As there was no cure, there was nothing for her to do but to go to bed and await the illness' development. Together we decided that she should remain at home rather than go to a hospital, and the task of nursing her became my sole and willing occupation. I brewed her tea and sponged her frail limbs; for hours at a time I sat by her bed, joining her in songs and prayers, and playing tarot. I believe I have not mentioned that my wife was devoted to the astrologer's arts. During her illness she taught me to read the cards, and prophesied a long life for me, which, in the circumstances, added to my melancholy. She was unenthusiastic about my proposal that her family be summoned, though she agreed that it would be appropriate at the end. Wishing nonetheless to provide her with a little more entertainment, I decided to invite Jean-Jacques to our rooms. I went out one afternoon, after alerting a neighbor that I would be absent for several hours, and found my old friend no longer at his usual café but at the one next door.

"Why?" I asked.

"Because the price of coffee has gone up 75 centimes and the proprietress has become most unfriendly."

Jean-Jacques, looking especially robust that day, carried an uncut copy of his new novel which he promptly autographed and presented to me. I explained the situation at home, and begged him to pay my wife a visit.

"I should be very angry with you, Hippolyte. You have kept me away from the princess so long! I wasn't going to eat her, you know."

"True enough. But you have an unsettling effect on people, dear Jean-Jacques."

"And now? I still do, I hope."

"My wife can no longer distinguish between pleasure and over-stimulation. Do come."

"I shall come very late."

"What about the curfew?"

"Let me worry about that."

I was delighted, and left him at once to return home. When Jean-Jacques arrived, about three in the morning, I was already dozing in the rocking-chair beside my wife's bed, where I now regularly slept. But when I opened my eyes at the sound of his knocking, I saw she was still awake, propped up on her pillows; the tarot cards were scattered on the quilt, and she was staring feverishly, fearfully at me. "It's a friend," I whispered to her reassuringly. "You'll see."

"She's not sleeping," I called to Jean-Jacques, as I pushed the coverlet from my knees. I left the bedroom and went to open the front door. Jean-Jacques, wearing the uniform of an enemy officer complete with combat ribbons and Iron Cross, bounded past me without a greeting.

"Sing out!" he cried gaily as he entered the room. I signalled to my wife not to be afraid. She began to sing a lullaby and Jean-Jacques accompanied her by dancing around the bed, his heavy boots resounding on the floor.

"It's perfect," I exclaimed; my wife agreed. "How did you know what to wear?"

"The very image of respectability, my boy," Jean-Jacques shouted, without interrupting his dance.

"But did I ever tell you that my father-in-law is an army officer?"

"What?" Jean-Jacques shouted.

"The Army! An officer!"

"The-very-image-of-respectability!" And with each word he stamped once from left to right.

"Long live victory," murmured my wife, moving further under the blankets until only her face was visible.

"And now, little lady, we're going to march." He grasped me by the shoulders and we goose-stepped up and down the room. I was filled with vivacity, and at a certain moment broke away from Jean-Jacques' powerful hold and ran to the side of the armoire.

"I declare war," I called out.

"You're dead," said Jean-Jacques calmly.

My wife burst into tears. I turned on him reproachfully. "Let's not make war. It frightens her."

"But I want to fight with you. After all, I was once a professional boxer."

"I know, I know. That's why it's foolish for me to fight with you." I began to feel apprehensive, for I thought Jean-Jacques might be serious.

"First, let me take off my respectability," he said in a determined voice, and began unbuttoning his neat olive-green shirt. My wife's head disappeared under the covers.

"But I'm dead. You said so yourself."

There was a low alarming sob from the bed.

"That's your advantage, Hippolyte. As having once been a boxer is mine."

He became impatient with the buttons, and lifted the shirt over his head. Seizing my opportunity, I reached for the chair next to the armoire, and struck him over the head with it. The moment he fell to the floor, my wife's head emerged from the blankets, her eyes now red with weeping. "Oh, oh," she cried.

"That's the penalty for impersonating an officer," I explained, drying her face with my handkerchief. Exasperation and anger at Jean-Jacques' eternal frivolity had left me speechless; I could not explain further, and only wanted to get him out of the apartment. "I must take him home now. I shall have to leave you for a while."

It would have been impossible for me to lift Jean-Jacques and carry him down the steep flight of stairs, so I went and roused our friend, the coal delivery boy, who lived in the next building. He agreed to assist me and we returned together. After I removed the incriminating costume and put Jean-Jacques into some old clothes of my own, we waited another hour until dawn. Then we brought him, still unconscious, downstairs, stuffed him into the cart which the boy used to make his coal deliveries, trundled him half across the city, and carried him up the stairs to his hotel room. I sent the boy back to the apartment to attend my wife until my return.

I believe I could have killed Jean-Jacques as he lay there. Surely that was the reason that I did not leave until I saw him recovering. He did not regain consciousness until noon; when I saw him turning in his bed and moaning and holding his head, I slipped out the door. I was exceedingly angry with him. Stopping to buy some food, I returned home. But when I entered my wife's bedroom, I saw to my dismay only the coal delivery boy lying, fully dressed, on the bed. He seemed frightened to see me, and blurted out that my wife seemed very ill when he came back, that he had summoned the neighbors who in turn had called an ambulance, and that she was in the city hospital. I hastened to the hospital, where the nurse confirmed the news of my wife's serious condition. I was allowed to see her for a few minutes, but she was in a coma. Three days later, she died.

I shall not speak, now, of my grief.

The task of making arrangements for her funeral presented somewhat of a problem to me. She would be buried in her family plot in our native city, with all the rites of the Church. But I also wanted a funeral service which would acknowledge the last years of her life in the capital with me. For this reason, without immediately wiring her family, I had her body placed in a casket and returned to our apartment. I then called on Professor Bulgaraux, to perform a private service. He agreed, on the condition that he could invite a number of colleagues and disciples. I did not invite Jean-Jacques, for I was still angry with him for the inconsiderate and emphatic way he had behaved in the last moments of my wife's conscious life. I did invite the coal delivery boy, and some friends who were actors. Lucrezia came with a young pianist, a recent enthusiasm. Monique arrived consumed with worry for her husband, who was a prisoner of war; I was moved that she had room for my bereavement, not realizing that she had amalgamated it with her own.

Professor Bulgaraux's lecture, or rather sermon, from which I shall give excerpts, did not fall short of my expectations. What

I give I am able to reproduce verbatim, including the peculiar style of punctuation, rather than rely on my memory, because he himself subsequently had it printed up as a pamphlet under the auspices of the Autogenist Society. It was entitled: "On the Death of a Virgin Soul."

He began:

"Friends and co-believers, mourners and speculators: Death is the most interesting event in life. It is comparable only to dreams, for there is no revision of a dream—only further dreams, and the interpretation of dreams. So there is no revision of death—only further deaths, and our reflections upon them.

"Now there are only two interesting—I might say satisfying— deaths: the death of a great criminal and the death of a virgin soul. For both deaths are the same—and bespeak that innocence to which all long to return.

"The secret of innocence is defiance. Criminal and virgin soul. The criminal defies the order of society—the virgin soul defies the order of nature. Both surpass their bodies in favor of—the will.

"Therefore the death of the criminal—and the death of the virgin soul—are willing deaths.

"We who are left in the common middle ground—dare we choose one of these seeming opposites which are—I tell you— it is no secret—equivalent?

* * * *

"Each one of us lives alongside his death each day. A tape, sometimes wider, sometimes narrower, which unrolls alongside our daily actions.

"Most—ignore death. But the criminal and the virgin soul live with their deaths. They cannot surprise them.

"The ways of disincarnation are—mysterious. Intelligibility cannot be explained. A fact—is a fact. Death—death.

"But life is—movement. Therefore—life is resurrection. Many have taught that first there is life—then death—then resurrection. I say: life—then resurrection—then death.

"In the Gospel of Dianus it is written, 'Live who must, die who will.'

"To the mourners, I say: Look at the grieving husband.*

"He does not grieve—does not condemn death. What would that avail him? Or anyone? For if we are as we are, then we cannot be other than we will be.

* * * *

"What was the life of this young woman? She was born—schooled—married. She obeyed her father and her husband. She died.

"You must have a vocation for such a life. You cannot choose it with the mind.

"The secret of life is vocation—which she had. It also takes a vocation to die well, which the criminal and the virgin soul possess.

* * * *

"In one of the Gospels of Dianus, a disciple inquires of his master, 'When shall we enter the Kingdom?'

" 'When shall you enter the Kingdom?' said the Master. 'When you make the two become one, and when you make the inside like the outside and the outside like the inside, and the upper like the lower and the lower like the upper! And if you make the male and the female one, so that the male is no longer male and the female no longer female, and when you put eyes in the place of an eye, and a hand in the place of a hand, and a foot in the place of a foot, and an image in the place of an image. Then you will enter the Kingdom!'

* * * *

* Here he pointed to me. I was sitting by the open casket, turning my wedding band between my fingers.

"How shall we interpret this teaching? The inside like the outside—The outside like the inside. Oh, virgins and criminals!

"Eye in the place of an eye—a hand in the place of a hand—a foot in the place of a foot—an image in the place of an image—

"The meaning is this. Acts of substitution constitute a life, until we reach the final substitution—for life, death.

"Where no more substitutions are possible—when we are pared down to our center—when we have found our beginning —there is death. Which is no death at all.

* * * *

"Seek not to decipher the end. Seek only to decipher your living selves. Death is the reward of our resurrection—death is our decipherment.

"We begin at the end—we end at the beginning. As the Master says, 'Blessed is the man who reaches the beginning; he will know the end, and will not taste death.'

"You will not taste death—you will be tasted by death. You will be complete—for you will be empty. You will be extreme —for you will be perfect.

* * * *

"When one has a picture taken, the photographer says, 'Perfect! Just as you are!' That is death.

"Life is a movie. Death is a photograph."

After the lecture Professor Bulgaraux's disciples crowded around the coffin for a last look at my wife and to embrace me. Professor Bulgaraux having hinted to me earlier that contributions to the society's research and publication fund had been scant lately, I gave him a check. I went out with Lucrezia and her escort for an aperitif and then returned to meditate.

I think I understood Professor Bulgaraux's sermon almost entirely; you might say that by now I was an adept at these ideas. But there was much that I did not agree with: not his characterization of my wife—I thought he caught her pale likeness beautifully—but the continual admonition to me not to grieve. It is too easy to be resigned to a loss borne by someone else. Besides, I had determined to allow my grief. However I did agree this much; there is a choice to be made, even in grief. I had scruples about my right to mourn. Any personal grief would have been inappropriate on my part, for my relationship in life to my wife was not a personal one, in the usual sense of the word. My relationship to her in death could hardly be different.

When, however, I accompanied my wife's body back to our native city, and stood in the cemetery with her family and mine, I shared fully in the communal grief. A provincial funeral is a more leisurely and weighty event than a funeral in the city.

My brother was unpleasantly distant to me, and I did not feel welcome in his house. Neither did I feel like accepting my in-laws' invitation to visit with them for a time. So in a few days I returned to the capital.

I said I would speak of my mourning, difficult as it is.

My grief expressed itself in many ways. I felt as if I had gotten loose in my skin. My armholes, the legholes, the hole for my head, eluded me.

I made a list of ways of dying. I got this far. Death by hanging, death by guillotine, death by peas up the nose, icicles through the groin, falling down an elevator shaft, crucifixion, the parachute that doesn't open, gangrene, jumping out of the dentist's window, arsenic in the onion soup, being run over by a trolley car, snake bite, the hydrogen bomb, Scylla and/or Charybdis, a broken heart, the stake, Russian roulette, syphilis, being tossed out of a roller-coaster, careless surgery, drowning, an airplane crash, sleeping pills, automobile fumes, boredom, tightrope walking, hara-kiri, rape by a shark, lynching, ultimatums, hunger, flying without wings, flying with wings (without a plane)—

Oh, how frail we are.

A childhood memory. I was three years old, still with long hair and wearing a white dress, playing with a hoop on the lawn in front of my house. Sunning herself on the lawn in front of the next house, which was separated from ours by a line of rose bushes, was our neighbor who was (as I had heard my mother say) a widow. I approached the bushes and stared at her. When she turned to look at me I asked, "How did your husband die?" In tones of unforgettable sweetness she answered, "His eyes closed."

That, reader, is grief. Such incoherence. You will understand why I do not continue further.

My business now was to reconstruct my life. But death, like violence, is an insidious example—hard to shake off.

I had formed more solitary habits in the months of caring for my wife. Her death did not seem sufficient reason to discontinue them.

It is remarkable that our way of living is not designed to respect a strong emotion or a single-minded idea, unless it takes the form of action. For, despite my avowed wish to be left alone, the callers continued to come, intent on their missions of consolation; not many, but enough. Monique was my principal visitor. Her widow's dress and veil (for she had just been notified that her husband had died in prison camp) matched my own black—though, sooner than she did, I returned to my habitual attire.

I soon tired of her company. I was impatient with the tender messages left under the door, with the dinners she prepared, with her way of tiptoeing loudly about the apartment. Neither her spasms of mourning—nor her jubilation when, that summer, the capital was liberated—were feelings I could share.

"How did your husband die, Monique?" I asked her when she hinted at staying the night with me.

"Oh, he was so good," she whispered, and began to sob.

When I challenged the sincerity of her grief, she became so indignant and abusive that I had to tell her to leave.

I do not think we greatly helped each other. She was both too sad and not sad enough to be good company for me. Monique was coarsely woven, and nearly indestructible, while my own fabric was becoming ever more tightly stretched. I remember that this image of myself became very important to me. When I resumed my old physical exercises, it was with this desperate image in mind. No longer idly solicitous for the good maintenance of my body, I now had a more pressing aim in view. I felt I had to keep myself limber or I would break. I urged my body to modify, to loosen, the expectant tautness of my mind. But the very veins in my arms and legs seemed clogged with grief.

Luckily for me, Monique soon busied herself in one of the many post-war committees for the restitution of injustices and the improvement of everything which were then springing up. Her calls became less frequent, and they usually entailed securing my signature for some petition or manifesto. I always signed, for despite the luxury of mockery which I allowed myself with Monique, her political sentiments (if one is to have political sentiments) were irreproachable.

Besides Monique, there were other friends whom I saw who were a little more skillful in their consolations. And there were several cold meetings between Jean-Jacques and myself, full of long silences. It is strange how little people mattered to me at that time, for my inner life was equally depopulated; even my dreams had deserted me. But I was used to being patient with myself, perhaps too patient. I played chess alone. My sexual pleasures were mostly solitary ones, with or without the aid of a mirror. I went to an occasional silent film. I waited for a dream.

FIFTEEN

Jean-Jacques had changed, there was no doubt about it. I don't know whether it was fame, middle-age, or financial stability which had altered his character. In any case he presented a decidedly lax, complacent appearance to me.

His complacency even extended to the rather grave political charges of collaboration with the enemy which, some people rumored, might be brought against him. It was thought that the selection of his last novel for the most exclusive of the yearly literary prizes, whose jury included a number of veterans of the Resistance, would do much to clear his name. But the charges continued to be voiced, and Jean-Jacques was twice called up for vague inconclusive questioning by the prefect of police, an ominous sign.

It was news of the difficulty Jean-Jacques might soon be in which impelled me to resume my relationship with him. For some months after my wife's death, I could not bear the thought of seeing him. I couldn't help holding him partly responsible for the distressing events of that fatal night, and the fact that he made no effort to see me after the funeral confirmed the unhappy revelation of his contempt for me.

But when I heard that he might be in serious trouble, I decided to call on him, and our friendship revived in a weary, guarded way. We used to meet at his rooms, or mine, or at some restaurant for lunch or dinner. Jean-Jacques had changed so much that he rarely spent any time in cafés now, except to meet someone such as a translator or a young writer with whom he had made a definite appointment.

His habits had changed in another way. Age, naturally, now made unseemly and unconvincing his nocturnal excursions in costume. Nevertheless I should not have supposed that Jean-Jacques had given up his philandering, promiscuous habits. Imagine, then, my astonishment when he told me one time when we met for dinner, about a year after my wife's death, that he had fallen in love, and for the first time in his life had taken someone to live with him. He described the object of his affections, a young Greek theological student, with such ardor that I could not fail to be persuaded of the change in him. Shortly after, I was introduced to the young man, whom I found stolid rather than charming. Dimitri had curly black hair and wore eyeglasses, and talked a great deal about his mother and about an obscure schism in the Orthodox Church on which he was writing his dissertation. An unlikely choice for Jean-Jacques! I was not surprised to learn later that he had left Jean-Jacques, but I was surprised that my friend was so dejected.

I have to admit that neither Jean-Jacques' lovesickness nor his new style of respectability moved me. It must have been a deep grudge which I bore him for his complicity in my wife's death, though I could not blame him for anything in particular. What had he done that night except try to be entertaining, as I had invited him to be? And he was still quite amiable, although he joked less, and seemed less eager to hear accounts of my latest dream.

Here is a final conversation, or rather two conversations, with

Jean-Jacques, which took place some eighteen months after my wife's death. I draw upon the entry in my journal.

"Dec. 5. While walking to meet Jean-Jacques today, I longed for an act which might be completed, for our recent meetings have been inconclusive.

"I thought of violence, because there could be no satisfying conclusion to a quarrel with him. He has always outtalked me.

"I thought of betrayal. I could go to the police and denounce him for the black market venture, the affair with the SS colonel, and the other things he unguardedly joked about with me. I wish I were capable of such an act. But I doubt that it would be good for Jean-Jacques to be locked up in a cell.

"Would that that venerable and happy custom, the duel, still existed in this country as a satisfying means of settling a quarrel, or merely a feeling of displeasure, between two men of honor who do not hate each other. As I walked I imagined this duel, but I could not find the weapon—sword? pistol? knives?—which would suit us. Our weapons have always been words, which wound me more than they do him—as in the following duel between us, which then took place in my mind. It was I who began:

Attack

I: You don't take your feelings seriously.
Jean-Jacques: They are too complex for that.

I: You are vain.
Jean-Jacques: I am a homosexual and a writer, both of whom are professionally self-regarding and self-esteeming creatures.

I: But you are merely acting the part of a homosexual.
Jean-Jacques: The difference is amusing, and not important.

I: You are a tourist of sensations.
Jean-Jacques: Better a tourist than a taxidermist.

I shot a look of triumph at my opponent, for I was pleased with my performance. But Jean-Jacques did not rest with defending himself. He proceeded to attack me.

Counter-Attack

I: You build so high that the bottom is bound to fall out of so unstable and fanciful a structure.

Jean-Jacques: You build so low.

I: You are a busybody.

Jean-Jacques: You have a passion for collecting advice and reprobation.

I: You are a villain.

Jean-Jacques: You are an impotent villain-worshipper.

I: You are frivolous.

Jean-Jacques: You have begun to bore me.

At this point, severely wounded, I retired from the imaginary field of honor. As I already knew, the verbal duel is generally without issue. Only physical violence or an act of unmerited generosity can finish it. Today, at any rate, my feelings were too sore to risk a closer encounter. Just as the verbal duel in my head was ending, I was passing a post-office. I stopped to send Jean-Jacques a *pneumatique* that I would not be able to meet him today, and spent the afternoon at a chess club instead."

By the evening of that day, I remember, my wounds—which were after all self-inflicted—had healed. The welcome spirit of objectivity had taken possession of me, and I could view the matter without pain. I saw that what was interesting about this imaginary conversation was that both speakers spoke the truth. Both weapons were sharp and well-aimed. I knew that I no longer amused Jean-Jacques—probably ever since I married, a decision which he was incapable of understanding. Jean-Jacques did not appreciate the subtle climaxes and revolution of my life; for him, it must have appeared that I had undertaken a journey on a treadmill, and from his point of view that description would be correct. My hits, however, were equally just. It was true that he was frivolous, vain, disloyal, and homosexual principally out of loyalty to the style of exaggeration. Altogether we had become a most ill-matched pair of friends.

The next day we did meet, for I went to call on him at his room. Jean-Jacques was at his writing table, soaking his feet in a pail of warm water, and cutting out pictures from a sports magazine with a razor blade. He looked sullen, and greeted me in a distracted manner. My own rancor had passed, and I remembered my old affection for him. But the impulse to violence, which I had stifled, was contagious. I observed that he wished to denounce me.

"Why don't you speak?" I said. His complexion was sallow, I noticed, and he seemed to have a bad cold.

"Why should I?" he replied sourly. "You can talk without me."

"But this morning I've nothing to say. I think I have come to do something."

"I don't believe you," he said, blowing his nose vigorously and then staring for a long time at the handkerchief.

"How did you spend your morning?"

"Writing letters. Tearing them up. Pissing in my pot. Deciding to grow a moustache."

"Come, come," I said, amazed at this maudlin fretful side of Jean-Jacques which I had never seen before.

"I'll tell you what's the matter. Why not? You are the hero of the play, a comedy, I have been working on for more than a year," he said. "Along with other things, of course. This morning I gave the play up. I can't compete with your nature."

"Maybe you can't write plays."

"Alas, no. My talent is intact. It's my subject," Jean-Jacques said to me. "You are a great comic fragment."

"Why a fragment?"

"Because no life has completed you," he replied. "You are a character without a story. You are a self-made *objet-trouvé*. You are your own idea, thought up by yourself." He blew his nose. "Unless," he added, "your character completes itself in those dreams you always speak about."

"No," I said sombrely, "my dreams annul me."

"And the way you pore over yourself!" he said sharply. "I have no objections to spending one's life before a mirror; I spend a lot of time there myself. But I can't approve of the timidity of your self-regard. You are in love with your dreams but don't possess them. Instead you hold back—hugging your dream-life, hanging over its cradle, deploring it, fearing it, perpetually hankering."

"No," I said, "I don't recognize myself in that picture. Except for one detail. The man in love with the idea of himself is forever seeking heroes before whom he can abase himself, since he alternates between self-esteem and self-condemnation. For me that hero has been you. However, I have renounced you."

"Well, well," Jean-Jacques smiled. "A declaration of independence, is it? My *objet-trouvé* is climbing down off my shelf?"

"Your words don't hurt me. Let's be friends."

"Now that the war is over and those glamorous brutes, our enemies, have departed, I want to leave the city for a while." He sighed. "I'm bored."

I knew his real reason for wanting to leave the city was to wait until certain unpleasant, and possibly dangerous, rumors and suspicions had died down. Nevertheless I took his remark seriously, knowing that Jean-Jacques, being so full of contradictions, could not tell a total lie about his feelings even if he tried. I began to explain to him how unnecessary it was to be bored, but he waved his hand in impatience.

"I have to borrow money from you, old Maecenas," he said.

"My writer's vocation summons me to the countryside." He grinned. "You know my customary sources of income. These would be cut off. I don't think I should take to seducing heavy-shoed farmhands or robbing parish poorboxes."

Another lie! I knew this to be untrue. Besides the small income which I had settled on him some years before, he had been making money from his writing; and such sources of income as prostitution and theft, which he had practiced years before when I first knew him, had long since been outgrown.

"Why should I lend you money?" I said, annoyed at his flippant way of taking my good-will toward him for granted.

"Why should you refuse me, my little dreamer?"

"Don't be affectionate with me. It doesn't suit you."

"I can't restrain myself, because we're saying goodbye for a while."

"If I lend you money, will you be less angry? Will you be honest with me from now on, even if we never see each other again? Will we have settled our accounts at last?"

"Yes," he answered gravely. "Why do you think I continue to be friendly with you?"

"Then I'll give you the money. Where will you go?"

He took his feet out of the basin and began drying them. "I have an urge to be a pilgrim," he replied. "I'm thinking of settling near the famous grotto in the south where the lame come to throw away their crutches and the tuberculars kneel in the sun to bleach their lungs."

He put on his shoes, then his coat, and took me by the arm. We walked to the door.

"I am sorry to part with you," I said.

"You don't need me any more," he replied languidly.

We went to my bank. I made arrangements to transfer a reasonable sum of money to Jean-Jacques in the form of a letter of credit. Then after the purchase of a train ticket and some luggage, I accompanied him back to his apartment to help him pack. I did not see him off, when he left two days later.

I was glad when Jean-Jacques went away, though I knew it was not the end of our friendship.

Oh, what a gloomy winter that was. Terrible cold, food shortages, mysterious fires and lootings in the neighborhood where I lived, old friends disappearing, reappearing, or being confirmed as dead. I fell ill and remained in bed for several months, tasting all the voluptuousness of illness. It was then that I returned fully to the contemplation of my dreams.

During the four years of my marriage and the two years following my wife's death, there had been many new dreams— with interesting variations, second, third, fourth editions of each. I remember particularly "the dream of the red pillow," "the dream of the broken window," "the dream of the heavy shoes," and "the dream of the arsenal." The man in the black bathing suit occasionally appeared to advise or to reprove me, or to make arbitrary demands upon my limited physical grace.

The first of these, "the dream of the red pillow," was a mild, pacific dream. I came before a judge who sentenced me to become overseer of a prison for delinquent children. My administration was a humane one. I sat in a revolving chair in the center of the courtyard, leaning back on a red pillow, and observed my charges systematically. The chair, my own invention, moved too slowly. Much went on behind my back, of which I was only partly aware. But as long as the children did no violence to each other, I chose not to interfere.

In "the dream of the broken window," I was in a film, acting the part of a housemaid. The director explained very carefully the part I was to play, and cautioned me not to say one word more than was necessary. I mopped the floor, polished the furniture, dusted the books, and scraped the wax from the inside of the candlesticks. You may imagine my dismay when I inadvertently broke one of the window-panes in the course of my exertions, for it was necessary to shoot the entire scene again.

In "the dream of the heavy shoes," I was looking for Jean-Jacques, who had been caught in an indecent act with the village idiot boy and had fled the country. I remember the rounded shoulders and dirty knees of the idiot boy, the torn coffee-colored shorts and dirty undershirt he wore, and above all the heavy leather shoes two sizes too big for him, in which he lumbered through the dream. I pleaded for Jean-Jacques before the authorities, and he was pardoned.

In "the dream of the arsenal," I was conscripted into preparing a huge bomb which was to be dropped upon the enemy. The man in the black bathing suit arrived to examine the progress of our work, and pointed out to us that we had constructed a searchlight instead of a bomb. He told us that he could smell a badly-executed task from a great distance, and that the stench of our irresponsible exertions had drawn him all the way from his headquarters several hundred miles away.

The subject of my dreams was often judgment and punishment. I suppose that I was punishing myself for the judgment which society, no doubt through oversight, had failed to inflict on me. Once, more than once, I had done something wrong. But I had failed to provide a minimal center of force against which others would react. My daily life had become weightless, and my dreams continued to mock me with their pictures of methodical and useless effort. The calmness I had happily elected in my life appeared in my dreams in the unwholesome light of bewilderment, dependence, malfunctioning, passivity.

There was one dream which gave me a clue in a different direction. This dream, the last, by the way which I shall mention without recounting it in full, I call "the literary dream." In the dream I am my famous namesake of myth and drama, vowed to celibacy. Frau Anders is my lusty step-mother. But since this is a modern version of the story I do not spurn her. I accept her advances, enjoy her, and then cast her off. Nevertheless I am punished. As the goddess in the opening of the ancient play declares: those who disregard the power of Eros will be chastised. Perhaps that is the meaning, or one of them, of all my dreams.

Thus, during my marriage and after, my dreams had not become less plentiful or less interesting to me. But I viewed them with greater detachment. I was now capable of asking myself if my dreams were a habit or a compulsion. One cultivates habits. One surrenders to compulsions. Perhaps a compulsion is only a stifled habit.

My dreams, which began as a compulsion, had settled into a habit; then the habit began to deteriorate, to parody itself. Not sensing the change, nor smelling their bad odor, the odor of decay, I rested complacently in what I now regarded as the ample bosom of my own poetry. Little alarmed me, though much saddened me. This restful state of affairs was, however, brought to an abrupt close by a dream I had, some two years after my wife's death, which was the only one of all my dreams that I could call a nightmare.

I dreamed that I was in a crowd, walking up a hill toward some kind of entertainment. The hill ended in a cliff or precipice. My companions began to descend by means of toe-holds in the face of the cliff, which they managed as easily as a flight of stairs. But I did not find the descent easy. I lingered, certain that I could not negotiate the steep descent, that I would become dizzy and fall. Finally I lowered myself a little way, then stopped and clung in terror to a sort of railing, unable to move up or down.

I remember thinking that I had tried this descent before, and already learned that I could not manage it.

The next moment, however, I was on the ground, milling about with the others who had made the descent. It was a sort of arena, surfaced with asphalt, but without seats and walled in on all sides like a handball court. In the center of this arena, quite apart from everyone else, stood three people, two men and a woman.

I immediately surmised, from their scanty costume and their bare arms and legs, that they were acrobats. Also, from the way they stood together, talking among themselves, completely absorbed in each other and indifferent to the crowd around them, I inferred that they must be foreigners.

They began to walk away from the center of the arena still talking to each other. But after taking only a few steps, one of them limped, stumbled, and then sat on the floor and examined his leg. I saw that he had a strange scar on his calf. Then I looked closer and saw his injury was more serious than I had thought: the scar ended in a disgusting cylindrical protuberance of flesh.

The man and the woman stood over him protectively, exhibiting great concern. I heard the other man say to himself, "No, he can't perform in that condition." He looked into the crowd, then singled out one of the onlookers and addressed him directly.

"Would you be so kind?" he said.

The onlooker made some diffident, non-committal reply.

"Please help," said the acrobat. "You can see how badly hurt he is."

The injured acrobat still sat, holding and scrutinizing his deformed leg. The woman stood next to him and watched the progress of the other acrobat's entreaties. This one, the man who entreated the onlooker for his assistance, was plainly the leader of the troupe.

"Well, all right," said the onlooker. "I'll help if I can. But I don't have much time."

"It will take only a moment," said the acrobat, and turned to smile at the woman and at his companion on the floor.

The onlooker asked what he had to do. "This," said the acrobat, drawing a knife from the pocket of his costume. "Just stand where you are."

The acrobat approached the onlooker with his knife and began to do something to him. He was drawing with the knife a number of vertical and horizontal lines on the onlooker's body and face. He drew a long line down the middle of his torso, one across the groin, another across the waist, and another across the chest. On the face he made a vertical incision from the hairline, down the nose, to the chin; and two horizontal incisions, one from the skin just above the left ear across the face just below the eyes to the top of the right ear, and another from the skin at the base of the left ear, across the face above the upper lip, to the skin at the base of the right ear.

I watched, extremely puzzled. Not only was there no blood, but the cooperative onlooker did not utter a word of pain or reproach. Yet I could see that the acrobat was not simply drawing with his knife, or just slightly marking the skin, but cutting deeply so that the flesh separated under his stroke.

The onlooker stood patiently while the acrobat worked silently and deftly with his knife. Having finished with the onlooker's face, he stepped back seemingly to admire his craft. Then, swiftly, he dug his fingers into the onlooker's face and pulled the severed and sectioned flesh away from the skull. I gasped with horror. "Won't someone stop him?" I was about to cry. When the acrobat withdrew his fingers, the onlooker's face fell into place, although the gaps in the face where the acrobat had made his incisions were still visible.

"Just testing," said the acrobat and smiled.

Since the onlooker was so calm, it now occurred to me that perhaps no injury was being done to him. No sooner did I think this than I myself was the onlooker. I was lying face down on the floor with my eyes closed, and I felt the knife tracing horizontal and vertical lines on my back and buttocks. It was not painful. It tickled a little, and actually, at moments, it was pleasant. Some twinges and harsh sensations made me accuse myself of being hypocritical, of pretending to enjoy what in fact I found tormenting. But I don't remember any pain.

Perhaps I really did fear what was happening to my body more than I admitted to myself, for I did not remain long in this role. Suddenly again a bystander, I was watching the acrobat make some final incisions on the original onlooker with his knife.

The acrobat addressed the onlooker, who was prone on his back and by this time unable to move without assistance or to speak. "There, I'm almost finished. Don't worry, there's only one thing more to do."

The onlooker seemed to understand and to take comfort in the acrobat's assurance that his ordeal was almost over. I felt reassured too, and leaned forward as far as I could without getting in the way to watch what the acrobat did next.

He took the body of the onlooker in his arms and stood it up, where it rested stiffly like a young tree brought to new ground to be planted. The onlooker's body remained upright, swaying slightly. A timid, hopeful expression in his eyes was the only sign of life in the rigid body.

"Just one thing more," said the acrobat in his soft, reassuring tone. "Please be patient. It won't hurt at all, and then you can go back to your friends." With his eyes the onlooker signalled his gratitude.

"Just one thing more," said the acrobat. "I can't tell you how grateful I and my colleagues are. You'll be glad you helped us."

I waited, full of hope that this ominous operation would soon be over, leaving the onlooker undamaged.

"Just one little thing more," said the acrobat.

Then with a rapid sure movement he grasped the sides of the onlooker's head. With one hand he pulled violently to the left, with the other to the right. First the skull was cleft, and then the onlooker's body, with only the faintest brief moan, barely more than a sigh, parted down the middle. The two cleanly separated halves of the body toppled stiffly to the floor.

The fate of the onlooker filled me with indignation, anguish. The onlooker had been so trusting, so compliant. And all the time the acrobat had intended to murder him. (I vaguely understood the purpose of the murder: the acrobat needed a body to replace the damaged body of his colleague.) He cared nothing for the onlooker, only for the little troupe of which he was the head. Outsiders were ignored, except when they served the acrobats' purposes.

Now I was sorry I had come down into the arena. I did not want to know of such cruelty and, turning my back on the scene, I awoke.

Never had I awakened from a dream with so great an impression of horror. For several days I inhabited the dream, and relived the feelings with which the dream had culminated. Indignation, however, was an emotion I knew to be perverse and profitless. I wanted to master my indignation. Yet I also thought that perhaps this outrage was salutary, an antidote to the phlegmatic state induced by my grief for my wife, and a necessary prelude to the calm I was seeking.

Of course it pleased me that as the dream repeated itself in succeeding weeks, I could watch the events in the arena with less emotion. Yet I could not accept this dream. I was not sure I understood it. How could I, when my life had been dismembered by my wife's death, just as the benevolent onlooker had been split in two by the acrobat.

It interested me to recall that for a while in the dream I had become the onlooker, the victim. Was my refusal to remain in this role courage or stupidity? Had I resisted something which I should have resisted—like the eye operation in "the dream of the mirror" or the bather's command to jump at the end of "the dream of the piano lesson"? Or had I misunderstood all my dreams, interpreting as persecution and betrayal what was in fact a lesson in liberation?

Dreams of horror and protest have their place, but surely are not our goal. Nor do we seek to be entirely, or mainly (as I was in this dream), spectators to great and terrible events.

A period of my life ended with this dream. I thought of leaving the capital. Since the war had been over, I had not once taken advantage of my freedom to travel. Jean-Jacques wrote me a friendly letter from his provincial retreat, urging me to visit him if I had nothing better to do. But I did have something better to do.

The fact is that I had not in recent years, despite the apparent contradiction of my marriage, wavered in my predilection for solitude. No more opportune moment could be imagined for my retirement. I was thirty-eight years old, unattached, unproductive, full of prejudices and uncompanionable habits. How could I hope to make a new life for myself with another woman? I would never find anyone as compatible, as yielding to my tastes, as worthy of my affection as my deceased wife.

But I did not want to go on living in the same apartment, which was redolent with memories of my wife and the odor of my own grief. I decided to look for more spacious quarters, in a neighborhood where I had not lived before. Then a marvellous idea occurred to me. There was that large house near the river which I had inherited from my father and furnished for Frau Anders. My former mistress had left the house shortly after I married; during the four years of the

Occupation the house was requisitioned and used for billeting enemy soldiers; since the liberation, it had stood empty—or almost empty, as I shall explain—and although in a state of considerable disrepair, it was eminently habitable. All things considered, the matter was easily arranged. But I must not omit to mention that when I informed my brother that I proposed to live in the house, he was strangely unfriendly to the plan. Even now I do not understand his reason, but I remember that he not only tried to discourage me (it was impractical; the house was too large; I was irresponsible; the repairs would be too costly) but gave me to understand that if I followed my plan I would be displeasing and even provoking him. I could not see the force of his arguments, particularly the one about the house being too large for me. (He had insisted rancorously, in a letter, that the house was large enough, counting the wings, to be used as a hospital or a school.) Counting on his not offering any legal obstacle to my plan, I decided to offend him and follow my own wishes.

Moving was simple, since I had few belongings. The day when I took possession of my new home was a clear winter morning with a light snowfall on the ground. I walked about the house, noting which windows needed new panes, collecting the wine bottles, old boots, socks, canteens, bricks, and torn canvas cots which littered the floors, piling all this in the garden, and, after clearing away the snow, lighting a splendid bonfire. The task of cleaning up was a pleasant one. Yet I mourned for my freshly painted walls, which I had never had the pleasure of living between, but inherited when they were disfigured, discolored, scrawled over, chipped, bullet punctured, peeling.

Once installed, I knew I had decided correctly, for I felt the peace and cheerfulness that only follows good decisions. A rigorously independent life in which I should have all the space I needed for my most extravagant and secretive projects was now possible to me. How easily the time passed, how comfortable I was in that unfurnished spaciousness after the confined and cluttered rooms of my dreams. And I had plenty to occupy me, for a period of time which lengthened from days to weeks to months to years. Six years I stayed in that house. I sewed and unsewed my ideas. I listened to my dreams. I thought of my wife. But, if I may trust my memory, I no longer lived in fear of the sudden vengeful arrival of Frau Anders.

For Frau Anders was with me, had in fact preceded me in the house. You will remember that my wife and I had sheltered her for some months during the war; and that after soldiers had searched our building several times and once our apartment itself, she had begged me to find her a better hiding-place; and that I had done so, and promised to describe this shelter in a later chapter. Well, the refuge I had devised for her—in the best traditions of detective fiction—was none other than her own house, then being used to billet enemy troops. I remembered a windowless back room in the basement adjoining the kitchen. The door to this room was the rear wall of a closet in the kitchen, and could be opened only by a trip lock which worked by lifting a shelf in the back of the closet. Thus the room was virtually safe from discovery. I warned Frau Anders that life here would hardly be pleasant, for she would have to bear the harsh noises around her and continual darkness. Late at night she could go into the kitchen, and steal a small bit of food, but she must be careful never to take enough of anything so that its loss could be noticed; and she could dispose of her excrement at a similar hour by going into the garden and burying it in the ground. Even after I had convinced her that she would be safe there, she was terrified of being caught when we went to the house. I consulted Jean-Jacques and we worked out a simple strategy. I had watched the house for some time, to determine the stations and number of the guards; there were two in the front and one in the back. We waited until the visit to the capital of one of the enemy heads of state, a day when most of the troops of the city were on parade. Then Frau Anders, Jean-Jacques, and I came to the house. I went to the front door, and engaged the guards in conversation. I said I wished to see a certain lieutenant, and refused to believe that no one of that name was billeted there. A few minutes were taken up this way before I was knocked down with a rifle butt, kicked twice, and thrown out. Jean-Jacques took on the guard in back, with better luck; I think he ended by making a rendezvous with him. In the meantime, Frau Anders had made her way into the house; and there she remained for the rest of the war.

The day the capital was liberated, I went to the house. It was with some difficulty that I finally got Frau Anders to answer, and it proved even harder to persuade her to emerge. She was a piteous sight. She had been in that dark room over two years without talking to a single person. Her voice was barely audible, her gaze unsteady, and she had lost all her teeth. She didn't seem surprised that the war was over; she said she always expected it would end some time. But when I invited her to come with me and stay at my place until she found one of her own, she refused. She said she was ashamed of appearing in the street without any teeth. I then suggested that she live in the house for a while, until she got used to a greater degree of freedom, and that I would come often and also send friends to visit her so that she would gradually become reaccustomed to human society. I followed this program faithfully, calling on her once a week. At my request Jean-Jacques went a few times, too; but then refused to go any more because, he said, she was hopeless and depressing. Still hopeful of her emergence, I took a dentist to the house who fitted her with a set of false teeth. But gradually I realized that she intended to stay where she was, if I would let her (and of course I had no intention of dispossessing her); she declared she was too old to live outside.

It was Frau Anders then, who lived in the house when I moved there, whose presence makes it not quite accurate to say that I was entirely alone in the succeeding six years. Nevertheless we rarely saw each other, for she lived in the basement and I in the upper two stories. She performed some elementary housekeeping duties for me, and had become sufficiently emancipated to go out and buy food or a newspaper. But other than the necessary conversations relating to the management of the house, in which at times she could become rather shrewish, we exchanged few words.

I do not want to give the impression that I had abandoned myself to the luxuries of melancholy and misanthropy. Perhaps it was melancholy which drove me into this spacious retirement. But once inside my castle, my melancholy lifted and was replaced by the vivacity which accompanies the assumption of any worthwhile task. Genuine isolation does not come easily to anyone, even to the most willing; I pursued my isolation rigorously. I wanted to learn if one could be really alone, and what was essential to remaining human. (Certainly I did not want to lose my humanity, my ability to be not alone, to go out when I wanted to—as poor Frau Anders had done.) I wanted a theatre in which I could imitate the singularity of my dreams.

Although I could have gone out, then, for the most part I did not. Frau Anders would market and run errands for me, if I was peremptory enough. When I did go out, it was not to be somewhere else. My occasional walks, for purposes of exercise, were entirely voluntary; I had shed all my roles except the biological one. It is the possession of a role which provides the impetus to go out in the world, to act at all. The more numerous roles, the greater the number of excursions. (In this way I understood Jean-Jacques' nightly wanderings, his agile transformations.) When I had learned to move with even greater agility, it did not seem necessary to move at all. For as any role can be condensed into an attitude, any act may be condensed into a posture. That is what I learned to do—to transform every act into a posture, and to link the postures with a subtle blankness.

I realize this thought is unclear but it is hard to explain an idea which is really a dance rather than a sequence of sentences. Take murder, for example. It now seems to me that Jean-Jacques murdered my wife. He did it with a dance, with a posture, with the mock threat to my own person. Since my wife's life depended on mine, seeing me about to be killed in a game, she playfully died with me. But her resources for surviving the game in order to play again were less than mine. And so she really died, while I did not.

SIXTEEN

I am not altogether sure of the sequence of events during the period in which I lived in that large house, and must rely partly on undated notes and letters and the journals which I kept then. I have had to arrange these in what seems the most likely order (my memory is not always of help), grouping together as belonging to the same period all documents written in blue ink, and to a later period those written in red. Several of the notebooks I have assumed to have been written consecutively.

The notebook which I have before me now is bound in leather and has a lion embossed on the front cover. It contains a series of numbered jottings written in red ink of which I will give just a few.

1. The dreams make me see myself as someone alien.
2. There is no knowledge of one's inner feelings, as there is of the outer world.
3. Despite the force with which I press myself against the line, I cannot jump outside the circle of my consciousness.

But I can step further inside. I can find a smaller circle within the larger circle, and climb into that.

4. If I cannot be outside myself, I will be inside. I will look out at myself as my own landscape.

9. If I give a serious answer, the question becomes serious.

10. The only interesting answers are those which destroy the question.

13. When I destroy the dreams, do I destroy myself?

16. I do not want to be appeased. I do not want to be comforted.

18. Oh, the great simplifiers!

21. Now I understand the mystery of the will. What is pain but the failure of will?

24. I don't want to have any convictions. If I am (or believe) something, I want to discover it through my acts; I don't want to act in the way I do because it accords with what I believe or what I am.

25. You do not decide anything. It decides you. You may act so as to provoke contempt. You may dehumanize yourself. But you may not decide these things, for then (despite all your efforts at abasement) you will not *feel* yourself an object of contempt and you will not be, what you desire, less human.

27. The first rule of the ascetic life is to appear comical. If only I were a hunchback!

31. The dreams which I now honor I first held in indifference and contempt.

32. I remain unfelt by myself, except in my terrible dreams.

33. My dreams will expel my character.

35. There are emotions which are still unnamed. I shall call them X, Y, Z.

39. My body failed me in my dreams.

42. I have put something into the world. Therefore I will take something out of it: myself.

46. Good and evil laugh at each other.

47. It may be said that I lack a sense of humor.

50. Life in slow motion. Life engraved with the point of a nail; and on the head of the nail, an indecipherable message.

51. Let the lights go out, so that a single light can shine.

52. Let the lion's roar be stilled, so that the bee's sting may be heard.

55. There are two paths, leading to two different goals. One is from event to knowledge: the well-celebrated path of wisdom. Another, from knowledge to event: the much advertised path to action . . . Are these all? Isn't there a third: from non-knowledge to non-event? And a fourth? From non-event to non-knowledge?

56. At first my activities exceeded my knowledge. Then, as I came to know less, I gave up action.

57. There was once a man who was waiting for something to happen to him; it never did. There was once a man who was waiting for nothing to happen to him; finally it did.

Let me tell you a dream which I had shortly after I moved into the house, which confirmed for me the correctness of my decision.

I dreamed I was in a dimly-lit cellar. There was a large coal bin in one corner and a furnace in the other. Most of the floor was occupied by stacks of newspapers, garbage pails, loose bricks, old suitcases, and two travelling trunks pasted over with torn labels from foreign hotels. That I was alone in the cellar did not appear unreasonable to me, for there was hardly room for anyone else. That I was loosely chained to a stake in the center of the floor also did not trouble me.

Beyond the length of my chain, across the cellar, was a stairway which led up to a door bordered with light. I regarded the stairs without feeling any impulse to climb them. The light was not intended for me. And hearing the distant noise of breaking glass, I was thankful to be where I was, safely away from the violence which I assumed to be taking place.

Nevertheless I knew that it was possible to be more or less comfortable, wherever one is. I was trying to make myself comfortable with the bricks. Although fettered, I had a small area in which to move freely, and perhaps build something. I assembled all the bricks within my reach. Then, after lying down once on the floor to measure my body, I placed the bricks carefully next to each other making a sort of bed out of them long enough for me to stretch out at full length.

But when I had lain on my bed of bricks, I found it was less comfortable than the floor. I dismantled the bed, retaining only a pillow of bricks, and settled myself to rest.

There was one small window in this cellar, but when I looked in its direction, the light hurt my eyes. A child's head appeared at the window, blocking the painful light. She was a pretty child, about four years old.

"It's a bear!" she cried, pointing at me. I smiled back, but this didn't seem right. Then I growled amicably. I knew I wasn't a bear, but didn't want to disappoint her.

The next thing I remember is eating a plate of rice. I was a bear now, or some sort of animal, for the way I ate was to gather the rice in my paws and rub it into my mouth. After I was finished I wondered who had brought the food and why I had not thought to detain him. I was lonely. I began to bang my bricks on the floor and shout. "Keeper!" I called.

The man in the black bathing suit appeared in the doorway at the top of the stairs. His bare muscular arms and legs were as forceful and athletic as ever. There was one addition to his costume, however: a rope knotted around his waist, to which a heavy keychain was attached which hung down to his thigh. As he descended the steps I watched him expectantly. What followed, though, far surpassed my hopes that he would stay for a while and talk to me.

"Unchain him," said the bather.

I was filled with joy at the prospect of leaving the cellar in the company of the bather. I would have been happy to go anywhere with him. Somehow I understood we were going to the park. In parks, I recalled, one receives consolation. The park is either a place to play or make love or talk. Any of these alternatives would have been delightful to me.

But I had forgotten that the park is also a place where one watches, and where one is entertained by spectacles. In the park I found myself on a small stage with a painted backdrop of trees. The audience before me, seated on folding chairs, consisted of nurses with baby-carriages and small children.

The bather was beside me on the stage, acting as the master of ceremonies. "Now he dances," he said.

I wished to dance for him! But my legs, which seemed made of wood or cardboard, refused to move.

The audience became restive. "There is no need to leave," the bather said. "He must dance."

I found, to my relief, that I was dancing. But the center of movement did not come from within me, but from wires attached to my wrists and ankles and to the nape of my neck. They were chains, really—familiar and cozy. I could not understand how I could now be a puppet, when just a moment before I had been an animal. But I knew that puppets could be as graceful as animals, and that dancing bears were ridiculous. It seemed better to be a puppet. I flung my arms and legs about rhythmically, straining to be worthy of the bather's approval.

"Perfect," said the man. A feeling of peace came over me, and my movements slowly subsided.

"Now we will show what else he can do," said the man. He beckoned to one of the children sitting in the front row who was clutching a large rag doll.

The child mounted the platform. "Bear," said the man in the black bathing suit, "kick the doll and caress the child." For an instant I wondered if he were addressing me. He repeated his command. I obeyed him immediately. But after doing exactly as he had directed, I found myself holding the doll in my arms; the child lay dismembered and bloody on the floor of the stage. Covering my face with my hands, I awaited the bather's wrath.

"That is innocence," said the man. "He can no longer be blamed."

"Who would dream of blaming him?" shouted one of the white-uniformed nurses, a stout blonde woman with a cheerful face. I realized that she was the nurse in charge of the dead child. Although her approval was not as important to me as that of the man in the black bathing suit, I was concerned about her feelings. She did not seem at all angry when she came forward and collected the child.

"He must kill," the bather called after her, as she left the stage. "But he intends no harm."

I nodded agreement. The children laughed. Their laughter raised a final small doubt in my mind; I wished to explain why I had been exonerated. "It is himself but not himself," I said, and this was the last thing I remember before I awoke.

I consider this dream in many ways the most important of all my dreams. For some time I had known that my dreams had a life of their own: they were not simply the subject of my attention, in the dialogue which I had opened up between my waking and sleeping life, but constituted a sort of dialogue among themselves. This dream was the reply to "the dream of the two rooms," my very first dream. In both dreams, there is the bather and a woman in white; in both dreams, I am asked to dance, I am chained and confined. But in the first, I cannot dance, my confinement is irksome, and the two personages of the dream are angry with me. In this dream, which I called "the dream of the puppet," when I am asked to dance, I am finally able to; my chains actually assist me, for they have become the end of wires which move my body gracefully; and I please the masterful personages of my dream. In the first dream, I am ashamed. In this dream I am not ashamed, I am at peace.

Incidents in my life, too, were illuminated by this dream. I thought back to my youth, soon after I had begun to dream, to that encounter long ago with a child in the park after the final conversation with Father Trissotin. I remembered how peaceful I had felt in that abandoned exchange of words with a child. It seemed to me that all my life had been converging on the state of mind represented in this dream in which I would finally be reconciled to myself—myself as I really am, the self of my dreams. That reconciliation is what I take to be freedom.

Do not think that I find this dream, or any of the others, unusual. For all I know, everyone has such dreams. What is unusual is the relation between my waking and my dreaming life. Under the pressure of my dreams, I came to adopt a style of living which cannot be called other than eccentric—except that 'eccentric' means literally 'out of or departing from the center,' while my life has, on the contrary, tended to revolve ever closer to the center, the very whirlpool of my dreams. But am I not quibbling? It is not distance from the center of one's self, one's dreams, which is meant by calling someone eccentric, but distance from the social center, the warm body of habits and tastes which are useful, amiable, and communally reinforcing. No, I will not disavow the label of eccentric.

Nevertheless there are labels which I do repudiate. I'm aware that any kind of eccentricity may be considered a psychological deformity; and that a narrative about someone of unusual tastes and inner experiences, as this one is, tends to be read as a psychological study. In a psychological study one takes dreams as evidence, as supplying information about the dreamer's preoccupations. I beg the reader not to avail himself of this simple way out, without at least considering my own example.

I am not interested in my dreams in order to understand myself better, in order to know my true feelings. I am not interested in my dreams, in other words, from the point of view of psychology. I am interested in my dreams as—acts.

I am interested in my dreams as acts, and as models for action and motives for action. I am interested in my dreams from the point of view of freedom. It may seem odd that, just at this point, in discussing a dream which presented me with so clear an image of my own enslavement, I should speak of freedom. I am aware of the alternatives. Were I to inspect my dreams with the purpose of "understanding myself," I would be considering my dreams from the point of view of bondage. I would then see how my dreams reflect my enslavement to my own character, its limited themes, its stale anxieties.

But one has only to declare oneself free in order to be, truly, free. I have only to consider my dreams as free, as autonomous, in order to *be* free of them—at least as free as any human being has the right to be.

Another notebook describes the routine of a model day in my new home. Remember, I spent six years there, and each day had to be filled with some activity. I invented a formula for awakening, getting out of bed, washing, dressing, eating, reading, exercising, going to sleep, so that their character as activities would be modified by my new understanding.

I have never wanted to be a specialist and I had not yet come to acknowledge the value of useful activity. But certain things have to be done daily, thrice daily, all one's life; and through repetition one inevitably acquires proficiency. What I wanted to do was to rid these acts of any practical aspect, to think of them as executed each in and for itself. Thus I converted my most menial daily acts into what might be called rituals, which

I performed faithfully, without any illusion that they were efficacious. I kept myself very clean, although there was no one to smell me. I was punctual, although I made no appointments.

I must emphasize that these rituals were, like all else in my life except my dreams, entirely voluntary. Once again, I must caution the reader not to reduce my acts to neurotic compulsions.

What are the features of ritual? First, and most obviously, repetition. Second, that this repetition proceeds according to a script in which every detail is fixed. Ordinarily, the goal determines the form of the act. The least form that achieves the goal which the person has in mind suffices. Say, I want to remove a candlestick from the shelf and place it on the table. It doesn't matter how I carry the candlestick, whether in my left or my right hand, whether I walk or run, or even whether someone else does it for me. All that matters is that in the end the object be where I want it. I will put it down emphatically. Further, the spot on the table doesn't have to be exactly specified. Anywhere on the table will do, so long as it doesn't fall off.

But if this act becomes a ritual the goal is absolutely precise. Equally precise are the means I take to arrive at the goal. There is only one correct way to transport the candlestick from shelf to table; only one place on the table where it may stand. The agent's intentions and wishes are irrelevant. He must not infringe upon the act by performing it in a personal and idiosyncratic manner. Ideally, he should move as in a trance.

Now I understood the most elementary but far from obviously intelligible feature of ritual—repetition. For why should any act need to be performed over and over in exactly the same way, which is laborious, unnatural, and difficult? Why should anything be repeated, ever? Why is once not enough?

Common sense tells us that the only good reason for doing something more than once is that it has not been consummated the first time. This is exactly what happens in ritual. The rules of ritual forbid precisely that which makes it possible for an act to be consummated or fulfilled: the break-through of personal emphasis, the uneven distribution of attention, a climax. Ritual, whose essence is repetition, is that act which is never done properly, and therefore must be repeated indefinitely. Ritual is that way of performing an act which guarantees the need of doing it again.

Consider my dreams. They consisted of acts which had to be performed repeatedly, hence their recurrence. Further, the emotional tonelessness of the dream after successive repetitions and variations had just this familiar quality of ritual: outward agitation contradicted by inner trance. The only task remaining to me was to execute the command of my dreams in my waking life, which is what I was attempting in that period of meditation in Frau Anders' house. I wanted my acts to become as automatic as they had been in "the dream of the puppet," for I had divined that once I moved in this way my dreams would be appeased, and the man in the black bathing suit placated.

Let me give you an example of how I learned to behave. It was a real event, in fact a situation of some danger to me— danger being more real than safety.

One night I was asleep in one of the rooms on the first floor when I was awakened by footsteps and a rustling noise in the corridor. I left my bed and went to investigate, taking care to arm myself with a poker from the fireplace. As I peered down the corridor, I saw a figure pressing himself against the wall. I pretended not to see him, and returned to my room. About twenty minutes later, hearing more noises, I rushed out into the hall and shouted at the intruder. He turned and faced me, a lean pimply youth in a black leather jacket.

"You better watch out," he said.

"I'm watching," I replied.

"This is a robbery!" He brandished a gun, and I dropped my poker.

I told him that he could have anything in the house which he put a bullet through, on the first try, at a distance of twenty paces. He looked at me incredulously, then laughed harshly. "I don't have enough bullets for all I want," he said.

I told him that I had a gun and he could use mine when his ran out. I followed him about the house, as he put holes in the officers' chairs and trophies in the salon, in each franc note of the cash I kept in a desk, in the gold balls in a room I set aside for the improvement of the senses, in a manicure set in a leather case, and in a few other articles of mine which he claimed.

At the end of his tour I complimented him on his marksmanship. He turned to me and said, "What if I want you? Is that part of the bargain, *maître fou?*"

I assured him that it was. "But you could only sell me if I am alive and in good condition," I added.

"Jesus!" he exclaimed. "What am I going to do with this junk?"

"The money is still good, the gold can be melted down, the furniture can be repaired."

He stared at me in a peculiar way and rubbed his eyes. "Christ! I think I'm dreaming. How did you get me to play this idiotic game? Nobody will believe me if I tell them about tonight."

"Don't regret what you have done," I said. "You've relieved yourself of a great burden. The burden of hiding and skulking. You have learned about disinterested violence, and I the secret of disinterested surrender."

He shook his head, laughed, and asked for a drink. We sat down and he told me about the three jail sentences he had already served—he was only twenty-two—and about his girlfriend, and the profession of house-breaking. A very decent fellow, really; I should be sorry not to have known him. About seven in the morning, he called a truck-driver friend who came and took the things he had chosen away.

You will remember that at the beginning of this narrative I formulated my researches into myself as a quest for certitude. A great philosopher, the first to make this the goal of his inquiry, found that all he could be entirely certain of was that he existed. He was certain he existed because he thought; denial of this was itself an act of thought. My quest led to the opposite conclusion. Only because I existed—in other words, thought—did the problem of certitude arise. To reach certitude is to learn that one does not exist.

Understand me, I do not deny common sense. I admit that I have a body, that I was born in such a place and at such a time. But it is never thoughts which are certain, only acts—acts cleansed of thought.

My dreams, although full of reflections and impressions, were a parody of thought, cleansing me of thought, and therefore of personal existence. Rather than being an obstacle to the original problem which I had set myself, they were the solution to it. Thus they deserved the fate of all solution: ladders which must be kicked aside after gaining the desired altitude. The discipline which I imposed on myself in Frau Anders' house was precisely an attempt to remove the dreams, by integrating them fully into my life—to dissolve the means, now that they had brought me to the end.

There is only one loophole in my argument, one chink in the armor I have fashioned for myself out of the union of my life and my dreams. I talk of certitude—even boasting to you, my reader, that I have achieved it. I am concealing something which I must admit, embarrassing or inexplicable as it is. While I talk of certitude, I remain uncertain of one important thing! It concerns Frau Anders, or to speak more carefully, of the woman for whom I furnished the house years before, whom I installed in it during the war, and whom I later joined there.

If that woman was not Frau Anders then a whole stretch of my memory is wrong. But surely, it was Frau Anders, whom I had generously given over to the care of an Arab merchant many years ago. It was she who returned two years later, mutilated and pitiful, whom I attempted unsuccessfully to murder. She, ever indestructible, on whom I conferred the house. It was Frau Anders who pursued me, wanted to marry me, drove me to marry, and lived for a while with me and my wife. It was Frau Anders whom I put into the house, under the very eyes of the enemy. It was she whom I joined there after my dear wife had died and the war was over, who kept me sullen company. It was the same woman, Frau Anders, whom I left in the house, subdued, lifeless, a ghost.

It seems perfectly simple, clear. And yet, I have other memories of the house in which I was entirely alone there. Is it possible that she was never there? How could that be? My wife would know whether she had lived with us or not during the war. But my wife is dead. The other witness is Jean-Jacques. He helped me put her there. But I am ashamed to ask him. I hardly see him now. He would find me foolish and senile, my memory fading. Indeed even if he should say yes; that does not solve the mystery, but rather compounds it. For I have still other memories, which cannot be reconciled with the past I have narrated. I distinctly remember being evicted from the house —by a Frau Anders who had never lived there.

I remember it as clearly as I remember everything else which contradicts it. I was in the room for the improvement of the senses—it was the sixth year of my tenancy—when the old woman who acted as my housekeeper came upstairs to tell me I had a visitor. (I willingly stipulate that this complaining querulous old woman cannot then have been Frau Anders. Who she was I do not know.) My housekeeper, whoever she was, could not have surprised me more if she had told me that there was a desert lion reclining on my living room carpet. I remonstrated with the old woman, for she had instructions to turn away all callers; but when I saw the malicious gleam in her eye, and learned from her that the visitor refused to leave, I decided to handle the matter myself. I went downstairs, and into the living room. Seated on a chair by the empty fireplace was a tall woman in her late fifties, tanned, wearing dark sunglasses and furs.

"Madam," I said. "Whom do I have the pleasure of addressing? You will excuse the bareness of my rooms, and the fact that there is no fire in the grate. I am not accustomed to receiving visitors."

"Don't you recognize me?" She took off her sunglasses and I examined the ruins of a vigorous handsome face.

"No, I don't," I replied irritably.

"Well, I barely recognize you, my dear, I must confess. You have become rather stooped and faded, your hair is quite grey, and, needless to say, you are almost twenty years older."

"If I am twenty years older, then so are you."

She laughed. "You were always rather clever, I remember that, in your mild stubborn way."

My heart began to pound. "Are you a relative?"

She laughed again.

"Only a relative of mine would dare talk to me with such impertinence and affectionateness."

"Don't you really know? Look at me closely. I am an old woman, though I don't feel old at all. Look at me. Dear Hippolyte."

A premonition came over me, and a thrill of pleasure and anxiety.

"You are someone who is happy."

"Evidently," she said. "Look at me."

Looking, I could stave off the knowledge no longer. "I know you."

"Do you? When did you see me last?"

"I let you precede me through a doorway."

"Oh," she cried, "don't remind me of that! I thought I should never forgive you, but I did, oh so quickly. Would I be here now if I didn't? Come, sit down. I shan't let you breathe a word about yourself, until I tell you all that's happened to me."

I didn't want to sit, because I didn't really believe in her, but she insisted. I saw that she had lost none of her old commanding manner, but the girlish desire to please which often contradicted it had gone. She told me to tell my housekeeper to bring us something to drink, and when I admitted that there were no amenities in the house, she produced a little flask of brandy from her purse. Then we began a long chat which lasted through the afternoon well into the evening.

After an hour I was convinced that it was no imposter. Who else could it be but Frau Anders? And I listened with laughter and amazement at her adventures. She had spent more than three years with the merchant—I had been right about that, there was no young son—during which time he had abused her cruelly. His ardor thrived on her terror. He had locked her up in a room in his house, visiting her thrice weekly between the hours of one and four in the afternoon, after which he left for the mosque. When her fear subsided, however, he grew tired of her, and sold her to a camel trader who took her further south with him into the desert. The trader used to beat her regularly; in one of his beatings she almost lost her left eye. After a year of lust and abuse, the trader left her with a water carrier in a desert village, and here Frau Anders spent more than a decade, quite happily.

At this point in her story, I interrupted. "You were happy?

By what means? What had replaced ill-treatment as a source of satisfaction for you?"

"There is a limit, Hippolyte," she replied, "even to the wish to be used by others." She explained that by this time, through poor diet, exposure to the desert storms, lack of baths, frequent beatings, she had begun to feel her age. She told me that she felt she had lost her sexual attractiveness, which I took to be a dignified way of telling me she had lost something of her sexual urge. She and the water-carrier, however, reached an understanding. He was an amiable and gentle man, mainly concerned with improving his lowly position in life, and Frau Anders agreed to help him.

"You can't imagine how enterprising I had become, Hippolyte," she said at this point. "You have no idea how it fortifies one's character to have to be concerned only with problems of survival."

"I do understand," I said with feeling.

"No, you don't. You can't. What does one worry about in this city, in any city? Psychological survival? But that's nothing. I mean real survival. In the face of marauders, starvation, jackals, cholera."

"You seem very well," I ventured.

"I am, I am," she said.

She continued her story. It was at this point that she had written to her husband and daughter, and received money from them and a formal quittance from her responsibilities to them. With the aid of the water-carrier, she took a survey of the village in which she resided. It was a community of some four thousand souls, consisting of shepherds, traders, and thieves. There was no farming, for it was the desert. Armed with her money, she offered the villagers material prosperity if they would crown her queen. They were sceptical at first, and explained to her that it was also against their traditions to be ruled by a woman. Woman is made for man's pleasure, man is made to govern and make war. While she waited for the village to concede authority to her, she set herself up in a little hut as a midwife and dream-interpreter.

"I'm a dream-interpreter, too," I interjected.

She ignored my remark and continued without pause. "You know. I told the village chief that his dream of seven camels meant seven years of drought. Unless they acknowledged me. They're remarkably credulous people, quite tractable under their manner of fierceness."

Finally she prevailed, and was crowned with all ceremony. Her birthday was made an annual feast of the village. After a year the water-carrier lost his position as chief consort, and was followed by a succession of dark young boys, but he, and each of her ex-lovers, was rewarded with a post in the village government. She negotiated with the government for an irrigation project, which brought farming to the village. The people prospered and looked upon her as a miracle-worker. The only price she exacted was reverence and obedience. Drawing on their obedience, she designed a model community: day nurseries to free mothers to work in the fields, a house of prostitution, a law-court, a theatre, a small army which she drilled herself. Under her direction, the village spent the war years pilfering from military installations.

"Catherine the Great," I murmured.

"Yes, I learned to respect Western comforts. There's nothing beautiful in dirt or poverty or disease. I've lost my ideals, Hippolyte," she said, "and good riddance. Life is simply a matter of survival. I'm not romantic anymore."

"Why did you leave?"

"One can't remain a queen forever. To retain one's authority one must abdicate or be martyred. I chose the former. That's why I am here. I have decided to spend the rest of my days here in the capital. And I have come straight to you."

"Why?"

"Don't be afraid, Hippolyte. I'm not going to rape you. My sexual days are over, as are my days of administration. Now I shall at last cultivate my spirit. But let me warn you, I am accustomed to being obeyed."

"By whom?"

"Why, by everyone," she said. "But I'll start with you. First of all, I want this house."

"My house?"

"I've checked with your brother. He agrees with me. It isn't good for you to remain here. It's too big for you."

"And not for you?"

"You'll see. I have more to fill it with."

"But I like it here. I am learning to be alone."

"Well, you'll have to be alone somewhere else. And besides, you're not alone. You have that hideous old woman, and she'll have to go."

"She's not with me. She's just here, too . . . What if I won't give you the house?"

"This will please you, I think. Jean-Jacques has given me a copy of the original plans which you drew up for the furnishing and disposition of the rooms. I see that you have never carried them out?" She looked around the modest and conventional decor of the room in which we sat.

I felt obliged to explain. "I had not the inclination. Besides, many other people occupied it. There were enemy soldiers here."

"Well, all that will be changed. You don't know it, but it was for me that you designed this house. For the last stage of my education."

"I repeat," I said angrily, "what if I don't give you the house? I happen to like it here. It's my home."

"You have to give it up. I have the plans." She reached in her purse, and produced them for my inspection.

"Would you throw me out on the street?"

"Nonsense! I'll give you time to find another place. Good heavens, I'll even help you. I have plenty of time, and much good will toward you, dear Hippolyte."

With these words Frau Anders stood up, gravely kissed me on both cheeks and made her way out of the house without letting me show her to the door. I remained in the room, dumbstruck, gazing around at my castle. Was it possible that she could deprive me of all this, my home, my refuge. I would act immediately. I would go to my brother, who, as the head of the family now, might speak with more authority than I. I would explain to him how necessary the house was to me, how I had just begun to know myself here, and that he must prevent Frau Anders from dispossessing me.

She had insinuated that I did not take proper care of the house. I thought desperately of painting it immediately; I would buy new furniture; every night there would be a fire in the grate. I rose from the chair in which I was sitting, caressed its back with the thrill of loss, and walked into the hallway, in time to see my old housekeeper darting down the stairs. She had apparently been eavesdropping.

Frau Anders returned the next morning. She brought groceries, and was accompanied by a Zulu whom she introduced as her masseur, and a darkskinned young lady with a shaved head whom she called her private secretary. To them, and to a carpenter who was also in attendance, she gave instructions for the repair and furnishing of the house. To me she gave a week to find a new place to live.

We had one more conversation of interest, in which Frau Anders allayed any suspicions which I had that she was evicting me in the spirit of revenge. As I had once dealt with her with a certain freedom, disposing of her for her own good, she explained, she now dealt with me in the same way for my own good. As I was right then, so she was right now.

I was not altogether convinced that she was right, but I

trusted her sincerity. The only thing that took me aback was that she spoke of love as her motive, self-love and love for me.

"I've learned to love myself, Hippolyte," she said. "I love my powdery smooth wrinkled flesh, my sagging breasts, my veined feet, the smell of my armpits. Every time I look into the mirror, I can't tell you how delighted I am that someone looks back, smiling, and that that someone is me. I want to embrace everyone, even beggars and school teachers. I love myself so much that I even love you, you strange brittle man."

"You won't live forever," I muttered glumly.

"Wait," she said. "Who can tell? I feel younger than ever. I shall die a baby, which is no death at all."

This was not self-love as I had understood it. No, I didn't understand her motives, but I knew she was sincere. This helped me to become resigned to her intervention in my life. And besides: she would use the house as I had not. It was made for her. She had always been a more worldly person than I; her retirement would therefore be more populated than mine, and need bigger living quarters.

SEVENTEEN

Voila que j'ai touché l'automne des idées.

Now I live in more modest quarters again. I no longer require the great number of rooms provided by the house from which I was either evicted or left voluntarily. It is some years since I left the house to the mistress of my youth—I trust it has done her as much good as it did me—and moved to where I have resided ever since, in order to lead the life which I described to you at the commencement of this narrative.

I receive friends occasionally. I still don't go out often. Yet I am not unaware of the life around me, nor incapable of assessing people correctly. The following anecdote will illustrate the change in me, as well as the fact that my seclusion is not as total as the reader may think, and that I have not failed to remain in touch with the principal events of our times.

Last Thursday I went out as I sometimes do to buy my evening meal. I bought a carp, and when I returned home and opened my damp package, I saw that the newspaper the fishmonger had wrapped the fish in had a picture of Jean-Jacques. My friend had been elected to the *Académie*, no less; he was one of the immortals! The article which accompanied his picture contained an account of his extremely controversial election to the *Académie*. It seemed that some members objected to his dubious political past, and of these a few even dared to try to revive the charges of collaboration which were bruited about, briefly, after the war—just before he prudently left for an extended residence in the south. But these voices were silenced by others, who instanced the austerity of his life, the versatility of his multiple careers, and the uncompromising courage of his art. Of such elements is literary immortality composed in our time!

I studied his picture in the paper for a long time. In the picture he was grizzled, well-dressed, and puffy eyed. I confess that I hardly recognized him. Not that we are not still friends. I had seen him only a year before, at a cocktail party given for him by his publisher, to which he had begged me to come. But I know that when I see him in the flesh, it is with the eyes of the past. Only in a photograph can I see him as he is in the present. And when I study the picture I ask myself, where is he? the great bully, the charming liar, the inconstant friend, the unprincipled coquette who amused and taunted me in my younger days, the frivolous Vergil who watched me descend into the inferno of my dreams. He is gone: aged, transfixed by the great stare of the public eye, frozen. Now he is utterly famous. Everyone laughs at his mockery, he can offend no one. His acts have been transformed into postures, but not out of his own will and in the privacy of his intimate life.

I suspect that when we see each other he barely recognizes me, too. For I have changed no less than he. But I and I alone have worked these changes in myself, a deeper change than any possible through the mere attainment of one's ambition. The greatest miracles of change are attained by the contracting of one's ambitions, as I learned in Frau Anders' house. There is a better method of changing the inferno into paradise than clambering laboriously up the rim. One can also climb down, climb into the devil's mouth, past the mangled bodies of traitors, through the gullet and into the devil's bowels themselves. The devil's asshole is the backdoor to paradise—if you will permit the indelicacy. In Frau Anders' house I was in the devil's asshole, a strait corner despite the apparent spaciousness of my residence. But one becomes easily habituated to a diet of excrement, to not complaining, and to standing still. The results were remarkable, as I have testified several times in this book. I emerged from that house—albeit that my emergence appears to me alternately as a rescue and as a cruel eviction— a new man, cleansed and purged of my dreams.

Now I am in a position to be able to help others again, though in an entirely different way than before, for now I am not interested in the inner but only in the outer man. I devote two days a week as an unpaid volunteer in a pauper's hospital, doing the work of an orderly and nurse. I am not sorry that I never adopted a profession, yet I regret the selfish employment of my time in my youth. My work in the hospital allows me to feel that I am making some recompense for my former idleness. Of course, compared with nursing as generally practiced by women, the tasks of a male nurse are less sentimental, more physical, sometimes janitorial. This is good work, requiring a nice mixture of improvisation, when one converses with the patients, and absolutely fixed routine, when one attends their bodies. And I have found, happily, few claims upon my pity, for the patients in this hospital, being destitute, really enjoy being ill, lying in warm beds, being cared for, shaved, and fed.

Once I even had the pleasure of seeing one of the patients whom I had attended during a bout of influenza, outside the hospital, disporting himself cheerfully at one of the public swimming pools along the river. His appearance was unusual, because he was a cripple. Imagine to yourself a bather whose legs were thinner than his arms, whose neck, around which hung a delicate silver chain with a cross, was thicker than his head. Seated on his enormous neck was a prizefighter's face: thick short brown hair cut close to his scalp, low fleshy forehead, flat nose, thick lips, wide jaw. From the neck surged great wings of shoulder blades, two enormous convex shields which marked his breasts, two stout trees for upper arms. His skin was smooth, moderately hairy, and deeply tanned. He wore a brief plaid Bikini around his tiny wasted hips, which revealed the diminutive bulge between his thighs that should have been so much larger. His legs were slender poles, in which one could barely distinguish the knees and the ankles. He could bend his left leg but the right was completely stiff, bent inward slightly at the knee and outward at the foot. His feet were no longer than his hands, which were not overlarge; and he had no movement in either ankle.

I was already sitting on a chair at the pool when he came in, propelling himself forward by means of a pair of unpainted wooden canes with black rubber caps. He recognized me, we exchanged greetings, and then he fell forward deftly onto the floor at the edge of the pool. His expression was relaxed, agreeable, often smiling—but it was not the painful ingratiating smile of the popular cripple, the cripple who has won his popularity by being nicer than anyone else in the crowd. He had come with four well-built young men in Bikinis, who proceeded to do handstands, wrestle with each other, dive in the water, take photographs of each other, and play the radio which they turned to the American Army station.

He entered the water by doing a rapid and faultless handstand from a sitting position, balancing firmly for a moment, then springing with his hands to dive into the pool, arms and head down, legs straight in the air. Once in the water, he swam quickly and singlemindedly back and forth across the pool half a dozen times. Then, without any dalliance in the water, he returned to the side, hoisted himself out entirely by means of his powerful arms, picked up his canes, and returned to the place where his companions were lying. After his swim, he sat, with his arms around his bent left leg, looking at his feet and wiggling his toes in time to the music on the radio. I noticed then that the little toe on each foot was thicker and longer than the middle three.

I was fascinated by the sight of my ex-patient, and full of admiration for his good spirits and his physical courage. It was then that I realized an important principle of life, which might be named the principle of the distribution of handicaps. It goes as follows. If you are a cripple, you require two indispensable friends. You need someone to consort with who is more crippled than yourself (to succor and to pity) and someone who is less crippled than yourself (to emulate and to envy). The truly unfortunate cripple is he who has not a friend of each type, shielding him on both sides against the mystery of health.

These are reflections which I believe I would not have been capable of when younger, more egotistical, and more impatient with my fellow men. But all that is changed now. In the end, there is no substitute for the vocation of service. I discover, with relief, that being good prohibits my dallying with the "interesting." Since I no longer dream, there is little that I find interesting about myself. Only other people interest me and I allow myself the pleasure of helping them.

Since my return to a more active life, I have learned that during those six years my friends believed I had been committed to a mental institution. The story circulated that my brother had testified for my committal, and produced a blueprint of the house I designed for Frau Anders as a map of my aberrations.

I first heard this story from an old school friend, now the

prosperous owner of a chain of hotels, on whom I went to pay a congratulatory call when I learned of the impending marriage of his only son. He received me cordially, but with such an air of solicitousness that I could not refrain from questioning him. With some embarrassment and hesitation about mentioning what he thought was a delicate matter, he told me that he'd heard I was ill. I was astonished, and, not understanding him fully, protested, "On the contrary, I've never felt better in my life. Didn't you know I have an exceptionally sturdy constitution?" Then his exact meaning became clear, but fortunately we were spared any prolonged discussion of the matter because his son entered the living room with his fiancée, and the rest of my visit was spent advising the family on the wedding preparations.

The fact that I made the groom and bride a handsome wedding present, a valuable family heirloom which I had in my possession, namely a rare and beautifully executed contemporary painting of the Emperor of the French, may indicate that I bore the father no ill-will for his rather unflattering idea of me. And when I subsequently realized, through timorous allusions to the event and muted congratulations on my recovery, that others of my friends believed the same, I did not feel it important to confirm or deny the story. Yet I would be dishonest if I did not admit that it troubled me. On the one hand, there was the fact that my memory, for the most part excellent, told me differently: I had not been in any institution, but in the house which I had inherited from my father, pursuing my solitude and the resolution of my dreams. On the other hand, as I have already explained, my memory does fail me on one important point. Moreover there are certain letters and journals which challenge my memory in its entirety. Perhaps it would be best for me to present some excerpts from these and leave the reader to decide for himself.

One notebook contains what I take to be a draft for the present narrative, begun some years ago and then abandoned. From its form alone I judge that it was begun prematurely; how else explain that for the most part the draft is in the third, rather than in the first, person? Certain transformations of the events of my life—I shall not anticipate, since in a moment the reader will see for himself—make me regard the entire document with suspicion. At one time I even doubted that I wrote it. But it is definitely in my handwriting, although occasional blottings and crossings out of the words indicate that I wrote in a condition of some strain.

Perhaps, in fact, it is just a novel. The list of possible titles alone takes up several pages, I notice—which indicates all the devotion of a literary ambition. Among the titles considered are: *My Curious Dreams, Poor Hippolyte, A Puppet's Manual, In My Father's House, A Reply to the Bather, Welcome Home, The Confessions of a Self-Addicted Man, Notes of a Dreamer on His Craft,* and—in a rare touch of what I hope is humor, but may be only self-consciousness—*Don't Believe Everything You Read.* There are also several pages of notes and admonitions to the writer, to the effect that the narrative should make quite clear the separation of the hero's dreams from his waking life, and draw the moral therefrom.

On second thought, I shall give only the synopsis of this projected narrative:

Ch. 1. The late birth and affectionate naming of Hippolyte. He is most comfortably born. His mother does not die until he is five. Little happens in his childhood, except church and a war and candy and school and the maid. He leaves home to go to the university.

Ch. 2. He, too, wants an honest career. Why not? But gradually he abandons his studies, and gives himself to apathy and to dreams.

Ch. 3. Life passes idly and without incident. Until, one day, he is kidnapped and locked up. The kidnappers treat him well, except for occasional bullying on the part of the athletic chief guard. He is rejected by a woman in white.

Ch. 4. Ransomed by his father, he returns to the city. Good resolutions, and the non-performance of them. He sinks into debauchery, and frequents unconventional parties. How he dreams!

Ch. 5. He seeks religious counsel, but does not find a priest to absolve him. Before entering the church, he watches a wrestling match.

Ch. 6. Hippolyte tries the ministrations of a psychiatrist, but not for long. Luckily, when he is at his wits' end, an elderly millionaire sends him on a trip. But no sooner does he leave his patron's house than he loses his way.

Ch. 7. He studies the piano and betrays a fellow student. He falls from a tree.

Ch. 8. Recovering from his injuries, he submits to an operation. The operation is successful; he returns home, where his father advises him to marry.

Ch. 9. He does not marry. A visit with some acrobats. They try to engage him to become one of them.

Ch. 10. He becomes a performer. The life of puppets and the behavior of bears. In this limited arena he finds peace. Disabled and sensitive, Hippolyte drones on.

You will observe that this effort to describe my dreams—dare I consider it an autobiographical novel?—has omitted my life; or perhaps it is the other way around. Somewhat more successful from the point of view of completeness, but still rather curious in my present estimation is another autobiographical sketch—in the form of a letter—which I found also among the papers of that period. The difficulty of assembling my dreams and my waking life in some order is better solved, but at a certain price, as the reader will see. I also have some doubts about the plausibility of the letter form itself. After all, to whom could it be addressed?

The letter is undated, and without salutation. It begins:

"Although I am aware of the unusual step I am taking, I wish to petition for a re-examination of my case. I can assure you that I do not take this grave step lightly, but have devoted several years to thinking about it before I was entirely convinced that it was within my rights.

"Aware as I am that you must have all the relevant documents at your disposal, I would still like to take the liberty of giving a brief résumé of my life and career, and what I consider the perhaps excessive consequences which I have incurred.

"My given name, Hippolyte, you will recall, as well as my unfortunate nickname, "the bear." On my dossier you will find when and where I was born, the youngest of three children. My father was a prosperous manufacturer. Nothing of special import marks my childhood, except the early death of my mother. I was raised and schooled in the city where I was born, and then went to live in the capital to study at the university.

"I had every hope of making an honest career for myself in one of the established professions. But a deplorable apathy overtook me, and I gradually abandoned my studies. My mind, vacant of useful occupation, countered by proposing to me a series of singularly repetitive dreams, in which I imagined myself mingling in a circle of strange and disreputable people, writers and artists, presided over by a rich middle-aged woman of foreign birth.

"For a while my life passed without incident (except for my dreams) in this state of uselessness and indecision, until, one day, incredible as it may seem, I was kidnapped and incarcerated for some time. How unfortunate I then deemed myself to be the son of a rich father!

"The kidnappers' retreat was located near a bathing resort

by the sea. I cannot complain of any ill-treatment on the part of my captors, beyond a certain amount of bullying. The chief guard was lame, but this did not establish any special bond of friendship between us. While in the house of the criminals, I fell in love with the mistress of the lame guard. She rejected me cruelly, thus permanently marring my still very impressionable erotic sensibility.

"After a short time, I was ransomed by my father, who bitterly reproached me for my idle life, and returned to the city. I wished more than ever to resume a normal course of activity, but I continued to be plagued by my dreams. A persistent figure in these dreams was an eccentric writer, of perverse and insincere sexual tastes, in whom I confided. Despite my resolutions, I did not return to the university. I sank into debauchery, and frequented unconventional parties, and at one of them almost raped my hostess in front of the guests. As if in punishment for my daring, my dreams brought these wishes fully into view. I began dreaming again about the foreign woman. I dreamed that I seduced her, and shamefully abused her sexually.

"In further dreams, however, I made an effort to break off with her. This encouraged me to think that there was some hope for me, and that I was not totally devoid of good feelings. I sought religious counsel, and was publicly shamed in a church where my sins had become known to the populace. Perhaps I did not make a confession in the proper spirit, for I was very much alarmed and upset when, upon entering the church I saw one of my kidnappers, the lame man, lurking in the courtyard. He did not menace me, but I was nonetheless troubled.

"My shaming in the church only hardened my heart, as it was revealed in my dreams, for the dreams about the writer began again. I dreamed that I accompanied him on his nightly excursions into perversion and debauchery.

"I will admit that some of my judgments upon myself are

retrospective; I have only learned in later years to look upon my dreams as important. At the time they occurred, I did not pay much attention to them. What concerned me was the real life I was leading. But since I have been instructed by you how the acts that are committed in dreams are even more weighty than those committed in our waking lives (because our dreams are free, whereas in our daily lives we act under compulsion; our waking lives proceed by the art of compromise, but our dreams dare all) I now estimate my dreams at their true value and I concur in the judgment which you have placed upon them. Please do not think that in raising a question about the severity of your sentence, I challenge the importance which you place upon my disreputable dreams.

"To continue: Not content with this defiance of all established laws, I confess that in my dreams, I persuaded the foreign woman to come away with me. I abducted her from the bosom of her family and took her to a city whose natives do not have the same scruples and tastes as civilized people. There I abandoned her.

"Can it be that these dreams pursued me because of my lack of occupation? I was extremely distraught. I even tried the ministrations of a psychiatrist, but I did not continue long with him. Luckily, when I was at my wits' end, an elderly millionaire took me under his patronage, and gave me enough money to travel and see the world.

"But even then, my dreams did not give me a respite but continued to offer me unwholesome moral alternatives, now in the form of the teachings of a savant of ancient religions. In my dreams the learned man persuaded me that the moral codes of the world were mere inhibitions, and that I belonged to a secret circle of the elect and emancipated. In keeping with these strange persuasions of my dreams, I imagined myself as part of the entourage of a wicked nobleman who committed unspeakable crimes, for which he was exonerated, even admired.

"Further dreams showed me about to seduce the daughter of the foreign woman of my earlier dreams, but refraining through a great effort of self-control. As a diversion from my troubling thoughts, I studied the piano, in which I excelled. But this, too, I had to give up; this musical study only gave further stimulus to my desire for unlimited and irresponsible self-expression. Thus, when one of my fellow students of the piano was ill, and being persecuted by our teacher, I refused to aid him.

"I then dreamed that I murdered the foreign woman, but as so often happens in dreams, my act was ineffectual. She pursued me in a series of horrifying erotic nightmares.

"Shortly after, my dreams took a more constructive turn. I dreamt that I had built a house to shelter the foreign woman whom I had criminally abused. This gave me a clue, and I determined to follow the good intentions of my dreams even as I unwittingly reflected their evil acts. Although by now past the age when it is becoming or seemly to be a student, I enrolled again in the university in the Faculty of Architecture. I thought I had shaken off the thoughts which were causing me trouble with my own conscience and with the authorities, but shortly after I began to prosecute these good resolutions I was called up before the tribunal, and narrowly avoided being sentenced to death.

"After this painful experience I returned to my native town, where my father advised me to marry. Unfortunately, I did not take his advice. Perhaps this was my worst mistake, for my dreams, as if in mockery, showed me many images of a blissful marriage with a young girl of good family and quiet mind. Had I ever married such a person, I might well have found happiness and led a useful life.

"I have tried, however, to show my willingness to serve society by a variety of endeavors, including administrative work in a penitentiary, and brief service in the army during the Second World War as a non-combatant artillery specialist.

"I therefore regard my subsequent re-imprisonment as an act of excessive severity, and press the authorities to reconsider their judgment. For the life of my dreams I am not ultimately responsible. My dreams were foisted upon me, and anyone can see that the selfish acts I commit in my dreams do not accord with the willing and submissive character I display in my waking life.

"The conditions in which I live in this institution, the dampness of the cellar, the fact that my bed is as hard as if it were made of bricks, that my only exercise is in the park where children and their nurses mock when they see me chained to the guard, seem decidedly excessive. The guard will inform you that I obey all his orders, even when I do not understand them.

"In the event that a pardon can be secured, or at least a parole, I venture to promise that I will dream no further.

"Yours respectfully, etc."

Let me say at once that this plaintive letter seems to me unquestionable proof of a certain period of delusion, during which my dreams became my real life and my real life the dreams. The reader knows that I do not now subscribe to the version of my life presented in the letter. But whatever the true version of my experiences, it appears that this letter of appeal won me a certain amount of peace. Or, if the letter is the true account, a pardon from my sentence. For I do not dream now.

The ancient philosophers were right in recommending the benefits of age. It is comfortable to be old. One has less to suffer, more to think about. For some, this peace results from the silencing of the sexual urge. For me, peace has come through the silencing of the involuntary impulses of my dreams. The painful difference between my dreams and waking life has not been dissolved, for I can still remember the difference and report it. But age has appeased and softened it. Without a great space of future before me, I can look back. And now the past as a whole, dreams and waking life alike, presents itself to me as fantasy.

The issue of my sanity cannot be easily dismissed, but after long consideration of the matter, I hold that I was not insane. Call it eccentricity if you like—but do not explain it away. The acts of the eccentric and the madman may well be the same. But the eccentric has made a choice, while the insane person has not; rather, he is abandoned to his choices, submerged in them.

I submit that I made a choice, admittedly an unusual one. I chose myself. And because of my absorption in myself and relative indifference to other people, my inward ear became acute enough to hear a mandate from myself which isolated me further from others. That mandate was, so far as I understand it, to live out to the fullest the meaning of privacy. In obeying this mandate I was of course aided by a temperament already predisposed to solitude. Well might I have appeared mad to those who judged by less inward standards. But how could I behave otherwise? The self within myself that was exposed in my dreams could only stammer and cringe. Public experiences have names. But the dedicated dreamer has no name for what he knows; if he acts on the nameless knowledge of the dream, he appears not to be acting, but falling into his acts, drowning in them.

Call it perturbation instead. Insanity and perturbation are two names, two judgments, for the same thing. We cure the insane. We quiet the perturbed. I am more quiet now.

More than quiet, I should say. I am fulfilled. For the true test of fulfillment is silence—as the meaning of fulfillment is not being filled, but becoming empty. Dreams filled my mind, I emptied them out. In order to accomplish this, it was necessary for me to give way to my dreams. And when they had done with me, they left me beached upon the shore of my old age.

The surgery that is endured, the room that is cleaned, the conviction that is expressed, the hand that is clasped, the class that is taught, the treaty that is signed, the dream that is interpreted, the object that is bought, the weight that is lifted—all these are events which do not, at least for me, have this fulfilling or emptying character. But the itch that is scratched, the book that is written, the hole that is dug, the bet that is won, the bomb that is exploded, the rage which ends in murder, the tears which are wept—these are what I should consider models of fulfillment and abolition. In this second list of acts, what is done is really concluded. And this, after all, is what everyone craves. To execute an intention amounts to abolishing a desire. The advent of anything brings with it mainly the problem of its disburdenment, its dissolution. The only thing remarkable about me is that I approached this task more comprehensively than most people do, thereby also narrowing my life more than most people care to do. For me, the very advent of myself suggested the problem of my own dissolution.

This is no small task! There is a great difficulty in concluding anything. Luckily, the conclusion of most things is not left up to us. For example, we do not have to decide when to die. We are awarded our deaths at random, without justice. This is the only true end of anything.

So my dreams, and my preoccupations with myself, came to an end at random. There was no intellectual symmetry in it. It was I who imported the meaning, by my own submission to the dreams and the way they narrowed my life. Perhaps, in a sense, my life itself ended with the passing of my dreams and their perturbations. But not really. I am a strong believer in posthumous existence. Is it not to the posthumous view that we all unconsciously aspire?—and that not only when we allow ourselves the hope of immortality. I have been more lucky than most. I have had both my life and after-life: this post-humous existence of mine prolongs itself in meditation and in the enjoyment of a well-cleared landscape. I have no expectations for the future. Far be it from me, however, to decide that the active part of my life is really over. Who knows if a new series of dreams may not someday be forthcoming, which will launch me on a series of speculations far different from those which I have experienced? Without expectations then, either of end or new beginning, I continue to live the life that is permitted me.

Now, as hard as it is, I must bring to a close what I have written. Since I must end, it should be without the effort to convince—as God, or Nature, does not try to convince us that it is time to die; convinced or not, we die. I shall conclude not by describing an act, nor with one of my favorite ideas, but with a posture. Not with words, but with silence. With a photograph of myself, myself as I shall sit here after finishing this page. It is winter. You may imagine me in a bare room, my feet near the stove, bundled up in many sweaters, my black hair turned grey, enjoying the waning tribulations of sub-jectivity and the repose of a privacy that is genuine.

ABOUT THE AUTHOR

SUSAN SONTAG is the author of two previous novels, *The Benefactor* and *Death Kit*, a volume of stories, *I, etcetera*, and several collections of essays, including the prize-winning *On Photography*. Her most recent books are *AIDS and Its Metaphors* and *The Way We Live Now*. In 1990 she received a five-year fellowship from the MacArthur Foundation. She lives in New York City.